*EVERYMAN, I will go with thee, and be thy guide,*
*In thy most need to go by thy side*

GEOFFREY CHAUCER was born c.1340, the son of a London wine-merchant. He served as page to the Countess of Ulster and later entered the household of Edward III. In 1360 he was captured by the French near Reims and ransomed by Edward. He married Philippa Roet, a lady of the Queen's chamber. He undertook several diplomatic missions, especially to Italy in 1372-3 and 1378. From 1374-86 he was Controller of Customs on Wool and Hides in the port of London; MP for Kent, 1386; Clerk of the King's Works, 1389-91. He died in 1400 and was buried in Westminster Abbey.

Chaucer's interests extended beyond literature to philosophy and science: he translated Boethius's *Consolation of Philosophy* and composed at least one treatise on Astronomy. Although he lived through one of the most remarkable ages of English poetry (the reign of Richard II), it was French, together with Latin, literature that mainly influenced him. He was also the first English writer to 'discover' the great Italian authors, Dante, Petrarch and Boccaccio. His earliest major poem, *The Book of the Duchess*, commemorates John of Gaunt's first wife, who died in 1369. It is cast in the form of a dream, as are also *The House of Fame* (unfinished), *The Parliament of Birds*, and the later *Legend of Good Women* (also incomplete). His masterpiece, *Troilus and Criseyde*, a narrative poem in five books, was completed c.1385. From c.1387 he worked on *The Canterbury Tales*, which remained unfinished at his death.

IAN BISHOP was educated at The Queen's College, Oxford. After graduating, he continued his studies in the field of medieval literature under the supervision of J.R.R. Tolkien. For many years he has taught medieval and post-Renaissance literature at Bristol University, where he is currently Reader in English. His publications include studies of two major fourteenth-century poems, *'Pearl' in its Setting* (1968) and *Chaucer's 'Troilus and Criseyde': A Critical Study* (1981), besides various articles and reviews concerning medieval literature.

# The Narrative Art
# of the
# *Canterbury Tales*

*A Critical Study of the Major Poems*

## Ian Bishop

*Reader in English*
*University of Bristol*

Dent: London and Melbourne
EVERYMAN'S UNIVERSITY LIBRARY

Typeset by Gee Graphics Ltd in 10 on 11½pt Sabon
Printed in Great Britain by
**The Guernsey Press Co. Ltd, Guernsey, C.I.**
for J.M. Dent & Sons Ltd
Aldine House, 33 Welbeck Street, London W1M 8LX

First published in Everyman's Library, 1988

British Library Cataloguing in Publication Data

Bishop, Ian
    The narrative art of The Canterbury tales :
    a critical study of the major poems.——
    (Everyman's university library).
    1. Chaucer, Geoffrey. Canterbury tales
    I. title
    821'.1      PR1874

No 285 Hardback ISBN 0 460 00285 6
No 1285 Paperback ISBN 0 460 01285 1

# Contents

# Preface

My thanks are due to Oxford University Press and Houghton Mifflin for permission to quote, throughout this study, from the text of Chaucer's works, printed in F.N. Robinson (ed.), *The Complete Works of Geoffrey Chaucer* (2nd ed., London, 1957). Since my book went to press, this edition has been superseded by the following: L.D. Benson (general editor), *The Riverside Chaucer* (based on *The Works of Geoffrey Chaucer* ed. by F.N. Robinson) (Houghton Mifflin, Boston, 1987). I have found nothing in this new edition that prompts me to alter anything that I have written here. Perhaps its most interesting innovation, as far as the text is concerned, is its adoption of J.A. Burrow's suggestion that the Tale of Sir Thopas should be divided into three 'fits' instead of two. However, in my discussion of that tale, I had already taken account of Burrow's suggestion — and its remarkable consequences (see below, p.53). Glending Olson's article, 'Chaucer's Monk: the Rochester Connection' [*Chaucer Review* 21 (1986), pp. 246-56], appeared too recently for me to be able to consider it in Chapter 1.

I am also grateful to Oxford University Press for permission to reproduce (with alterations) my article '*The Nun's Priest's Tale* and the Liberal Arts' from *The Review of English Studies* n.s. 30 (1979), pp. 257-67; to the editors of *Medium Aevum* for permission to reproduce (with alterations) my article 'The Narrative Art of *The Pardoner's Tale*', which appeared originally in *MÆ* 36 (1967), pp. 15-24 (and subsequently reprinted elsewhere); and for permission to reproduce excerpts from my article, 'Chaucer and the Rhetoric of Consolation', from *MÆ* 52 (1983), pp 38-50. My thanks are also due to Penguin Books, Ltd., for permission to reproduce brief extracts from my essay, '*Troilus and Criseyde* and *The Knight's Tale*', from Boris Ford (ed.), *The New Pelican Guide to English Literature*, Volume 1, Part 1: *Medieval Literature, Chaucer and the Alliterative Tradition* (Penguin Books, 1982), pp. 174-187.

My colleagues, Professor J.A. Burrow and Dr Myra Stokes, read an earlier draft of this book and offered helpful corrections and suggestions. I am particularly grateful to Dr Stokes who, once again, very kindly undertook to correct the proofs of a book of mine. I also wish to thank the editorial staff of J.M. Dent & Sons for much careful and patient advice. Any faults that remain are entirely my own responsibility.

I.B.B.
Bristol, 1987.

# Abbreviations

| | |
|---|---|
| CA | John Gower: *Confessio Amantis* |
| CFMA | *Classiques Français du Moyen Age* |
| ChR | *Chaucer Review* |
| EC | *Essays in Criticism* |
| EETS | *Early English Text Society* (e.s. = extra series) |
| ES | *English Studies* |
| JEGP | *Journal of English and Germanic Philology* |
| MÆ | *Medium Ævum* |
| ME | Middle English |
| MED | *Middle English Dictionary* |
| MLN | *Modern Language Notes* |
| MLQ | *Modern Language Quarterly* |
| MLR | *Modern Language Review* |
| N & Q | *Notes and Queries* |
| OE | Old English |
| PBA | *Proceedings of the British Academy* |
| PL | J.-P. Migne (ed.), *Patrologia Latina* |
| PMLA | *Publications of the Modern Language Association of America* |
| PP | William Langland: *Piers Plowman* |
| PQ | *Philological Quarterly* |
| RES | *Review of English Studies* (n.s. = new series) |
| SAC | *Studies in the Age of Chaucer* |
| SP | *Studies in Philology* |

## Abbreviated Titles of Chaucer's Works

| | |
|---|---|
| CT | *The Canterbury Tales* |
| CYT | The Canon's Yeoman's Tale |
| FrankT | The Franklin's Tale |
| GP | The General Prologue (to *The Canterbury Tales*) |
| HoF | *The House of Fame* |
| KnT | The Knight's Tale |
| LGW | *The Legend of Good Women* |
| MancT | The Manciple's Tale |
| MerchT | The Merchant's Tale |
| MilT | The Miller's Tale |
| NPT | The Nun's Priest's Tale |
| PoF | *The Parlement of Foules* |
| PhT | The Physician's Tale |
| ReeveT | The Reeve's Tale |
| SqT | The Squire's Tale |
| TC | *Troilus and Criseyde* |
| WBP | The Wife of Bath's Prologue |
| WBT | The Wife of Bath's Tale |

# Chapter I

# Introduction: 'The Book of the Tales of Canterbury'

Many lovers of Chaucer's poetry encounter his work for the first time through a reading (perhaps a prescribed study) of the General Prologue to *The Canterbury Tales*. After being conducted through its famous gallery of portraits, we learn — from the mouth of the Host — how the author intends to present to us his anthology of tales. We are led to suppose that we are about to begin a more or less continuous narrative concerning a pilgrimage from Southwark to Canterbury, in which the various pilgrims entertain each other, and compete with one another, by telling stories, recorded in their own voices. Many of us will have been encouraged in this way to go on to read 'The Book of the Tales of Canterbury' (as it is called in some MSS) from beginning to end – though probably omitting the two prose 'tales' (The Tale of Melibee and The Parson's Tale). There can be no better way of reading the *Tales* for the first time.

One result of such a consecutive reading, however, will be to reveal certain discrepancies between the plan for the whole work, which is sketched in the General Prologue, and that which is executed in practice. The experienced reader will now realize that what he has before him is a compilation of (mostly) narrative compositions, loosely set into a (not altogether consistent) narrative framework by means of an incomplete series of linking passages. He will probably have discovered that certain tales and interludes move or delight him rather more than others, and he may indeed have been struck by a passage at the end of the Prologue to the Miller's Tale where the author seems to invite the reader to make his own selection of tales for his edification or delight. At the same time, he may have found that his reading of the 'complete' text has stimulated him into making some intriguing and illuminating comparisons between various items and passages, some adjacent, others remote from one another.

The authority and significance of the passage from the Miller's Prologue will be considered later in the present chapter. For the moment I will merely remark that I suspect that most of us, when we return to *The Canterbury Tales* after our first reading, accept thereafter the invitation to make our own choice, though without losing sight of the implications of the sequential arrangement of tales. Such a pragmatic and discriminating approach is the one that I propose to adopt in this critical study, which is concerned mainly with exploring the character and achievement of those tales that seem to me to be the most rewarding. Tastes change notoriously from one age to another. The evidence of the MSS suggests that one of the most esteemed of the tales during the century after Chaucer's death was the prose Tale of Melibee. The reasons for this preference constitute an interesting historical question; but it is not the kind of historical question that I am principally concerned with here. It seems unlikely that Melibee will again be held in such high regard, and I am content to accept — with a few important reservations — what is, in effect, the verdict of most twentieth-century readers as to which tales are the most worthwhile. By this I mean the verdict that is implied in the choice of tales that are given special attention in universities, schools and colleges, as indicated, for example, by those that are issued in separate editions for the purpose of assisting detailed study.

However, I am rather less content to accept some of the theories that have been advanced in recent decades concerning the way in which some of these tales are to be understood and appreciated; and I would question a number of currently cherished assumptions about what Chaucer is doing in these poetic narratives. This is not to deny the debt that I owe to the labours and discoveries of scholars and to the guidance and stimulus that I have received from many critics — a debt whose magnitude is very inadequately indicated in the footnotes to this volume. The following chapters comprise a series of interlinked, yet largely self-contained, essays in which I re-examine these narrative poems and suggest some fresh ways of approaching them. These discussions are founded upon a close reading of Chaucer's poetry — though not so close as to exclude from view everything except the words on the page immediately before the reader's eyes. Individual tales will be considered in relation to their immediate context (where one can be established), and will continually be compared one with another, and also with other works by Chaucer. In addition, I shall make comparisons with works by other medieval writers where this seems to me to be especially helpful for an understanding and appreciation of Chaucer's achievement.

What this study will not attempt is to offer any novel theory concerning the overall design of this heterogeneous and incomplete compilation: I do not claim to know what Chaucer's final intentions were in this matter. However, since several scholars and critics have proffered such theories, and since their speculations often affect the way in which they read and estimate particular tales, it is necessary to review briefly some of their conclusions.

In the earlier part of the present century, most attempts to identify the peculiar quality of Chaucer's achievement made great play with the 'dramatic' possibilities of the *Tales*. *The Canterbury Tales* differs from other 'framed' collections of stories[1] precisely in the way in which particular tales are juxtaposed and interrelated, as well as in the way in which they are assigned, with varying degrees of propriety, to the pilgrim narrators, whose portraits are exhibited in the General Prologue. From this sober observation of fact, it was tempting for commentators to proceed to the more imaginative position from which the Prologue appears as a static review of the dramatis personae who, as the account of the pilgrimage advances, become involved in a drama of conflicting temperaments, opinions and prejudices, often revealed in the tales which they choose to tell.

In order to sustain the momentum of this 'roadside drama', some commentators were obliged to read between the lines of Chaucer's verse, to postulate various unrecorded 'nods and winks' between the pilgrims, and to supply the fictitious narrators with undeclared motives and unspoken thoughts.[2] More recent scholars have criticized such supplementations of Chaucer's text, and have noted the naïve literal-mindedness that is often apparent in such speculations. When discussing the structure of the *Tales*, they have tended to look for a more abstract principle of unity.

The reaction against the 'roadside drama' theory was heralded by the suggestion that the pilgrimage should be regarded symbolically rather than literally: the journey to Canterbury is an image of the Christian's passage through this life on what the Parson calls 'thilke parfit glorious pilgrymage / That highte Jerusalem celestial' (X, 50-1).[3] But the theory that has proved to be most influential during the past thirty years is that which sees the structure of *The Canterbury Tales* as an example of 'Gothic form' – a notion that has been taken over from certain modern historians of later medieval art.[4] According to this theory, the structure of the *Tales* depends upon significant juxtaposition of parts (as in a medieval cathedral) rather than upon organic development.[5] The Gothic cathedral has also furnished some more particular images that have been offered as models for structural principles that may be observed in Chaucer's book. One of these is the rota (as in the 'wheel' or 'rose' window);[6] another is the labyrinth (as seen, for example, in the maze on the floor of the nave at Chartres).[7] The scholar who proffered these two models also suggested that the interlace pattern, so common in medieval art, may indicate another structural principle that contributes to the unity of the *Tales*. This suggestion is somewhat more plausible, as *entrelacement* was an important structural principle in the longer French romances of the previous century.[8] A 'key' of a different kind has been fashioned from the four categories of change which certain medieval commentators detected in Ovid's *Metamorphoses*: natural, magical, moral and spiritual.[9] The most recent theory finds a structural principle in the idea of 'self-correction' on Chaucer's part. The Man of Law's Tale is regarded as a Christian 'correction' of the pagan Knight's Tale and of the fabliaux that follow it. But it is seen as merely the first of a series of such 'self-corrections' that culminates in Chaucer's Retractions at the end of the *Tales*.[10]

It is no part of my purpose to discuss the merits of these competing theories. What I would observe is that all of them — whether their expositors are of the old persuasion or the new — attempt to demonstrate in effect that *The Canterbury Tales* is greater than the sum of its parts. Many readers will instinctively sympathize with the intention that underlies such demonstrations. But we must beware of at least two potential dangers that are inherent in any such attempts.

The first of these concerns the possible effect upon our appreciation of particular tales. The quality of the whole work must depend upon the quality of its parts; but the quality of the constituent parts of *The Canterbury Tales* is, in truth, uneven.[11] Consideration of a particular tale's intrinsic qualities can all too readily be set aside by a commentator whose dominant interest in that tale is to show how it contributes to his cherished theory about the overall design of the *Tales*. This is not just a matter of a willing or unwitting suspension of 'aesthetic' judgment: it may involve the neglect of those aspects of the narrative 'process' that happen to contribute nothing to the external scheme, or it may even result in a distortion of a tale's intrinsic significance in order to make it conform. As a fourteenth-century commentator might have put it: there is a danger that such practices may result in the misrepresentation of a tale's *sensus* (its 'story line') or a distortion of its *sententia* (ME, *sentence*) — its inner significance.[12] In saying this, I am not overlooking the fact that sometimes extrinsic considerations of context may affect or re-direct a pre-existing story's *sentence*. This is especially true of the kind of narrative known as an *exemplum* (which I discuss in Chapter 4) — a story that is used to support or illustrate an argument. Yet, even in such cases, there is no excuse for neglecting to consider the conduct of the narrative on its own terms.

The other problem that must not be ignored in any attempt to examine the structure of the *Tales* is both more technical and more fundamental. It is also very complicated, and I can do no more than glance at it here. The arrangement of the *Tales* with which most readers are familiar today is that of the Ellesmere MS (now in the Huntington Library, San Marino, California). This is the order adopted by F. N. Robinson in his edition of Chaucer's works.[13]

Robinson divides *The Canterbury Tales* into 'Fragments', numbered from I to X (alternatively styled 'Groups', lettered from A to I). The breaks between Fragments indicate places where there are no linking passages of narrative or dialogue between tales. The recent publication of an edition of the *Tales* based upon the Hengwrt MS (in the National Library of Wales, Aberystwyth)[14] may have prompted many readers of Chaucer to re-examine the way in which modern editors reach decisions about the relative authority of the fifty-five MSS that are more or less 'complete'.[15] Hengwrt is probably the earliest of the surviving MSS and its text is considered to be the closest to Chaucer's; but its order of tales differs somewhat from that of Ellesmere; and it does not contain certain items and passages which appear in that manuscript. Furthermore, as the result of recent work on the text of the *Tales*,[16] there is now very considerable uncertainty about Chaucer's final intentions regarding the arrangement of constituent items — if, indeed, he ever had any final intentions. The present is, therefore, hardly the most opportune moment for attempting to view *The Canterbury Tales* as an example of 'significant form'. At the same time, it should be observed that there are certain fairly constant features in the ordering of tales in those MSS that are considered the most authoritative. These particulars include the integrity of Fragments I, III, VI and VII. Another is the fact that these MSS begin with Fragment I (General Prologue, tales of the Knight, Miller, Reeve, and the Cook's abortive tale) and conclude with Fragment X (the Parson's Tale — usually followed by Chaucer's Retractions). For the purposes of the present study, it will be convenient to refer to the text of Robinson's Second (1957) Edition, and to its numbering of Fragments, if only because this is still the edition that is most widely accessible.

Neither of the objections I have raised need undermine the feeling that *The Canterbury Tales* is greater than the sum of its parts. At the same time, it may be thought prudent for a critical study to focus its attention — as I propose to do — upon the achievement of constituent parts rather than to speculate about Chaucer's final intentions for the design of the whole. Yet it would be perverse to ignore the setting in which the tales are placed. I shall therefore consider next how much — or, indeed, how little — of a context can be established for particular tales, and how far this will affect our reading of them.

Towards the end of the General Prologue (I, 790-5), the Host, Harry Bailly, proposes a story-telling competition, whereby each of the twenty-nine pilgrims shall tell two tales on the journey to, and another two during the return from, Canterbury. The pilgrim whom the Host judges the winner will be rewarded with a supper, paid for

by the rest of the company, when they return to his own hostelry at
the sign of the Tabard in Southwark. In the event, most of the
pilgrims relate only one tale apiece, some tell none at all. The pilgrim,
Chaucer, is allowed a second chance after the Host prevents him
from completing the Tale of Sir Thopas; he responds with the prose
Tale of Melibee. A bonus, unforeseen in the General Prologue, is
afforded by the arrival (in Fragment VIII) of the Canon's Yeoman,
who supplies a further tale. The Canon's Yeoman's Prologue and
Tale is one of the items that is absent from Hengwrt; but there seems
to be no good reason for doubting its authenticity. It may be that it
was unavailable to the compiler[17] of Hengwrt, but had been
rediscovered by the time that Ellesmere was put together. However
that may be, Ellesmere provides twenty-three tales (including the
Squire's Tale, also left incomplete) plus the Cook's Tale which
breaks off when it has hardly got under way.

Chaucer evidently did not devise a diary or time-tabled itinerary in
the way that Dickens did for his description of the peregrinations of
the Pickwick Club, whose members traversed much of the same
terrain as Chaucer's pilgrims, and who, like them, were (occasionally)
entertained by tales en route. There are sporadic indications of time;
two of them involve fairly elaborate calculations. But they do not
make it possible for us to discover how many days the journey took.
In the Introduction to the Man of Law's Tale (II, 1-14), the time is
reckoned as 10 a.m. on 18 April. At the beginning of the Parson's
Prologue (X, 1-12) the pilgrims are entering the outskirts of an
unnamed village at 4 p.m. on a day which — according to certain
scholars who have attempted the necessary astrological calculations
— could not have been later than 17 April![18]

As for the itinerary, a few towns and villages along the Canterbury
road are named, as having been reached, or as being in prospect.[19]
But on only two occasions does the Host draw the pilgrims' attention
forcibly to them. The first introduces the double reference to
Deptford and Greenwich (I, 3906-7). The Host's remark, 'Lo Grene-
wych, ther many a shrewe is inne!', seems to be a private joke on
Chaucer's part. It reminds me of the uncomplimentary remark by the
author of Sir Gawain and the Green Knight about the denizens of the
Wirral. Both remarks indicate the poet's personal involvement in the
respective localities.[20] The other reference occurs in the Prologue to
the Monk's Tale, when the pilgrims have evidently reached the spot
where Mr Pickwick was later to raise his telescope to his eye. The
Host exclaims: 'Loo, Rouchestre stant heer faste by!' (VII, 1926). It
may be worth our while to dwell here for a moment — precisely
because Chaucer does not. For, if ever there was an opportunity for
him to establish a significant relationship between the contents of

particular tales and his topographical scheme, it occurs here.

Rochester not only marks the mid-point of the journey from Southwark to Canterbury, but also stands at the only major river crossing en route, guarded to this day by its formidable and elegant Norman keep (the particular object of Mr Pickwick's scrutiny). It was also a cathedral city, its church of St Andrew being served by a house of Benedictine monks. Moreover, it had its own modern 'martyr', who was himself a pilgrim. St William of Perth, a baker, was murdered at Rochester in 1201, while on pilgrimage to the Holy Land. He was buried in the cathedral, and his miracle-working relics attracted rich offerings from pilgrims, rivalling those donated at the shrine of Becket himself at Canterbury. With the proceeds the monks were able, throughout the thirteenth century, to replace the Eastern half of their Romanesque church with a building in the Early English Gothic style.[21]

After the Host draws attention to the proximity of Rochester, the Monk narrates his seventeen 'tragedyes' which reiterate the theme that, when men reach the zenith of Fortune's wheel, she casts them down into ultimate misery. Fragment VII is then concluded with the Nun's Priest's Tale of Chauntecleer. Inserted into this beast-fable is a lengthy anecdote (derived ultimately from Cicero or Valerius Maximus) about two fellow pilgrims who seek a night's lodging in a 'toun' which is large enough to possess a 'west gate' (VII, 3035), and is eventually called a 'citee' (3044). But the city was so crowded and accommodation was so limited ('so streit of herbergage' — 2989) that they could not be housed together. One of them found room in an inn, but the other had to sleep in a 'stalle / Fer in a yeerd, with oxen of the plough' (2996-7), where he was murdered for his gold, and his corpse was concealed in a dung cart so that it might be smuggled out through the city gate. These conditions are similar to those that must have obtained in Rochester, crowded with the two-way traffic of pilgrims to Canterbury and travellers to the Channel ports. Its local saint was a murdered pilgrim and, moreover, its reputation as a haunt of thieves and criminals who preyed upon travellers still flourished in Shakespeare's day.[22] Here, indeed, might be a warning to pilgrims, about to seek lodging for the night, not to let themselves be separated from their 'compaignye'.

If the modern visitor cares to venture into the choir of the cathedral, he will see, prominently displayed on the N.E. pier (and pointedly placed opposite the bishop's throne), a thirteenth-century wall-painting. It depicts the tall figure of Fortune, standing within her wheel, as two figures climb up among the spokes, and a king, poised at the top, is about to be precipitated downwards in the manner of the subjects of the Monk's 'tragedyes'. It is worth bearing in mind that the Monk is the only one of Chaucer's pilgrims who would normally have access to the solidly walled-in choir; the others being confined to the nave, which was used as a parish church until 1423.[23]

Here, one might have thought, were particular, associative reasons — both literal and symbolic — for the poet's making something of the pilgrims' arrival at Rochester. But the framing narrative makes nothing of it whatsoever. After the Host remarks that Rochester stands 'faste by', the narrator seems to pass it by — almost as if he were motoring at 70 mph down the M2 by-pass (which, in fact, follows fairly closely a subsidiary pilgrim route). Not only is there no account of the pilgrims at Rochester, there is not even a mention of their arrival at Canterbury.

It is often taken for granted that the Parson delivers his penitential discourse, the last of the tales in the MSS, as the company approaches Canterbury. It is assumed that Chaucer had altered (what may have been) his original plan by the time he reached the Parson's Prologue, and that he intended to conclude his narrative at the end of the outward journey. One scholar has argued that this would conform with the usual practice adopted in medieval accounts of pilgrimages.[24] Others have seen symbolic propriety in the progress from the tavern to the cathedral that would result from such a change of plan. There are indeed fairly cogent reasons for making such an assumption. Nevertheless, it should not be forgotten that it is an assumption. There is no explicit reference, in Fragment X, to the proximity of Canterbury; it is not even certain in which direction the pilgrims are supposed to be travelling. Indeed, at least one commentator has argued that some of the tales are intended for the return journey.[25] The literal-minded reader may also wonder what has become of the short-story competition. Has it been abandoned; and if so, when and where?

Such queries and conjectures about what Chaucer might have done serve at least to emphasize how incomplete, shadowy and uncertain his framing narrative of the pilgrimage is. My excursus about the pilgrims at Rochester serves another purpose also. It demonstrates how readily a would-be commentator may be beguiled by a little 'background' knowledge into fabricating a theory that has no secure foundation in the foreground of the author's text. Once an idea suggests itself it may easily become obsessive. The notion of Chaucer's 'Rochester tales' — which could, indeed, be taken considerably further[26] — might burgeon into a general theory that topography does, after all, provide the structural principle upon which *The Canterbury Tales* is based! Few notions would seem more preposterous to several recent commentators. So, before such an incipient hypothesis has a chance to develop, it is advisable to indicate how weak its foundations are. Two observations will suffice to expose this weakness. In the first place, the Wheel of Fortune was one of the most ubiquitous of medieval commonplaces. Secondly, the ancient anecdote about the two travellers is introduced by Chauntecleer, not as a warning against treacherous inn-keepers in crowded cities, but as one of eight *exempla* that he cites to prove the prophetic nature of dreams. Yet I would maintain that this hypothesis is not much less plausible than several which commentators have offered in all seriousness when attempting to demonstrate some significant principle of unity in the *Tales*. Its misdirection of the *sentence* of Chauntecleer's *exemplum* is hardly less wilful than are several 'accommodations' that have been perpetrated in order to establish a theory concerning the overall design of Chaucer's book.

We move on to somewhat surer ground when we consider two other aspects of the structure: the relationship between tales within particular Fragments, and the assignment of tales to narrators. I shall first consider these two aspects together with reference to Fragment I, and then separately in relation to certain other Fragments. Fragment I consists of the General Prologue and the tales of the Knight, Miller and Reeve, together with the abortive Cook's Tale. A formal discussion of the General Prologue falls outside the scope of the present study, which is concerned mainly with the achievement of the tales. In any case, there is little I can add to the illuminating scholarship and criticism that has been devoted to that famous portrait gallery.[27] The Knight's Tale was probably composed before Chaucer set about compiling *The Canterbury Tales*.[28] It suits the Knight in so far as it is about chivalry; but in as much as it tells a story of rivalry in love it would seem better suited to his son, the Squire.[29] Nevertheless, it is the middle-aged Theseus who emerges as the dominant human figure in the tale. Yet, on the other hand, the Knight is presented as a devout crusader[30] on whose lips such a consistently pagan story might not seem appropriate. The style is generally dignified, but Chaucer alters its register frequently,[31] not in order to reveal various traits of the narrator's character, but in accordance with the requirements of the action as the poet conceives of them.

The following of the Knight's Tale by the Miller's is a bold stroke on Chaucer's part. The contrast is emphasized by the various correspondences between the two tales which have been noticed by commentators.[32] Regarded naturalistically, the Miller's requiting of the Knight may be seen as representing the 'lewed' [uneducated] drunkard's misunderstanding of the profound performance of his predecessor. But, although a Miller might have recited the bawdy anecdote on which the tale is based, no Miller — whether drunk or sober — would have been capable of composing the Miller's Tale. The world of the Miller's Tale is no less the creation of a poetic imagination than is that of the Knight's. By delegating the narration of both the juxtaposed tales, Chaucer implies the limitations of both their visions of life, while allowing his imagination freedom to exploit the potentialities of the different literary genres with which they are associated.

The ostensible relationship between the Miller's and Reeve's Tales is more superficial. Because the principal butt of the Miller's fabliau is a carpenter, the Reeve (who was also a carpenter) thinks it is directed against him personally (cf. I, 613-14; 3914-15). So he retaliates with his story of the discomfiture of a proud Miller — caused not, however, by a Reeve, but by two clerks. Indeed, in both these fabliaux, it is the clerks who triumph. For the fabliau was a genre composed for the entertainment of the upper classes, and educated men, at the expense of their social inferiors.[33] What Chaucer has done is to take characters who would normally be the butts of such stories and make them act as the narrators. A psychologically-minded critic might argue that the Reeve is so incensed against the Miller that, in order to put him down, he is prepared to betray the artisan class to which they both belong. I doubt, however, if that is what Chaucer intended.

These two fabliaux are further linked by the fact that they are set in the university towns of Oxford and Cambridge respectively. No reader of these tales can henceforth afford to ignore the late J.A.W. Bennett's erudite and fascinating monograph on *Chaucer at Oxford and at Cambridge*,[34] in which he demonstrates the remarkable extent to which the examination of historical rolls and records can illuminate these works of fiction.[35] Professor Bennett also observes:

> Not only are our two tales tied to these university localities, they are bound to each other in a tight warp and woof of parallels and contrasts, verbal echoes and reflections.[36]

He proceeds to give ample illustration of this assertion. Yet it seems to me that the main effect of the parallels and echoes is to draw our attention to the much more profound differences between the tales. It will not suffice to account for differences in tone between these fabliaux purely in terms of the contrasted characters of their narrators: the relatively good-natured Robyn, and the older and sourer Osewald.[37] The different visions of life that Chaucer offers in these transformed fabliaux are, in their way, as remote from each other as are the worlds of the Knight's and the Miller's Tales.

The only Group whose structure in any way resembles that of

Fragment I is Fragment III, consisting of the Wife of Bath's Prologue and Tale, and the tales of the Friar and Summoner. The latter are paired on a similar basis to that which binds the tales of Miller and Reeve in permanent enmity. Yet, again, it is the difference between these two satirical tales that is so striking. Fragment I begins with a Prologue that includes, within its gallery of portraits, an objective description of the Wife of Bath. Fragment III begins with a Prologue that approaches the length of its predecessor, but is monopolized by the Wife of Bath, who now conducts her own *apologia pro vita sua*. There are parallels between her Tale and the Friar's,[38] just as there are between those of the Knight and the Miller. The bachelor knight in her tale encounters a benign fairy, disguised as a hideous hag; the summoner in the Friar's Tale, on the other hand, encounters a devil, dressed in green, who calls himself a bailiff. Both of these supernatural characters have designs upon the respective protagonists. Even in the Wife's tale the existence of evil 'fairies' is already envisaged with the reference to the incubus, some of whose functions have been usurped by the friar who has exorcized him (cf. III, 865-81). These correspondences, however, are far less significant than those between the tales of Knight and Miller. Within certain other Fragments there are meaningful relationships between some juxta-posed tales: for example, between those of the Monk and the Nun's Priest in Fragment VII. However, I have yet to be convinced that relationships which commentators have noticed between the tales of the Physician and Pardoner (in Fragment VI)[39] or those of the Second Nun and Canon's Yeoman (in [Robinson's] Fragment VIII) are more than superficial or adventitious.[40] Attempts to establish such relationships seem to me to distract attention from the essen-tial qualities of the individual tales rather than to enhance our understanding and appreciation of them.

Dryden was the first notable critic to comment on what has come to be regarded as the most original principle of Chaucer's compilation:

> All his Pilgrims are severally distinguish'd from each other ...
> The Matter and Manner of their Tales, and of their Telling, are
> so suited to their different Educations, Humours, and Callings,
> that each of them would be improper in any other Mouth.
> (Preface to *Fables Ancient and Modern*).[41]

Our previous glance at Fragment I will have shown that, in certain respects, Dryden's claim is somewhat exaggerated. This also applies to tales in the other Fragments: some were evidently composed before the compilation was devised;[42] some have apparently been taken out of the mouth of one narrator and assigned to another speaker;[43] several are appropriate, in a general way, to the 'education' and 'calling' of their teller, but not especially to his 'humour'; a few are tailored for particular individuals.[44] There is still much argument among scholars and critics concerning the last of these classes. The Prioress's Tale is obviously appropriate for a nun. But is it suitable for the Prioress as she is described in the General Prologue? And, if so, does it intensify, or does it modify, the suppressed irony of that portrait?[45] Again, it is obvious that the tales of the Pardoner and the Wife of Bath are closely involved with the prologues in which these narrators are made to reveal their own characters. Yet the relationships between these tales and their respective prologues are, it seems to me, of a different order. The Pardoner's Tale (by which I mean specifically the *exemplum* of the three rioters seeking Death) is capable of standing alone; and has indeed been acclaimed as one of the most powerful short stories in English. Its relationship to the Pardoner's Prologue, and to his nefarious designs, affords an added dimension of irony which, however, in no way affects the quality of the tale itself. I believe that those critics are mistaken who think that the manner in which the tale is told reflects the idiom of its speaker, or who think that its telling is intrinsically contaminated by the character of its narrator. Indeed, I maintain that the full force of Chaucer's ironical presentation of the Pardoner depends upon the integrity of the tale.[46] On the other hand, the Wife of Bath's Tale is permeated by the spirit of the narrator of its Prologue; its self-indulgent digressions continue to exhibit the prejudices and preoccupations of Dame Alys. It has sometimes been claimed that the hag's discourse on old age, poverty and 'gentillesse' is an authorial intrusion that does not suit the character of the fictitious narrator. I shall argue that, on the contrary, it is an essential part of Alys's narrative strategy.[47] Without the support of the Prologue, much of the *raison d'être* of the Wife of Bath's Tale would disappear, whereas the Pardoner's *exemplum* can stand unsupported by its framework.

Although the reader would (I think) be puzzled by the Wife of Bath's Tale if it had survived without its Prologue, he would certainly not dismiss it as an inferior piece of writing; for it is manifestly a brilliant and entertaining performance. But what I have said about this tale raises the question of to what extent a poor or indifferent story may be redeemed by its propriety to the 'Education', 'Calling', and 'Humour' of its narrator. A particularly pertinent instance here is afforded by the Manciple's Tale. As a re-telling of the 'just so' story (ultimately derived from Ovid's *Metamorphoses*) of how the formerly white and melodious crow became raucous and black, Chaucer's performance may seem heavy-handed, needlessly digressive and uncertain in direction. However, it has been argued that it becomes much more interesting if it is regarded as illustrating — in effect — the 'education', 'calling' and 'humour' of its narrator. Although I agree with this opinion, I do not think that, when read in this way, the tale is metamorphosed into one of Chaucer's most accomplished narratives. As I shall show in Chapter 8, it cannot compare in brilliance and profundity with the Nun's Priest's Tale — that other astonishingly oblique re-telling of a traditional fable (where, incidentally, the character of the fictitious narrator is of minimal interest).

A similar rescue operation has been undertaken — quite needlessly and officiously, in my opinion — on behalf of the Squire's Tale. This tale (as Milton regrets) leaves 'half told / The story of Cambuscan bold'. According to some critics it is tactfully interrupted and curtailed by the Franklin, who thereby prevents the company from being bored any further by the efforts of an inexperienced young narrator who cannot properly master his material. I do not think the Squire's Tale is meant to be such a twin of the burlesque Tale of Sir Thopas. It is indeed appropriate for its youthful narrator; but it participates in his enthusiasm for the world of romance without any suggestion of ridiculing him.[48]

The critical estimation of the Franklin's Tale has tended to fluctuate in accordance with divergent opinions of its narrator's character. In my student days my teachers thought that the Franklin would be a far more congenial high-table companion than would the Clerk of Oxenford. They welcomed the 'humane' and 'modern' marital arrangement between Dorigen and Arveragus, and admired the dénouement in which the principal characters acted like 'gentlemen all round'. A later, leaner, and possibly less privileged generation of academics condemned the Franklin as a glutton and a snob. Recalling perhaps Goneril's use of the word 'epicurism' (Lear, I, iv, 267), these moralists have looked askance at 'Epicurus owene sone' (I, 336), while forgetting how Chaucer balances this remark against the statement that 'Seint Julian he was in his contree' (I, 340). The manner in which his tale is concerned with 'gentillesse' came to be regarded as betraying the narrator's uncomfortable awareness of the fact that he stands a little lower than the 'gentry'.[49] The Franklin's adoption of the genre of the 'Breton lai' was derided as an attempt to impress the pilgrims of superior rank by relating what he mistakenly believes to be a 'refined' and fashionable kind of tale.[50] It has been argued too that the marital compact, described at the beginning of the tale, would have been regarded as absurd by Chaucer's contemporaries[51] as it is contrary to the teachings of the medieval church about the proper subordination of wives to their husbands. The most sophisticated of this generation of critics admires the way in which Chaucer presents the Franklin as a simple-minded narrator who does not recognize the disturbing implications of the tale he tells.[52] In view of such extreme disagreements among critics, it may almost be an advantage to forget about the Franklin, for the moment at least, and to approach the tale as Chaucer's own essay in the genre of the 'Breton lai'.

There is another kind of relationship between the parts of 'The Book of the Tales of Canterbury'; for Chaucer himself appears to encourage comparisons between remote, as well as adjacent, constituents. In the General Prologue Chaucer follows his portrait of the worldly Merchant immediately with that of the unworldly Clerk of Oxenford. The contrast is emphasized, not merely by contiguity, but also by a verbal echo. It is stated that the Merchant's conversation was 'sownynge alwey th'encrees of his wynnyng' (I, 275) — although he was actually in debt — whereas it is stated of the Clerk that 'sownynge in moral vertu was his speche' (I, 307). But the more or less idealized portrait of this Clerk of Oxenford sets up an exemplar that we are obviously meant to keep in mind when we read the description of Nicholas, the clerk in the Miller's Tale — a comparison which is also enhanced by close correspondence and verbal echoes.[53] Similarly, the expert dealings and business efficiency of the merchant of St Denys, in the Shipman's Tale, is thrown into relief by comparison with the operations of his peer in the General Prologue — especially as both accounts exploit references to the technical language of commerce.[54] I have already commented upon the relative superficiality of the (undoubtedly intended) correspondences between the adjacent tales of the Wife of Bath and of the Friar. In Chapter 5 I shall suggest that far more illuminating are the correspondences between the tales of the Friar and the Pardoner — even though these tales are not contiguous.

The fact that Chaucer appears to encourage comparisons between both remote and proximate elements brings me to the question of the presence of 'themes' within the *Tales*. The most discussed theme in the compilation has been that of marriage. Discussion began in the early years of this century with G. L. Kittredge's theory of a 'marriage debate' between certain of the pilgrims. According to Kittredge,[55] the argument was inaugurated by the Wife of Bath with her thesis that what women most desire is 'maistrye' or sovereignty over their husbands and lovers. This is eventually answered by the Clerk of Oxenford in his story of the 'patient' Griselda. The Merchant adds his own animadversions in both the Prologue to, and in the body of, his tale about the cuckolding of the elderly Januarie by his young wife, May. A humane and reasonable conclusion to the discussion is reached in the Franklin's description of what Kittredge regards as an ideal marriage compact between Dorigen and Arveragus.

Kittredge's theory proved to be very influential for several decades; but it rests upon assumptions that do not meet with universal acceptance today. In the first place, it assumes that what we now know as Fragments III, IV and V were planned by Chaucer as a deliberate sequence. But, as already noted, recent textual criticism suggests that we are in no position to make such a confident assertion about the poet's intentions as to the ordering of these particular tales. Secondly, Kittredge assumed that these three Fragments constitute a *dramatic* sequence. In order to demonstrate this hypothesis, he was obliged virtually to try to 'sink' the inconveniently intervening (but stubbornly buoyant) tales of the Friar and Summoner, and to discount the Squire's Tale as an interlude on the theme of romantic love. Thirdly, in order to establish dramatic continuity, Kittredge was compelled to 'read between the lines' of Chaucer's verse and to indulge in imaginative supplementation of the text. So he imagines the Clerk as taking notice of the Wife of Bath's assertion (III, 688-91) that no clerk can speak well of 'wyves'. From then on, the Clerk is imagined as 'listening without comment, and biding his time'[56] until the Host invites him to tell his tale.

What Kittredge's critics object to is not his assertion about the importance of marriage as a theme, but the way in which he employed the 'dramatic principle' in order to construct a debate. Indeed, one of the ways in which they sought to undermine his theory was by pointing out that at least seven other tales are entitled to be enrolled as members of the 'marriage group'. For my own part, although I do not believe in the presence of a formally organized debate, I nevertheless think that the instinct which led Kittredge to associate these four tales was reasonably sound. Indeed, two of the tales — those of the Merchant and Franklin — are even more closely related than Kittredge realized: they may, in fact, be regarded as unidentical twins. In Chapter 6 I discuss the four tales in sequence, although on an entirely different basis from Kittredge's, and without any sugestion that they contribute to a debate among the pilgrims, or that they comprise an exclusive group.

The theme of marriage no longer maintains the monopoly that it once enjoyed. Recent scholars have detected a plurality of themes in Chaucer's collection; and they have increasingly come to recognize the importance of his employment of different genres. The combination of the two approaches is well illustrated in Helen Cooper's recent study, *The Structure of the Canterbury Tales*. Dr Cooper sees

Chaucer's collection as similar, in some respects, to a medieval *summa*:[57] she regards it as an 'Encyclopaedia of Kinds' (Chapter 3); and she also observes the way in which it works out variations on a number of themes. Among the themes that Dr Cooper identifies are: 'Brotherhood and Friendship'; 'The Girl with Two Lovers'; 'Female Saints and Wykked Wyves'; 'Fortune, Providence and Suffering' (Chapter 6). I entirely agree with her insistence on the importance of recognizing Chaucer's deployment of literary 'kinds'. But I think that the whole question of specifying and isolating 'themes' should be approached with caution. The situation is similar to that which is encountered when we consider attempts by commentators to perceive relationships between contiguous tales within Fragments: some of the variations on the selected themes are indeed genuinely significant, whereas others are somewhat factitious. There is a danger that one will be tempted to pursue relatively superficial or merely accidental manifestations of a theme from one item to another throughout the compilation; and, in so doing, may fail to distinguish the intrinsic harmonies and sequential developments that determine the individual character of a particular tale. It is partly in order to avoid this danger that I propose to work outwards from an appreciation of the peculiar characteristics of individual tales. However, since one of the most effective ways of bringing out the individual qualities of a particular tale is to compare it with others that have something in common with it, I shall discuss tales together under various headings. Because I agree that *The Canterbury Tales* may be regarded as an 'Encyclopaedia of Kinds', the basis of this grouping will be largely generic. Indeed, one of my main concerns will be to illustrate the extraordinary variety among tales that belong to the same genre. To a more limited extent my grouping will be thematic and stylistic. I would emphasize that this arrangement is not offered as a contribution to the debate about the structure of the *Tales*; I review the tales in this way merely for the convenience of making apt critical comparisons. Nevertheless, the arrangement is partly the result of following up the implications of a remark that Chaucer himself makes.

As we see in the following quotation, there is one place where Chaucer appears to invite the reader to search for examples of his own favourite genres and to choose the 'mateere' that suits his taste, as an alternative to accepting the tales in the order in which the compiler offers them. The Miller's Prologue concludes with the poet's apology for including this tale and others of its kind:

M'athynketh that I shal reherce it heere.
And therfore every gentil wight I preye,

For Goddes love, demeth nat that I seye
Of yvel entente, but for I moot reherce
Hir tales alle, be they bettre or werse,
Or elles falsen som of my mateere.
And therfore, whoso list it nat yheere,
Turne over the leef and chese another tale;
For he shal fynde ynowe, grete and smale,
Of storial thyng that toucheth gentillesse,
And eek moralitee and hoolynesse.
Blameth nat me if that ye chese amys.
The Millere is a cherl, ye knowe wel this;
So was the Reve eek and othere mo,
And harlotrie they tolden bothe two.
Avyseth yow, and put me out of blame;
And eek men shal nat maken ernest of game.

(I, 3170-86)

At first this passage may seem to be wholly disingenuous. Few readers will be deceived by the poet's plea that he is merely the innocent compiler whose duty, like that of a legal witness, is to repeat the exact words (however distasteful he may think them) of the various narrators. This piece of extenuation is of the same order as the designedly unconvincing arguments which are put into the mouth of Alceste, in the Prologue to *The Legend of Good Women* (G, 338-52), to defend Chaucer against the charge of having defamed womankind in writing *Troilus and Criseyde*.[58] Moreover, Chaucer has lavished as much art on the composition of the Miller's and Reeve's Tales as on that of the Knight. He also wishes, presumably, that the carefully contrived correspondences and contrasts between these tales will not escape the notice of his more perceptive readers. At the same time, he seems to recognize quite genuinely that some tales may be too strong for the stomachs of certain readers and that, in any case, not every tale will appeal 'to every gentil wight' every time he opens the book. Whereas the imagined pilgrim audience must sit through the whole performance, not knowing whether the next act will bring embarrassment, boredom, edification or delight, the reader is offered the freedom of Chaucer's newly constituted library.

At present, however, I am interested in this passage mainly for the way in which it functions as an index of genres and 'mateeres' to be found in Chaucer's book. My discussion of the tales is arranged, to a considerable extent, in accordance with the division that the compiler points to here. Chapter 2 is concerned with tales 'of storial thyng that toucheth gentillesse'. It is principally concerned with making a fresh approach to, and a detailed re-appraisal of, the Knight's Tale. It also re-examines more briefly the Squire's Tale and 'Chaucer's' Tale of Sir Thopas. The Franklin's Tale also comes into this category, but I reserve detailed examination of it for a later chapter, which will afford an opportunity for making some more incisive and revealing comparisons. These tales are usually termed 'Romances'. But I prefer Chaucer's own description, because there has recently been some argument about the application of the term: everyone seems to know what everyone else understands by it, but no two definitions are identical.[59] Chapter 3 is concerned with tales of 'harlotrie'; that is, the principal tales that develop the traditions of the fabliau. (In this case, detailed treatment of the Merchant's Tale — the most untypical of these fabliaux — is reserved for discussion in Chapter 6 in what I regard as a more illuminating context.) This chapter concentrates mainly on the Miller's Tale, but also argues that its companion piece, the Reeve's Tale, has been underrated and, in some respects, misunderstood. Chapters 2 and 3 emphasize the wide variety that the poet achieves within each of these genres.

Chapter 4 considers Chaucer's use of one of the most prolific of medieval narrative types: the *exemplum*. He does not mention it in the present list, perhaps because exemplification is a mode rather than a genre, and because almost any kind of story may serve as an *exemplum* — or *ensample* (as Chaucer calls it). The Monk's Tale comprises a collection of seventeen *exempla*; but the finest of Chaucer's stories that is introduced as an *ensample* is, of course, the Pardoner's narrative of the quest for Death.

Chapter 5 is organized on both a generic and a thematic principle. The tales of the Friar, Summoner and Canon's Yeoman all involve the exposure (and ridicule) of a villain through the mouth of a hostile narrator — whereas the Pardoner had shamelessly boasted of his own vicious practices. Thematically too, discussion of these tales about the avid search for material reward — 'The Quest for Meed' — follows logically upon that of the Pardoner and his tale. The implications of this theme go beyond the bounds of venality satire. It is a prominent subject throughout 'The Book of the Tales of Canterbury'; and it is one that accords well with the framing narrative about pilgrims who are seeking the shrine of the 'blisful martir' in the hope that he will 'quite' them their (spiritual) 'meede' (cf. I, 770). It is also a subject that received profound treatment in the writings of two of Chaucer's greatest English contemporaries: Langland and the anonymous author of *Pearl*. I have already referred to Chapter 6, 'Chaucer's "Wyves" and the Art of Persuasion', as covering the tales included in the traditional 'marriage group', although it discusses them on a different basis from Kittredge's —

and, moreover, one that is stylistic rather than thematic. There is a contrast between Chapters 5 and 6, in so far as the former deals with a major theme of public morality, whereas the latter gathers together the principal tales about intimate, personal relationships. My two final chapters are focused upon the most successful examples of tales of 'moralitee and hoolynesse'. Chapter 7 concentrates mainly on the most intriguing tale of 'hoolynesse', the Prioress's Tale, whereas Chapter 8 leads, through a consideration of the Manciple's Tale, to an analysis of Chaucer's most sophisticated comic masterpiece, the Nun's Priest's Tale. Both of these fables embody characteristically oblique attitudes towards the practice of extracting 'moralitee' from works of fiction.

Alternatively, the grouping of tales in the following chapters may be regarded sociologically. Chapters 2 to 5 are concerned with the three 'estates' of medieval society: the tales discussed in Chapter 2 are about members of the military or knightly class; those in Chapter 3 are mainly about members of the commons; Chapters 4 and 5 deal with tales that are narrated by members of the clergy or their associates. Chapter 6 is preoccupied with women, Chapter 7 with children, and Chapter 8 with animals and the characters they assume in moral fables.

It is not my intention to make a dutiful survey of every item that is included in *The Canterbury Tales*. Among those that will not receive detailed critical attention are the Tale of Melibee and the Parson's Tale. There are three reasons for omitting discussion of these particular items. They are not 'tales' except in the very basic sense of 'something that is told'; they are both in prose; the Tale of Melibee adheres much more closely to its original than do any of the other 'translaciouns' among the *Canterbury Tales*. Chaucer's prose translation is a subject that still requires detailed investigation that would be beyond the scope of the present study.[60]

Mention of Chaucer's use of prose in the tales that are not discussed leads naturally to consideration of his writing of verse in those that are the subject of this study. His use of verse is something that is apt to be taken for granted, partly because it was the more common medium for narrative in Chaucer's own day, and partly because a good many modern British readers have been familiar since their schooldays with one or more of these tales in rhyming verse. Yet no writer of fiction today would normally employ this medium; nor do serious poets think of themselves as raconteurs. Narrative verse is sometimes composed for the amusement of children, and that which is addressed to adults is usually of the facetious kind associated with light entertainment. Perhaps it is partly for this reason that a certain popular modern verse rendering of *The*

*Canterbury Tales* so often succeeds in making Chaucer — one of the most adult of English poets — sound merely schoolboyish:

> And certainly he was an excellent fellow.
> Many a draught of vintage, red and yellow,
> He'd drawn at Bordeaux, while the trader snored.
> The nicer modes of conscience he ignored.
> If, when he fought, the enemy vessel sank,
> He sent his prisoners home; they walked the plank.[61]
>
> (cf. I, 395-400)

Fortunately editors have made Chaucer accessible in the original, not only to students, but also to any reader of poetry who is prepared to look no further than the margin and the foot of the page for basic assistance.[62] Editions intended for students, and for the general reader, wisely make the minimum of fuss about the poet's metrics. They supply rudimentary precepts concerning pronunciation, grammar and scansion. They formulate simple rules for the sounding of final *e*, for elision, and for 'alternative stress'.[63] When describing Chaucer's 'rhyme royal' stanza or his handling of the couplet, they refer to his line indifferently as decasyllabic, five-stress, or iambic pentameter. I have no intention of disturbing the smooth surface of these waters. Those who have done so, by propounding 'unorthodox' theories about Chaucer's prosody,[64] are generally regarded as spoilsports who hurl boulders into the middle of the pond in order to rock the boats of those taking their innocent pleasure there. Yet, whatever one may think of these theories, their proponents have certainly made some of us think again about the problems involved in defining Chaucer's metres — not to mention the difficulty Chaucer must have experienced himself in trying to accommodate within a metrical form a language that was undergoing rapid change.

The technical basis of Chaucer's poetry is not my concern here. What I would describe is something that is more elusive. Any critical study must be based upon a close reading of the text. In the case of Chaucer especially, it should be based upon a reading of the text aloud in order to demonstrate how the poet, through the placing of words in his metrical scheme, insists upon particular intonations, inflections of voice, modulations of tone, and rhythmical patterns. It is almost impossible to represent on paper such delicate instances of the way in which sound enhances the sense. Even to attempt to do so would involve so much minute analysis and unwieldy periphrasis that it would be impossible to demonstrate such effects in the illustrative passages that are quoted from Chaucer's text in subsequent chapters. So I shall conclude this preliminary chapter by offering a detailed analysis of just three short passages — chosen almost at random — in order to give some idea of what Chaucer gains from composing his narratives and dialogues in verse. The first excerpt is written in the 'rhyme royal' stanza; the other two in couplets.

The first example is the stanza from the Prioress's Tale that tells how the seven-year-old schoolboy came to learn the Marian antiphon that invokes the Virgin as 'Loving mother of the redeemer':

> This litel child, his litel book lernynge,
> As he sat in the scole at his prymer,
> He *Alma redemptoris* herde synge,
> As children lerned hire antiphoner;
> And as he dorste, he drough hym ner and ner,
> And herkned ay the wordes and the noote,
> Til he the firste vers koude al by rote.[65]
>
> (VII, 516-22)

The diminutive scholar's achievement is beautifully encapsulated within the single stanza. The long sentence may, at first, appear to represent a straightforward learning process, that advances from modest beginnings (emphasized by the repeated 'litel'), through the *crescendo* of confidence in the fifth line, to the achievement in the final, clinching couplet. It is indeed appropriate that his memorizing of the complete 'firste vers' should coincide with the stanza's concluding line — even though 'vers' may refer to a single line of Latin verse rather than to a stanza.

But the process is, in fact, not quite so straightforward. The boy is diverted from the task he ought to be performing (the learning of his prymer) into that of mastering the words and music of the anthem. It is the singing of the older children in the next class that distracts him from his appointed task. This is unobtrusively emphasized by the pattern of rhyming words. In the 'A'-rhyme of the initial quatrain, 'lernynge' is displaced by 'herde synge'; and the 'B'-rhyme causes the boy's 'prymer' to be replaced by the older children's 'antiphoner'. The fifth line — 'And as he dorste, he drough hym ner and ner' (i.e. 'nearer and nearer') — involves a cautious adventure that gradually approaches the security of the final couplet, whose new 'C'-rhyme celebrates the completion of the boy's transference of his concentration (cf. 'al by rote') from the reading of his 'prymer' to the words and musical 'noote' of the 'antiphoner'.

To subject this little stanza to such a cumbersome analysis is to 'break a butterfly upon a wheel'. But it does reveal how exquisitely and subtly constructed the stanza is. I now move from this delicately

fashioned passage to one that is designed to sting. In the Reeve's Tale
we are introduced to a supposedly celibate village parson who
marries off his illegitimate daughter to the local miller. They, in turn,
produce a legitimate daughter, whose clerical grandfather has great
plans for her future. He will provide her with a sufficient dowry to
enable her to marry into 'society'. Chaucer also tells us where the
money was to come from:

> This person of the toun, for she was feir,
> In purpos was to maken hire his heir,
> Bothe of his catel and his mesuage,
> And straunge he made it of hir mariage.
> His purpos was for to bistowe hire hye
> Into som worthy blood of auncetrye;
> For hooly chirches good moot been despended
> On hooly chirches blood, that is descended.
> Therfore he wolde his hooly blood honoure,
> Though that he hooly chirche sholde devoure.
>
> (I, 3977-86)

The use of the conjunction 'therfore' at the beginning of the
penultimate line of this quotation seems to imply that the last two
couplets constitute a syllogism. But they do nothing of the kind.
Chaucer is adept at constructing counterfeit syllogisms for satirical
purposes. The mere motion of a syllogism is suggested by verbal
parallelism and internal rhyme. The phrase 'hooly chirches good'
(i.e. 'property') in 3983 is echoed in the next line by 'hooly chirches
blood'. The latter phrase then reappears in a blandly elliptical form
in the line that carries the pseudo-conclusion: 'Therfore he wolde his
hooly blood honoure'. The 'chirche' has been shoved aside — or,
rather, it has been pushed down into the pendent, second line of the
couplet, where it appears, shorn of its rightful 'good'. The effect can
be properly appreciated only when the lines are read aloud with the
necessary alterations of the voice-pitch on the key words — 'hooly',
'chirche', 'blood'. Behind these lines is the notion of the perversion of
the Apostolic Succession. The only kind of succession that the church
allows its ministers is that of ordination. From the time of the
eleventh-century Pope Gregory VII, the spiritual quality of the
succession was protected by the insistence on clerical celibacy. The
parson in this tale diverts the church's endowments into the founding
of a dynasty of flesh and blood.

The final example is the Prologue to the Nun's Priest's Tale, which
is really an epilogue to the Monk's Tale, as it is mostly occupied by
the reactions of the Knight, and then the Host, to the Monk's series
of 'tragedies'. The contrast between the characters of the Knight and

the Host is brought out strikingly by their different manners of speech; and their peculiar speech inflections are caught by the placing of particular words, phrases and clauses within, or across, the sequence of couplets. Certain authoritative MSS, such as Hengwrt, contain only a small part of this passage;[66] but if any lines *sound* authentically Chaucerian it is these.

The Knight's interruption of the Monk is polite, but firm:

'Hoo!' quod the Knyght, 'good sire, *namoore* of this!
That ye han seyd is *right ynough*, ywis,
And *muchel moore*; for litel hevynesse
Is *right ynough* to muche folk, I gesse.'

                       (VII, 2767-70 — my italics)

His firmness is evident from the calculated repetitions and echoes — especially in the phrases I have italicized. The *enjambement* between the second and third lines enacts the sense of superfluous excess by causing the phrase 'And muchel moore' to spill over into the opening of the next couplet. The Knight is one who has mastered the art of public speaking, and who knows how to exact obedience without giving offence. This is also evident from the way in which he continues by modestly expressing his personal preference ('I seye for me' — 2771) for 'comedy' (i.e. stories with happy endings) over 'tragedy'. A further simple repetition helps him to conclude his speech with a cadence that is firm, modest and soothing:

'Swich thyng is gladsom, as it thynketh me,
And of swich thyng were goodly for to telle.'

                             (VII, 2778-9)

His addressing the Monk by the polite, pronominal form 'ye' (2768) contrasts sharply with the Host's wilfully impolite use of the familiar 'thou', when he eventually turns to the Nun's Priest at 2808-10:

Thanne spak oure Hoost with rude speche and boold,
And seyde unto the Nonnes Preest anon,
'Com neer, thou preest, com hyder, thou sir John!'

In this context, the word 'rude' means pretty well what it means today. There is a marked anti-clerical streak in the Host, which he is able to indulge with impunity when addressing a clergyman of inferior status. The Host's command to the priest is conveyed in a line with a strongly marked caesura, which is preceded by four monosyllabic words and succeeded by a variation upon them. In the second half-line 'neer' is replaced by 'hyder' and 'preest' by the contemptuous nickname for a priest, 'sir John'. The line is so constructed that, when read aloud, the repeated 'thou' sticks out like a finger rudely pointing at the object of the Host's jocular contempt.

Perhaps the most skilfully written part of the Knight's speech is that which, in effect, carries his definition of 'comedy' (in the medieval sense of the word):

> 'And the contrarie is joye and greet solas,
> As whan a man hath been in povre estaat,
> And clymbeth *up* and wexeth *fortunat*,
> And there abideth *in prosperitee* . . .'
>
> (VII, 2774-7 — my italics)

A sense of climax is induced by the sequence of three phrasal verbs, in which the number of syllables in the adverbial element gradually increases, as indicated by the italicized words. This may be classified as a rhetorical figure; but it sounds completely spontaneous. A similarly telling sequence was later used by one of Chaucer's most distinguished admirers, in the opening lines of *Absalom and Achitophel*:

> In pious times, e'r Priest-craft did begin,
> Before *Polygamy* was made a Sin;
> When Man on many multipli'd his kind,
> E'r one to one was cursedly confin'd . . .

In the third line, Dryden generates a lively impression of multiplication by gradually increasing the number of syllables in the alliterative series. His master-stroke arrives with the anti-climax in the frustrated fourth line, which never manages to progress beyond the repeated monosyllabic *one*.

When the Host takes it upon himself to second the Knight's objection to the Monk's Tale, his manner of address is altogether different. Indeed, it is not until 2788 that he addresses the Monk direct, echoing the opening words of the Knight but adding a characteristic imprecation: 'Sire Monk, namoore of this, so God yow blesse!' Until then, he speaks of the Monk in the third person, holding him up to the other pilgrims as an object of ridicule:

> 'Ye,' quod oure Hooste, 'by seint Poules belle!
> Ye seye right sooth; this Monk he clappeth lowde.
> He spak how Fortune covered with a clowde
> I noot nevere what; and als of a "tragedie" —
> (Right now ye herde), and, pardee, no remedie
> It is for to biwaille ne compleyne

That that is doon, and als it is a peyne
(As ye han seyd) to heere of hevynesse.'
                              (VII, 2780-7 — I have altered
                                Robinson's punctuation)

Whereas the Knight speaks in carefully modulated sentences, the Host's colloquial stream rushes ahead, deflected into a swirl of oaths, asseverations and parentheses: '(As ye han seyd)' — one can see him bowing deferentially to the Knight whom he is bound to respect and is anxious to flatter. But the impression of the Host's uncontrolled utterance is created by very disciplined writing on the part of the poet, especially by the studied way in which he ensures that the ends of clauses hardly ever coincide with the ends of lines. The normal tendency of such sustained *enjambement* is to encourage fairly sophisticated, periodic syntax. But Chaucer frustrates any such tendency by his reiterations of the conjunction 'and' (always in the middle of the line) and so causes the torrent of the Host's outburst to advance in spurts.

If the reader wishes to perfect his technique in reading Chaucer's poetry aloud (or for making it resonate within his 'mind's ear') in such a way as to bring out his modulations of tone and transitions of mood, he may find that the opening lines of the Wife of Bath's Tale (III, 857-81) afford a particularly challenging and rewarding 'test piece'. The narrator's gradual insinuation, into the deceptively nostalgic Arthurian *incipit*, of her teasing satire against the Friar is wonderfully conveyed by the verse's changes of tempo and continually shifting rhythmical patterns.

# Chapter 2
## 'Of Storial Thyng That Toucheth Gentillesse': The Knight's Tale and its Chaucerian Affinities

### I

Before Chaucer compiled *The Canterbury Tales*, all his major poems were concerned with the subject of sexual love. The quality of human love that especially interested him was that which is nowadays usually designated by the medieval French term, *fine amor*. Although the application of the term was variable (and not confined to sexual love),[1] it is generally understood to suggest the idea of love as an end in itself, a passion that can both refine and destroy. It is often associated with the ideal of *gentillesse*, which Chaucer so ardently cherished.[2] There is no limit to the 'servyse' that the 'gentil' lover is prepared to undertake for his lady's 'worship', though he can never hope to 'deserve' any reward from her; if she chooses to love him, it will be the result of her own gracious 'mercy'. Sexual love thus acquires a religious dimension; for this notion of 'servyse' is analogous to the Christian doctrine of the insufficiency of human merit, and the need to rely upon divine grace for salvation. The characteristics of the 'gentil' lover are set forth most appreciatively by Chaucer's Criseyde in the lines in which she tells Troilus what first caused her to take pity on his suit. She says that she was not moved by his royal status or his military prowess, but because she found in him 'moral vertu, grounded upon trouthe':

> 'Eke gentil herte and manhod that ye hadde,
> And that ye hadde, as me thoughte, in despit
> Every thyng that souned into badde,
> As rudenesse and poeplissh appetit,
> And that youre resoun bridlede youre delit . . .'
>                                            (*TC*, IV, 1674-8)

But these are (ironically enough) almost the last words she speaks to him before she leaves Troy for the Greek camp, where she eventually succumbs to the advances of the nobly born, but far from 'gentil', Diomede.

In a passage towards the end of *Troilus and Criseyde* (V, 1772-85), Chaucer fears that he may have incurred the displeasure of his female readers by telling (in what is by far the longest of his continuous narratives) the story of a woman who was 'untrewe' in love. So, in the (unfinished)[3] *Legend of Good Women*, he performs an act of penance for this 'sin' by writing the lives of Cupid's 'seintes' (cf. *CT*, II, 61), ladies from classical mythology and history who remained faithful in love, even unto death. In the sophisticated Prologue to this collection of stories (his only such compilation outside *The Canterbury Tales*) he dreams that he finds himself in the presence of Cupid, who is angry with him for having translated the *Roman de la Rose*, 'That is an heresye ageyns my lawe', and for having written *Troilus and Criseyde* (*LGW*, G, 255-6). Referring particularly to *Troilus*, the god asks 'what eyleth the to wryte / The draf of storyes, and forgete the corn?' (*LGW*, G, 311-12) — having just given the poet an impressive bibliography of decent and honourable stories about women which he could readily have come by, instead of going out of his way to perpetuate the memory of one of the few women celebrated for being 'false' in love.

In the passage in *Troilus* where Chaucer apologized to the ladies for having written about the 'untrewe' Criseyde, he declared that he would rather have celebrated 'Penelopeës trouthe and good Alceste' (*TC*, V, 1778). He had already mentioned, earlier in this same final book (*TC*, V, 1527-33), Alceste's supreme self-sacrifice to save her husband from death. The Cupid of the *Legend* evidently regards this as a spark of grace in the renegade; and so he appears before Chaucer accompanied, not by his mother 'Seynt Venus' (cf. G, 313), but by Alceste herself, who acts as intercessor for the defendant. In his defence she gives a list of his 'good works', which mentions *The House of Fame*, *The Book of the Duchess* and *The Parlement of Foules*. The catalogue also includes his narrative about

> '. . . al the love of Palamon and Arcite
> Of Thebes, thogh the storye is known lite'
>
> (G, 408-9)

as well as the Life of Saint Cecilia, which Chaucer incorporated into *The Canterbury Tales*. The Life of Saint Cecilia became the Second Nun's Tale; the story of Palamon and Arcite became (with minimal adaptation) the Knight's Tale. Alceste's statement that the story of Palamon and Arcite 'is knowen lite' seems to imply that Chaucer is to be congratulated for discovering Boccaccio's *Il Teseida*, the principal source of his acceptable narrative,[4] just as he is to be reprehended for having gone out of his way to employ the same poet's *Il Filostrato* as the chief source for the offending *Troilus* – though Chaucer, of course, never acknowledges Boccaccio as his source for either piece.[5]

The intentionally superficial level on which the Prologue to *The*

*Legend of Good Women* operates is evident from its attitude towards *Troilus* on the one hand and the story of Palamon and Arcite on the other. No account is taken of the challenge which Chaucer had accepted by writing in *Troilus* about a 'false' heroine, where, by presenting her from the inside as well as from the outside, he had produced a far more understanding portrait of a woman than is to be found in the essays in feminine hagiography of which Cupid approves.[6] Conversely, Alceste fails to recognize that Chaucer's version of the story of Palamon and Arcite is, in some respects, no less outrageous in its attitude towards the religion of Cupid and his mother than is *Troilus*. The god of love's role in the Knight's Tale is as ambivalent as that of his namesake in the offending *Troilus*. Moreover, the portrait of Venus is decidedly less flattering than that which emerges in Book III of *Troilus*: in the Knight's Tale she is the unstable 'geery Venus' (I, 1536) who is presented as a trouble-maker.[7] Yet it is easy to understand why devotees of romance fiction should have been expected to favour the story of Palamon and Arcite in so far as it tells of the conflicting claims of love and friendship, eventually reconciled, but only after the intervention of death. One of the frustrating features of *Troilus* is that the love story proper concludes inconclusively with the discarded lover on the battlefield skirmishing with Criseyde's new lover, Diomede. The hero is eventually killed — quite irrelevantly as far as the love story is concerned — by Achilles. In the Knight's Tale, however, Emelye is fought over in the 'listes roially' by the officially organized retinues of Palamon and Arcite. The victorious Arcite receives his fatal injury as the result of being thrown by his horse during his lap of honour. As he dies in his lady's arms, he generously urges her that, if she should ever think of marrying, she should: 'Foryet nat Palamon, the gentil man' (I, 2797). Emelye, like Criseyde, is the creature of a plot that requires her to transfer her favour from one man to another; but the plot allows her to do so in a manner that wins public approval.

The first of the Canterbury tales is, therefore, concerned with a subject that Chaucer's readers would have expected him to treat and, moreover, it is one whose sentiment the most conservative among them could approve. This affords one reason for considering it, in the first instance at least, in relation to his previous compositions. Another is that it is so much longer than the other Canterbury tales that it has the dimensions of a separate poem, able to stand on its own; and it was, in any case, probably written before the great compilation was devised. I have elsewhere discussed it side by side with *Troilus and Criseyde*,[8] Chaucer's other major 'translacioun' and re-creation of a narrative poem by Boccaccio. Here I propose to approach the Knight's Tale through a work with which it has affinities of a different kind. This is another of the compositions of which Alceste approved: the 'love vision', *The Parlement of Foules*.[9]

Yet, once again, Alceste's choice of a work to commend to Cupid is a little surprising. For the argument of this poem suggests that those who make 'servyse' of Venus and Cupid their *summum bonum*, or 'supreme good', are likely to end in misery. Erotic love is here viewed indeed as 'the loveris maladye / Of Hereos' that drives Arcite almost to madness in the Knight's Tale (*CT*, I, 1373-4). In the poem's concluding episode — that of the 'parlement' of birds itself — *fine amor* is viewed in an altogether different perspective. Moreover, it is a perspective that Chaucer derived — at least in part — from that portion of the *Roman de la Rose* which provoked Cupid's denunciation of the whole poem as 'an heresye ageyns my lawe'.

After declaring that his knowledge of love is derived exclusively from books, the narrator begins the 'dream allegory' of the *Parlement of Foules* by describing how he had been reading a book 'a certeyn thing to lerne' (20). One therefore assumes that he was searching for information about some aspect of love. So it is surprising to be told that his 'olde bok totorne' was the 'Dream of Scipio', the only surviving portion of Cicero's *De Re Publica*, preserved for posterity in Macrobius's commentary upon it. Cicero, the Roman philosopher and champion of the dying republic, was concerned there, not with personal love, but public duty — with what will result in 'commune profyt', as Chaucer calls it (47). From the celestial vantage point of a 'sterry place', the younger Scipio's ancestor, Africanus, shows him how insignificant the Earth is 'At regard of the hevenes quantite'; earthly life is only a kind of death. But man's soul is immortal and can reach a place of eternal bliss, provided he devotes his life to the public good or 'commune profyt'. The only reference to sexual love, in the course of Chaucer's synopsis, is a negative one: Africanus declares that breakers of the law 'and likerous folk' (79) will, after death, be whirled about the earth in punishment for many aeons until, their purgation completed, they too will be admitted to 'this blysful place'. In other words, Africanus seems to be saying that, if you wish to reach heaven by the direct route, you should have nothing to do with the cult of Cupid, and the art of love.

Chaucer is dissatisfied with the ascetic *sentence* of this treatise: he retires to bed

> Fulfyld of thought and busy hevynesse;
> For bothe I hadde thyng which that I nolde,
> And ek I nadde that thyng that I wolde.

(89-91)

He falls asleep and his quest 'a certeyn thing to lerne' is continued in a dream. But in the dream everything is transformed and he is now granted 'that thyng that [he] wolde'. Africanus appears and transports the dreamer to the gates of a park, which would, I think, have reminded Chaucer's original readers of the park of Deduit (Mirth) that Guillaume de Lorris describes near the opening of the *Roman de la Rose*.[10] But the differences are as important as the similarities. Guillaume is concerned with the difficulty of access to the exclusive realm of *fine amor*, symbolized by the fact that his paradise of love is surrounded by a high embattled wall, whose only entrance is through an obscure wicket-gate. The entrance to the park in Chaucer's poem is, on the contrary, through conspicuous, broad double gates. The only restraint appears in the text of two contradictory legends inscribed above the respective gates: whereas the one invites the postulant to enter into 'that blysful place / Of hertes hele' (127-8), the other warns him to avoid this haunt of Disdain and Frustration ('Daunger'), this place of sterility, where 'the fish in prysoun is al drye' (139). There is evidently no difficulty in entering into the service of Cupid: what concerns Chaucer is the question of whether it is worthwhile. His attitude is, in fact, much closer to that of Jean de Meun, the detached, amused, semi-philosophical author of the 'anatomy of sex' that comprises the continuation of the 'art of love' with which de Lorris had begun the *Roman de la Rose*. It is, presumably, this latter portion of the work which the Cupid of the *Legend of Good Women* had in mind when he condemned the poem as 'an heresye ageyns my lawe'.

The ambivalent character of passionate or (as we would say) 'romantic' love is confirmed as soon as the dreamer passes through the portal into the garden. At first he finds himself in a paradisal landscape, a veritable *locus amoenus*,[11] but, as he approaches a temple of brass, the atmosphere becomes somewhat sinister and sultry. In a dark corner of the temple Venus lies half naked and — even more provocatively — half clothed in a transparent dress: 'Ther nas no thikkere cloth of no defense' (273). On the wall there hang, as trophies, many broken bows of 'maydenes' (of either sex) who have wasted their time in the service of 'Dyane the chaste'. On the other side are painted the figures of those whom tyrannic love has destroyed. They are all practitioners of *fine amor*, who pursued the 'servyse' of Venus and Cupid as their be-all and end-all. They include Dido, Piramus and Thisbe, Cleopatra, Tristram and Isaude, and — significantly — Troilus.

Without commenting on the meaning of this episode, Chaucer passes to another part of the park, where the various species of birds (representing different types and social classes of men) are assembled, on St Valentine's Day, to choose their mates. The choice is a straightforward business for all of them except for the three principal practitioners of *fine amor*. In the Knight's Tale two rival princes seek the hand of a beautiful lady; here three 'tercelet' eagles vie for the claw of an exquisite 'formel' eagle, whom the goddess Nature (president of this 'parlement' of assembled birds) displays in the palm of her hand. These 'gentil' eagles are as obsessive in their love as are Palamon and Arcite; the unsuccessful wooers must remain single for the rest of their lives, because, according to the ethos of *fine amor*, nobody who is genuinely in love could ever contemplate transferring his affection to another lady.

The goddess Nature had appeared in the latter part of the *Roman de la Rose*,[12] but she is derived ultimately from the personification in Alain de Lille's poem, *De Planctu Naturae*,[13] or, as Chaucer calls this product of the twelfth-century 'School of Chartres', 'the Pleynt of Kynde' (316). She is the Creator's deputy or 'vicaire'; she is responsible for the physical aspect of creation, both of the macrocosm and of the little world of Man, whereas God reserves to Himself the creation of Man's immortal part. In Chaucer's poem she is responsible for creating the archetypes of the various species; but she also oversees the functions of procreation that keep these species in perpetual being. Nature is virtually a composite figure, made up of an aggregation of the individual natures of the various species; for a creature to obey her promptings is simply to act in accordance with the Divinely ordained principle of its own being — with what, in the Middle Ages, was known as Natural Law. In Alain's poem, Nature laments that, whereas all other creatures obey her decrees, Man alone offends against them. Perhaps Chaucer's purpose in representing classes of human beings as species of birds is to offer a vision of mankind still innocent in its sexual practices — still observing Natural Law by ensuring that Venus and Cupid subserve the purposes of God's deputy.

Nature exhibits a universal tolerance: she can appreciate the refined sensibilities and protracted pleadings of the 'gentil' eagles; but, at the same time, she sympathizes with the impatience to fly away with their mates that is so vociferously expressed by the humbler birds, such as the duck, goose and cuckoo. For Nature always listens with one ear 'to murmur of the lewednesse behynde' (520) — to the comments of the uneducated backbenchers in the parliament. It is not Nature, but various birds of 'gentil' rank, practitioners of *fine amor*, who ridicule the unrefined, yet commonsense, sentiments which the humbler birds utter in their suitably forthright, colloquial idioms.

This concept of Nature allows a certain amount of fresh air to dispel the hot-house atmosphere of the cult of Venus and Cupid, who are always ready to establish a tyranny in men's hearts. At the same time, the attitude of this 'vicaire of the almyghty Lord' (379) towards sexual love is far more benevolent than that which Africanus adopts from the lofty remoteness of his 'sterry place'. For her, love is a contributor to 'commune profyt'. As a creator himself, Chaucer has considerable empathy with this viceroy of the Creator, as may be seen in his delight in coarse and ugly natures (for example, in the description of the Miller in the General Prologue of the *Canterbury Tales*) as well as in human counterparts to the beautiful 'formel' eagle. Commentators have long recognized in the variety of attitudes and idioms to be heard in the human aviary of this poem a foreshadowing of the performances of the different narrators of the *Tales*. However, in order to approach the Knight's Tale specifically, we must confine our attention to the contributions made by the 'gentil' birds to Nature's 'parlement'.

The pleas of the three rival eagles are, like the characters of Palamon and Arcite, differentiated but equally balanced.[14] Nature stipulates that the formel must give her approval as to 'whoso he be that shulde be hire feere' (410). The goddess's use of the term 'feere' [mate] implies that Chaucer regarded equality between the spouses as the natural state of affairs. But the first tercelet, who is of royal blood, insists on debasing himself, as befits a practitioner of *fine amor*: politely 'correcting' Nature, he states that he would 'serve' the formel as 'my soverayn lady, and not my fere'. He is prepared to be torn to pieces, if ever he proves to be unfaithful to her, or if he should be an 'Avauntour' — that is, 'one who boasts of his lady's love', a most heinous crime in a cult which insisted upon humility and discretion. He recognizes that he has no claim on her, apart from what he voluntarily grants him through her 'mercy'. Nevertheless a competitive note is struck when he asserts: 'And syn that non loveth hire so wel as I' (435). The second eagle, 'of lower kynde' (i.e. of lower rank), takes up the challenge and points out that he has served her longer than his rival. But he is likewise careful not to insist on any right to her:

> 'And *if* she shulde have loved for long lovynge,
> To me ful-longe hadde be the guerdonynge.'
>
> (454-5)

It is, however, the third eagle who is the most interesting. He is able to claim neither the rank of the first, nor the length of service of the second; but he is gifted with intelligence and skill in forensic rhetoric.[15] He begins with a prologue or *exordium*, in which he emphasizes the disadvantages of speaking last:

> 'Now sires, ye seen the lytel leyser heere;
> For every foul cryeth out to ben ago
> Forth with his make, or with his lady deere;
> And ek Nature hireself ne wol not heere,
> For taryinge here, not half that I wolde seye,
> And but I speke, I mot for sorwe deye.'

(464-9)

He is employing a standard 'topic' of the *exordium* known to rhetoricians as *captatio benevolentiae*, or attempt to secure the good will and sympathy of one's audience.[16] This eagle is careful not to draw attention to the advantage of having the last word. His advantage appears in the first line of the next stanza, when his aggressive instinct comes into its own as he swoops upon the argument of his immediate predecessor: 'Of long servyse *avaunte* I me nothyng.' He thereby insinuates that his rival is guilty of one of the worst crimes against the ethos of *fine amor*. His whole procedure is an example of what the author of the *Rhetorica ad Herennium* (I, vii) calls 'insinuatio' — a feature of the indirect *exordium*.[17] Having disposed of the opposition, the eagle makes the positive point that depth of feeling rather than length of service is what matters in love. He too adds a disclaimer, declaring that, in making this point, he is not referring to any merits or rights of his own.

The narrator declares that he has never heard 'so gentil ple in love' as these three exhibitions, and the falcon, who is elected as spokesman for the birds of prey, observes that it is impossible to 'preve by resoun' which of the three loves the formel best, their arguments being so well balanced. He concludes:

> 'I can not se that argumentes avayle:
> Thanne semeth it there moste be batayle.'

(538-9)

This is precisely the solution that will be proposed in the Knight's Tale; but it is interesting to see that it is here rejected. Clearly, Chaucer considered the chivalric practice of fighting tournaments for a lady's favour an outmoded procedure. Eventually Nature decrees that the formel shall choose for herself — a privilege that is hardly accorded to Emelye in the Knight's Tale. The goddess Nature does, however, direct the formel's attention particularly to the royal eagle. The formel shows that same reluctance to serve Venus or Cupid for the present as does Emelye when she prays in the temple of the chaste Diana.[18] Such maidenly modesty was regarded as becoming by Chaucer's contemporaries. This can be seen even more clearly in the account of Virginia, the tragic victim in the Physician's Tale, whom Nature (once again appearing in person) introduces as her masterpiece, whom she has created 'to the worshipe of my lord' (*CT*, VI, 26) — i.e. God Himself.[19] In the *Parlement* Nature readily grants the formel's request for a year's postponement of her decision.

The poet's view of Nature is not a sentimentalized one. The 'merlioun', himself a bird of prey, denounces the cuckoo as 'Thow mortherere of the heysoge [hedge-sparrow] on the braunche / That broughte the forth' and, more wittily, as 'wormes corupcioun' (611-14). Nor, in spite of the chorus of rejoicing as the birds fly off with their mates, is the conclusion one of unalloyed contentment: two of the eagles are doomed to a life of perpetual disappointment and sorrow. Nevertheless, the vigorous delight that the poet takes in representing the courtship rituals of such a variety of birds offers a vision of life that may lead one to think of the final scene of this ode for St Valentine's Day as if it were Chaucer's Song of Innocence.

It is usually thought that the *Parlement* precedes *Troilus* in the Chaucer canon. However that may be, when one turns from the former to the latter, it is as if one were to turn from Chaucer's Song of Innocence to his Song of Experience — in the sense of a different 'vision' of the same world. We pass from comedy to 'tragedye'; we abandon the walled insulation of a dream-garden for the walled insecurity of a besieged city; we exchange the maternal goddess, Nature, for the meretricious goddess, Fortune; we move from an idealized vision of mankind (as innocent as the birds in its love-making) to the representation of weak, flawed humanity. The Knight's Tale, in spite of its 'happy ending', likewise participates in this harsher vision of life. In it we hear slightly less about Fortune than we do in *Troilus*, but we hear considerably more of the pagan gods, who are conceived of both anthropomorphically, as members of the classical pantheon, and astrologically, according to the medieval tradition whereby seven of them lend their names to the planets, capable of exerting an 'influence' upon human affairs. Arcite seeks the patronage of Mars, Palamon that of Venus and, as we have noted, Emelye that of Diana. These divinities were already active in Chaucer's Italian source. But the most remarkable, and alarming, of these powers is one who had no part to play in the *Teseida*: the role of Saturn in bringing about Arcite's death is Chaucer's own invention.

Almost as significant as this additon to his principal source is one of Chaucer's minor excisions from the *Teseida*. When Boccaccio's Arcita dies, his soul flies up to a celestial vantage point, similar to the one from which Scipio looked down upon the Earth — indeed, this distant 'despising' of worldly vanity was, by the fourteenth century, a well-established rhetorical 'commonplace' or *topos*.[20] The *Teseida* passage is Chaucer's principal source when he introduces his famous version of the *topos* at the end of *Troilus and Criseyde*, where Troilus's soul looks down upon 'This litel spot of erthe', and he 'fully gan despise / This wrecched world' and laughs at those who mourn his death (V, 1807-27). The 'tragedye' of *Troilus* ends almost where the comedy of the *Parlement* begins. At the end of *Troilus*, Chaucer uses this heavenward flight to usher in his Christian epilogue, addressed to potential lovers among his audience of 'yonge, fresshe folkes, he or she'. In the Knight's Tale, however, Chaucer disclaims any knowledge of the destination of Arcite's soul, declaring 'I nam no divinistre' (cf. I, 2809-15). Not only does this story of pagan antiquity[21] remain uncontaminated by any Christian intrusions, it also refuses to hold out any hope of compensation, in an after-life, for troubles endured in what Theseus calls 'this foule prisoun of this lyf' (I, 3061).

Before we explore the poem's profounder implications, we must remember that it is offered, in the context of the *Canterbury Tales*, as entertainment: in a passage that has obviously been inserted — or ' in eched' — for the occasion, the Knight enters into the spirit of the game when he exclaims: 'Lat se now who shal the soper wynne' (I, 891). To adopt the terminology of medieval literary analysis, we must appreciate the tale's *sensus*, or superficial meaning, before we can proceed to examine its deeper significance, or *sententia*. But what manner of entertainment does it afford? G.L. Kittredge described *Troilus and Criseyde* as 'the first novel, in the modern sense, that ever was written in the world'.[22] Although this description is, in many important ways, inadequate, it does at least provide the modern reader with a familiar way into that poem; once inside, he can modify his definition of its genre in accordance with his experience of the work. Similarly, it is possible to approach several of the Tales as if they were 'short stories'. But a reader is likely to be perplexed and disappointed if he approaches the Knight's Tale as a short novel or a 'long short story'. In *Troilus*, there is quite as much introspection as in any psychological novel. Indeed, almost the whole of the significant part of its slow-moving action is secret, even when one or both of the lovers are present at a social gathering or public meeting.[23] The public neither knows nor cares about their relationship. The Knight's Tale is an altogether more extrovert performance. From the moment when Theseus and his hunting party interrupt the secret duel between Palamon and Arcite in the grove, the love affair of the rival knights becomes as much a matter of public concern and spectacle as is the altercation between the three eagles in *The*

*Parlement of Foules*. Theseus cannot avoid regarding their love dispute in the context of 'commune profyt'.

*Il Teseida* is the earliest example of a Renaissance vernacular epic: not only does it contain the same number of books as Virgil's *Aeneid*; it even has the same number of lines (if one excludes from the count the interspersed sonnets).[24] In reducing Boccaccio's twelve books to four well contrasted and balanced parts,[25] Chaucer is tending towards the compactness of drama. Indeed, the tale's dramatic potentialities were recognized in the Elizabethan age, when no fewer than three plays were made from it, although the only one to have survived is *The Two Noble Kinsmen* by Fletcher and Shakespeare.[26] But, although the shaping spirit that formed the Knight's Tale may be moving in that direction, it has a long distance to travel before arriving at true drama. Several critics have spoken of an element of pageantry in the tale,[27] but it is much more dramatic than a pageant. A different modern theatrical analogy may be provisionally more illuminating.

I have often regretted that nobody has made the Knight's Tale into an opera. A Visconti or a Zeffirelli would find plenty of scope for his talents in the challenge of its *mise en scène*, with its crowd scenes, its detailed ceremonial, splendid processions and the tournament, in Part IV, inflated into a miniature battle within the confines of an arena. The designer of symbolic multi-purpose sets would find a challenge in the fact that the grove in Part II, the 'theatre' in Parts III and IV, and the funeral pyre in Part IV, are all supposed to be located on the same spot.[28] The 'disposition' of scenes and speeches has something of the formality of an opera arranged in graded 'numbers' — arias, duets, ensembles and choruses. Again, just as the conventions of Grand Opera can transcend the limitations of naturalistic representation, so, at the end of Part I, in what is virtually a male 'duet', Arcite (from one side of the stage, as it were) utters a formal 'complaint', while 'Upon that oother syde Palamon' (I, 1275) pronounces a parallel 'complaint' — even though the former is at large in Thebes, while the latter is still imprisoned in Athens. Arcite advances from complaining about the irony of his own situation, now that physical liberty has banished him from his daily sight of Emelye, to a lament for the irony of the human predicament in general (I, 1223-74). A similar universalizing development occurs in Palamon's closely corresponding complaint (1281-98; 1303-33): 'O crueel goddes that governe / This world with byndyng of youre word eterne . . .'. Both laments are based upon passages from Boethius's *Consolation of Philosophy*, though not from the parts that offer consolation. The formal balancing of these 'complaints' is symptomatic of the fact that any attempt to distinguish between the two

cousins on moral grounds is bound to fail, since it is an essential part
of the poet's design to show that neither can be said to *deserve* his
fate; the fortunes of the one might easily have been the fortunes of
the other. Perhaps the most one dare say is that Palamon (whose
patroness is Venus) would have to be sung by a tenor; Arcite (the
protégé of Mars) by a bass!

At several points in the tale one is aware of the presence of a
chorus, applauding, or weeping at, the 'gentil' behaviour that is
exhibited before their eyes. The cousins are not even allowed to settle
their secret duel in the grove without being interrupted by Theseus,
his Queen and her sister, Emelye, and a whole hunting party, in order
to provide a moving ensemble as a concerted finale for Part II. When
Theseus eventually decides that it is time for Emelye to marry
Palamon, he does not take the young people aside to sound them out;
instead he makes the proposition in a public assembly. The Duke's
speech on the subject is set up as the crowning 'number' of the whole
work. As he is about to address the 'parlement' he acts as one who is
conscious that the spotlight is trained upon him:

> Whan they were set, and hust was al the place,
> And Theseus abiden hadde a space
> Er any word cam fram his wise brest,
> His eyen sette he ther as was his lest.
> And with a sad visage he siked stille,
> And after that right thus he seyde his wille . . .

> (I, 2981-6)

But the most memorable solo performance is, of course, the speech of
the dying Arcite, with its unforgettable poetic *rallentando*:

> 'What is this world? what asketh men to have?
> Now with his love, now in his colde grave
> Allone, withouten any compaignye.'

> (I, 2777-9)

Finally, it is worth observing that, just as some of the finest operas
are based upon notoriously feeble plots, so the plot of the Knight's
Tale is one that might be regarded as unworthy of a second-rate
romance.[29] It tolerates such contrivances as disguise, divine intervention, and (most notoriously) coincidence — the particular instance at
I, 1663 ff. eliciting from the narrator a blustering and quite unconvincing attempt at justification. Yet Chaucer's poetic imagination and
his power of expresssion altogether transcend these mechanical
defects.

## II

The story of 'al the love of Palamon and Arcite' begins with a prologue in which neither of the cousins and 'sworn brothers' participate. The back-drop for the scene is the Temple of Clemency outside Athens — appropriately enough, as Theseus is about to perform his first act of 'pitee'. A company of Theban widows, dressed in black and standing two by two, has been waiting for the return of the Duke from his conquest of the land of Femenye, where he has acquired a bride, in the person of its Amazonian Queen Ypolita. As the triumphal procession enters (from the left) the eldest of the widows (leader of the chorus) approaches the Duke. Theseus is the first (as he is also the last) character to speak in the poem. As soon as he hears of the impious and inhuman atrocity committed against the corpses of the widows' former husbands, 'No neer Atthenes wolde he go ne ride' (968), but, having despatched Ypolita, her young sister Emelye, and attendant ladies to the city (*exeunt* right), he turns the body of the procession round, and immediately marches to Thebes (*exeunt* left). I have added 'stage directions' in order to indicate how imaginatively Chaucer uses spatial direction for dramatic effect — far more so than Shakespeare does in the corresponding scene (Act I, Scene i) of *The Two Noble Kinsmen*.[30] The war with Creon takes place 'off stage', as it were. Theseus orders the two knights of the Theban royal house, found lying side by side on the battle field, to be imprisoned 'Perpetuelly, — he nolde no raunsoun' (1024). The harshness of this sentence shows the serious-ness with which he regards the tyranny of Creon and his adherents. Theseus is not waging war — as often happened in fourteenth-century Europe — as a game of hazard that would yield plunder for the victors and wealth in the form of payments for ransom. He has conducted this campaign in the spirit of a crusade. Moreover, he recognizes in the young Palamon and Arcite a potentially long-lasting threat to his realm. And, indeed, when Palamon later escapes from prison, he does plan to make war against his former captor (1482-4). The Duke's lack of mercenary interest in the captives is confirmed when he later releases Arcite 'withouten any raunsoun' (1205).[31]

The true Act One, Scene One, discovers the two Theban knights some years later in Theseus's prison tower, its gloom relieved by the prospect of the garden into which Emelye enters a-Maying: 'And as an aungel hevenysshly she soong' (1055).[32] Palamon's first sight of her is framed by a harsh and formidable surround: 'A wyndow, thikke of many a barre / Of iren greet and square as any sparre'

(1075-6). It is not surprising that the prisoner thinks he sees a vision of Venus, and kneels down to petition her to deliver them from captivity. When Arcite catches sight of her he immediately employs the language of *fine amor*, hoping for her 'mercy and hir grace' (1120). There then develops the quarrel that converts them from 'sworn brothers' into deadly rivals.

If we compare this altercation with the pleas of the three eagles in *The Parlement of Foules*, we may observe in detail the difference between 'Innocence' and 'Experience'. The sudden vision of feminine beauty so excites the two males, caged together for so long, that it induces a pathetically childish squabble. Palamon claims 'I loved hire first, and tolde thee my wo / As to my conseil . . .' (1146-7). Arcite retorts that 'paramour I lovede hire first er thow', since Palamon merely reverenced her as a goddess whereas 'myn is love, as to a creature'. It will be remembered that the second eagle based his case upon the length of his 'servyse' — an argument which was indeed taken seriously by practitioners of 'courtly love'. Palamon's claim reads like a parody of this argument, since his 'servyse' exceeds Arcite's by only a few seconds. Palamon already thinks of her as '*my* lady' at 1143, and continues to do so during the encounter with his cousin in the grove (1588). By the end of the tale he can in truth claim length of service — longer than that of almost any lover in romance. As Theseus observes to Emelye:

> 'Syn he hath served yow so many a yeer,
> And had for yow so greet adversitee,
> It moste been considered, leeveth me;
> For gentil mercy oghte to passen right.'
>
> (3086-9)

The adroitness of the argument with which Arcite seeks to undermine his cousin's claim to priority is comparable to the way in which the third eagle succeeds in turning his predecessor's own argument against him. But it is less damaging, since it amounts to nothing more than a quibble – as ridiculous as Palamon's original claim. Yet Arcite eventually perceives the absurdity of the contention, as is evident from his allusion to the fable of the dogs striving for the bone; and he returns to a recognition of the hopeless situation of the two of them, when he blankly concludes: 'Heere in this prisoun moote we endure' (1185). Ironically enough, within a few lines he has been released from prison as the result of the good offices of Perotheus, the friend of Theseus 'syn thilke day that they were children lite'.

This episode is important, not only on account of its contribution

to the action, but because, at the moment when the cousins become
deadly rivals, it celebrates a friendship so indissoluble

> That whan that oon was deed, soothly to telle,
> His felawe wente and soughte hym doun in helle.
>
> (1199-200)

Part I concludes, as we have seen, with the poetic 'duet' which,
though lacking the drama of the earlier exchanges between the
cousins, is far more profound in its appreciation of the ironies of the
human condition.

  Most of Part II is set in the grove. Seven years have passed; the
newly escaped Palamon enters and conceals himself in the bushes.
Then (with characteristically 'operatic' improbability) Arcite (disguised as Philostrate) enters 'to doon his observaunce to May' (1500).
The text is quoted of the 'roundel' that 'loude he song ayeyn the
sonne shene' — perhaps it is set to the same tune as Emelye's May
song in the prison scene. After a while his mood changes and he falls
into a 'studie' (1530). He laments Juno's continued hostility towards
the royal house of his native Thebes; and he bewails his hopeless love
for Emelye — only to be surprised and denounced by one who
declares: 'I am Palamon, thy mortal foo' (1590). Instead of disposing
of his unarmed rival, Arcite generously offers to provide victuals and
weapons for Palamon. Darkness descends, and, when the lights go
up again, Arcite returns, and there follows one of the great moments
of romantic pathos that would appeal especially to a 'gentil'
audience:

> Ther nas no good day, ne no saluyng,
> But streight, withouten word or rehersyng,
> Everich of hem heelp for to armen oother
> As freendly as he were his owene brother.
>
> (1649-52)

Then they fight like wild beasts, only to be interrupted by Theseus,
the Queen, Emelye and attendant courtiers and huntsmen. The
improbability of this second unexpected meeting, or 'unset stevene'
(cf. 1524), causes the narrator to surpass himself in disingenuous
protestation (1663-72).

  One of the most interesting features of the famous episode that
follows is the way in which Theseus's changes of mood are
represented poetically by carefully modulated shifts in linguistic
register. These modulations may be heard from the moment when
this upholder of order sees, against the rising sun, silhouettes of two
men fighting 'withouten juge or oother officere' until that when he

finally decrees that they shall settle their suit for Emelye 'in a lystes roially' (cf. 1712-13 and 1884). For a second time he allows himself to be moved by the supplications of women. He first reflects, in appropriately ethical terminology for a 'governour':

> 'That lord hath litel of discrecioun
> That in swich cas kan no divisioun.'
>
> (1779-80)

But his idiom becomes altogether more colloquial when he observes that their quarrel was due to love: 'Who may been a fool, but if he love?' (1799). He continues to muse:

> 'But this is yet the beste game of alle,
> That she for whom they han this jolitee
> Kan hem therfore as muche thank as me.
> She woot namoore of al this hoote fare,
> By God, than woot a cokkow or an hare!
> But all moot ben assayed, hoot and coold;
> A man moot ben a fool, or yong or oold, —
> I woot it by myself ful yore agon,
> For in my tyme a servant was I oon.'
>
> (1806-14)[33]

But essentially these lines convey the amused tolerance of a middle-aged man for the impetuosity of youth.[34]

Theseus is here presented as the humane ruler. His motive for clemency is expressed in Chaucer's favourite line (it is echoed, for example, in CT IV, 1986 and V, 479): 'For pitee renneth soone in gentil herte' (1761). His humanity is confirmed when, near the beginning of Part IV, he modifies the original arrangements for the tournament so as to prevent 'destruccioun' of those of 'gentil blood' and 'to shapen that they shal nat dye' (2533-60). This move effectively answers the charge, brought against him by some critics, of being throughout the tale a ruthless political opportunist. A scheming politician would hardly wish to produce the situation where a discontented rival survives alongside the married victor. Indeed, this possibility evidently so worried the authors of *The Two Noble Kinsmen* that they adopted the barbarous expedient of making Theseus insist that the cousins shall agree that the one who is defeated shall be executed.[35]

At the conclusion of Part II, the benevolent and enlightened Duke appears to be master of the situation. Meanwhile Part III is devoted almost entirely to the gods. Its design is as significant as that of the

amphitheatre which Theseus constructs to accommodate the lists.
First come the descriptions of the oratories (within the theatre),
dedicated to the deities most immediately concerned with the issue in
hand: Venus, Mars and Diana. When Palamon and Arcite bring their
supporters to Athens, their respective champions, Lycurge and
Emetreus, are made the subjects of two scrupulously balanced
descriptions. Then follows the account of Emelye's visit to Diana's
temple, flanked by accounts of the visits of her suitors to the temples
of their respective patrons. All this is preceded by a description of
the Duke's architectural design, and succeeded (in a concluding
passage of similar length) by an episode that is dominated by the
appearance of a god to whom Theseus had not erected an oratory
within the compass of the amphitheatre that seems to symbolize his
notion of an ordered universe.

The three descriptions of the oratories call forth some of the most
memorable lines in the poem. The description of the temple of Venus
has the same disturbing quality as that of her temple of brass in *The
Parlement of Foules* — partly because both are based upon the same
passage in Book VII of the *Teseida*. But it is the account of the
Temple of Mars in Thrace, depicted upon the walls of his oratory in
the 'theatre', which is the most chilling. The depicted temple is placed
below a forest

> In which ther dwelleth neither man ne best,
> With knotty, knarry, bareyne trees olde,
> Of stubbes sharpe and hidouse to biholde.
>
> (1976-8)

The temple is like a prison: the description of its door reminds one of
the prison window through which the cousins caught sight of Emelye
(though the temple is windowless):

> The dore was al of adamant eterne,
> Yclenched overthwart and endelong
> With iren tough; and for to make it strong,
> Every pyler, the temple to sustene,
> Was tonne-greet, of iren bright and shene.
>
> (1990-4)

Elsewhere in the tale, martial combat is invested with a certain
glamour, as in the summons to arms (2106-16), and in the use of the
poetic diction of the alliterative 'gestes' and romances to describe the
thrust and clangour of the tournament (2602-16). But the relentless
catalogue (1995-2040) of various forms of violence and death places
the profession of arms in a less attractive context: 'The smylere with

the knyf under the cloke'; 'The colde deeth, with mouth gapyng upright'; 'The careyne in the busk, with throte ycorve'. In Mars' 'divisioun' are also to be found less prestigious occupations, such as those of the barber, the butcher and the smith.[36] The barber is included because of his surgical activities; but it should also be remembered that Arcite later pledges to Mars:

> 'My beerd, myn heer, that hongeth long adoun,
> That nevere yet ne felte offensioun
> Of rasour nor of shere . . .'

(2415-17)

The climax comes with the lines:

> And al above, depeynted in a tour,
> Saugh I Conquest, sittynge in greet honour,
> With the sharpe swerd over his heed
> Hangynge by a soutil twynes threed.

(2027-30)

The reader may well remember, as he ponders these lines, that Theseus himself has been dignified with the title of 'Conqueror' since the very opening of the tale (862).

It has sometimes been argued that, in praying to Mars rather than Venus, Arcite is more interested in winning the tournament than in marrying the lady. But a careful reading of his petition will show that this is not so (see especially 2383-405): the love of the two suitors is equally intense. The most interesting prayer is that of Emelye to Diana (2297-330). As we have observed,[37] her wish to remain a virgin votaress of the goddess of chastity would have seemed to Chaucer's contemporaries the proper sentiment for a young lady to cherish. Moreover, it is appropriate that an Amazon should desire to continue to follow the queen and huntress, chaste and fair, 'in the wodes wilde'. Since she does not desire to subject herself to a mortal man, 'to ben a wyf and be with childe', it is perhaps a mistake for her to invoke Diana to help her 'For tho thre formes that thou hast in thee'. For one of the tripartite goddess's manifestations is as Lucina, to whom women in labour cry (cf. 2083-6). But Emelye's reluctance to marry is motivated by something more than a proper maidenly modesty. She is genuinely distressed by the strife between the cousins on her account; her greatest desire is that Diana shall 'sende love and pees betwixe hem two'. Finally, she asks that, if she is destined to marry, may Diana 'sende me hym that moost desireth me'. The solution (advanced in *The Parlement of Foules*), that the lady should be allowed to choose for herself, is evidently as unthinkable in this antique society as it is in certain Asian communities today.

The promises of success made by Venus amd Mars to their respective protégés being mutually exclusive, strife breaks out in heaven which Jupiter (symbol of justice and order) is unable to resolve. So it falls to his father, Saturn, the oldest of the gods, and the most wide-ranging of the planets, to find a solution. As the narrator remarks, reconciliation is contrary to Saturn's nature (2451). But he is not required to act 'agayn his kynde'; he merely produces one of his characteristic 'accidents', by commanding Pluto to send a fiend to frighten Arcite's horse, so that it throws its rider and causes his fatal wound. Saturn embodies a primitive, arbitrary malevolence. He is the bringer of famine and pestilence (through the exercise of his 'influence' or *influenza*), and produces other incalculable 'disasters'. This planet is the planner's bane. He declares his nature in his address of comfort to his grand-daughter, Venus (2453-78). It is one of the most powerful speeches in the poem; and it offers no comfort whatsoever to mortal men. It confirms the alien character of the gods, already delineated in the 'duet' at the end of Part I.

At the beginning of Part IV, Theseus is permitted a little more glory. The detailed description of the preliminaries of the great tournament culminates in the appearance of the Duke at a window, 'arrayed right as he were a god in trone' (2529). As one watches this manifestation of Theseus, the 'Conqueror', it is difficult to forget the precarious exaltation of 'Conquest, sittynge in greet honour' . . . 'al above, depeynted in a tour' (2027-8). When viewed in the shadow of the transactions of Part III, Theseus's posture looks like an act of unwitting hubris. In spite of the Duke's detailed plans for preventing 'mortal bataille' (2533-65), Nemesis follows when Saturn contrives the death of the victorious Arcite. Theseus's humane and even-tempered scale of cosmic order and harmony is untuned by this seemingly senseless accident. He can be comforted only by 'his olde fader Egeus', who knows 'this worldes transmutacioun . . . Joye after wo, and wo after gladnesse'. In other words, the aged man's bleak philosophy of *contemptus mundi* —

> 'This world nys but a thurghfare ful of wo,
> And we been pilgrymes, passynge to and fro.
> Deeth is an ende of every worldly soore.'

$$(2847-9)$$

— is the only one that appears to allow for the activities of the most ancient of the 'gods'.

The brief sample that we are given of Egeus's speech has sometimes been condemned as platitudinous. Certainly it consists of commonplaces; but, then, so does the celebrated final speech of Theseus. Before we can hope to understand Chaucer's procedure, it is necessary first to appreciate precisely with what kind of commonplaces we are concerned, and also the ways in which they are employed. The influence of certain passages from *The Consolation of Philosophy* upon Theseus's final speech has long been recognized. Boethius's treatise is concerned to offer general consolation against the onslaughts of Fortune. But the Knight's Tale also draws upon a much more ancient and specific type of consolation: the consolation for death, or *consolatio mortis*.[38] In classical Greek and Roman times a repertory of 'topics' of consolation, or *solacia*, was established for the practical purpose of comforting the bereaved. In the Christian era the old 'topics' were suitably adapted to conform to the aspirations and dogma of the new religion. For example, one of the standard *solacia* of antiquity, especially appropriate when the deceased was cut off in youth, was the argument that Theseus eventually applies in the case of Arcite:

> 'And certeinly a man hath moost honour
> To dyen in his excellence and flour,
> Whan he is siker of his goode name
> . . .
> Than whan his name apalled is for age'
>
> (3047-53)

This argument was known as the *solacium* of the *'opportunitas mortis'*. Its Christian counterpart is the argument that, by dying young, a man avoids opportunities for committing sin, and so is more assured of salvation than if he had lived longer. This is one of several Christian *solacia* that are used in *Pearl*, where the anonymous poet is concerned to console himself for the apparently meaningless death of his daughter before she was two years old. In the fourteenth century, the use of such 'topics' is not restricted to works of fiction. In 1348 Edward III's fifteen-year-old daughter, Joan, died of the plague when she was travelling to join her fiancé, the Infante of Castile. Letters from the English King to the Spanish court have survived. They too are heavily dependent upon the standard Christian *solacia*.[39] However, as the Knight's Tale is set in pagan times, Chaucer employs only *solacia* of the antique kind, just as he had deliberately kept his narrative free from Boccaccio's account of the heavenward flight of Arcita's soul and, consequently, of anything corresponding to the Christian conclusion of *Troilus*.

The other preliminary point that needs to be emphasized is that, in classical and medieval rhetorical practice, 'topics' may be used in two

ways; they may either be employed at their face value, or deployed
tactically (and sometimes disingenuously) as a means of persuasion.
These commonly held beliefs, probabilities, or 'stock responses' were
used by rhetoricians as the counterpart to the self-evident propositions that a logician employs as premises when constructing a
syllogism. Aristotle had applied the term 'enthymeme' to the
rhetorician's kind of syllogism (though the term subsequently
acquired several different meanings).[40] When 'topics' are used
disingenuously the argument becomes what Chaucer elsewhere calls
a 'sophyme'.[41] Egeus employs the 'topics' associated with the
*consolatio mortis* at their face value, whereas his son deploys them in
order to induce his hearers to adopt a certain course of action
(though I am not, of course, suggesting that Theseus's speech is
disingenuous).

Like the old man in the Pardoner's Tale, Egeus has seen all that
this world can offer and he has no longer any relish for it. He has
acquired the unsophisticated wisdom of old age that is no longer
embarrassed by the fact that the great truths are often the great
platitudes: for him the simplicities of traditional wisdom have
replaced the ingenuities of dialectic.

When Theseus, in his final address to the 'parlement', refers to
Arcite's having departed 'out of this foule prisoun of this lyf', it is
obvious that his father's philosophy of *contemptus mundi* has
impressed him. Yet there is something in the Duke, still in his prime
of life, that forbids him to resign himself altogether to such an ascetic
position. As a 'governour' and active ruler of men, he cannot yet
afford to turn his back upon life and clothe himself in his shroud. By
the time he addresses the assembly, he has made a fresh attempt to
'save appearances'.[42]

In order to avoid misunderstanding this speech, it is necessary to
assign it to the correct branch of philosophy. Because it begins by
referring to 'the Firste Moevere of the cause above' (2987), it may
appear to be an exercise in Metaphysics and an attempt to argue
from First Principles. But what Theseus offers is a 'longe serye' (3067)
— a lengthy argument — that consists not of a succession of syllogisms, but of a sequence of 'topics' which he regards as constituting
the links in 'the faire cheyne of love' (2988) made by the 'Firste
Moevere' (whom Aristotle identified with God). There is no logical
demonstration of the operation of a principle of love in the universe.
As an example of metaphysical thinking, or as a theodicy (such as
*The Consolation of Philosophy*), it is unsatisfactory. It can no more
'justify' the tragedy of Arcite's death than can the teleological scheme
of 'gods' and planetary 'influences' earlier in the poem. Moreover,
there is an apparent inconsistency in the poem's cosmology that

becomes evident in Theseus's speech. In Part III, where Jupiter is represented as one of the seven planetary 'gods', he is impotent, being unable to resolve the strife between Venus and Mars. But Theseus elevates Jupiter, the symbol of justice and order, above the system of the planets, raises him above the Primum Mobile (the outermost sphere of creation) and identifies 'Jupiter the kyng' with the 'Firste Moevere' Himself (3035-8), who first made 'the faire cheyne of love' that binds all the elements of creation in harmony. If the Knight's Tale were a treatise on metaphysics or cosmology, the apparent discrepancy between these two 'models' would require rigorous examination.

But Theseus's speech is not a statement of the poet's own philosophy of cosmic order; he is presented as a wise pagan ruler who must do what he can with the concepts that are available to him. The speech belongs to the domain of Politics rather than that of Metaphysics; it involves an exercise of — to adopt Aristotle's distinction — the practical rather than the speculative intellect. As a statesman, he has the responsibility 'to maken vertu of necessitee' (3042) and to practise conscientiously the art of the possible within the far-from-perfect environment of 'this wrecched world adoun' (2995). An effective monarch must act in the belief that the world is ultimately governed by 'Jupiter the kyng', the symbol of justice and order. Since the 'influence' of the planet-god, visible in the sky, has evidently been unavailing, Theseus optimistically transfers his character and function to a remoter, more mysterious, invisible Power.

The Duke argues that stability exists only in the realm of eternity. In the contingent world everything goes by 'progressiouns' and 'successiouns' (3013-14); the cycle of birth, life and death continually revolves. Between 3017 and 3066 he draws strength and comfort from his repertory of *solacia*, and applies them to the particular case of Arcite. As a result of prolonged mourning for the dead knight, the cycle has been halted at the point of death. His reason for summoning the 'parlement' is to urge a renewal of life through the marriage of Palamon and Emelye. The purpose of his lengthy exposition is to dispose the minds of these two mourners (but especially Emelye) to accept this proposition; he is also anxious to gain public approval for the match.

Mention of the Duke's political role raises another problem. At 2973-4 it is stated that one reason for his promoting the marriage of his sister-in-law to the surviving Theban knight was his desire

To have with certein contrees alliaunce,
And have fully of Thebans obeisaunce.

This has caused certain critics to take a cynical view of the proceedings. But, for any hereditary monarch, the dynastic implications of marriage must be paramount. In *The Parlement of Foules* sexual love was considered in the context of the 'commune profyt': Nature presumably is considering the good of the community when she directs the formel's attention to the royal eagle. I have already referred to letters from Edward III to the Castilian royal family upon the death of his daughter. The king is evidently concerned about the frustration of his plans for cementing by marriage the alliance between the two realms; but, at the same time, the depth of his personal grief is no less apparent.[43] At the end of the Knight's Tale there is a felicitous confluence of dynastic considerations, of the expected 'romantic' ending, and of the fulfilment of Arcite's dying wish — thus bringing about a kind of resolution of the conflict between love and friendship.

Time, not Eternity, is the effctive consoler in this narrative. We have already seen how Theseus urges Emelye to accept Palamon because 'he hath served yow so many a yeer'. 'Servyse' is to be expected of a 'courtly lover' during his probationary period of courtship. 'Palamon, the gentil man' — as Arcite calls him in his dying speech (2797) — goes further and continues his 'servyse' after marriage:

> And Emelye hym loveth so tendrely,
> And he hire serveth al so gentilly,
> That nevere was ther no word hem bitwene
> Of jalousie or any oother teene.
>
> (3103-6)

Yet this account of Palamon's continuing 'servyse' may cause the reader to recall the words that Arcite addressed to Emelye earlier in his final utterance: 'I biquethe the servyce of my goost / To yow aboven every creature' (2768-9). Even as one responds to the general rejoicing at the final curtain, it is difficult to exorcize Arcite's spirit completely from one's mind. Perhaps I am not the only reader to sense the presence of his 'goost' as an unbidden guest at the wedding festivities, and to catch an echo from yet another part of his most unforgettable speech:

> 'What is this world? what asketh men to have?
> Now with his love, now . . .
> . . . . . . . . . . . . . . . . . . . . . . . . . . . . . . . . '
>
> (2777-8)

## III

Another tale in which a knightly wooer continues his 'servyse' of his lady after marriage is that of the Franklin (cf. V, 744-52, 791-8). The narrator sets the action of his 'Breton lai' in an even more indeterminate period of pagan antiquity than that of the Knight's Tale. The Franklin assigns the tale to its proper genre in his Prologue (V, 709-15); but it transcends in subtlety and seriousness all the other English examples of a type of romance that had been virtually invented by Marie de France in the twelfth century.[44] It conforms to type in so far as it is a (comparatively) short romance, concerned with love and involving magic. But neither the benign fairies of *Sir Launfal* nor their sinister counterparts from *Sir Orfeo* are here.[45] The magician is an enterprising 'clerk' of Orleans University, who treats his clients to a demonstration and a business supper, before driving a hard bargain with them. Yet even he is eventually affected by the story's pervasive spirit of 'gentillesse' and voluntarily forgoes his fee. I postpone detailed discussion of this tale until Chapter 6, which also includes a consideration of another tale that has its roots in a type of story that has affinities with the 'Breton lai': the Wife of Bath's Tale. Moreover, it too 'toucheth gentillesse', though in a somewhat oblique manner.

In Ellesmere, and certain other MSS, the Franklin's immediate interest in 'gentillesse' is elicited by the Squire's Tale, which breaks off after only two lines of its Pars Tercia (V, 671-2). It is not clear whether we are supposed to think of it as being interrupted by the Franklin, who realizes, from the Squire's prospectus of forthcoming adventures (V, 661-70), that it would be impossibly long for narration on the pilgrimage. What is certain is that the older man praises the Squire, 'considerynge thy yowthe', for his 'wit', his eloquence, and for speaking 'so feelyngly'. The reference to the narrator's 'yowthe' has been seized upon by several critics who have described the performance as 'a young man's tale'—in the disparaging and condescending tone which that phrase often carries. The tale has been regarded as a deliberately botched performance, designed by Chaucer to expose the immaturity of its not very competent narrator. This opinion of the tale seems to me to be altogether misconceived. I agree, on the contrary, with the favourable view of its narrator's competence taken by a recent critic, who also argues — but in no condescending sense — that, in this tale, 'Chaucer has assembled a picture of a young man's imaginary world'.[46]

Before examining the characteristics of the narrator, it is first necessary to observe that this fragmentary tale may be seen as Chaucer's response to a type of fiction that is the opposite of the compact 'Breton lai'; namely, the protracted, aristocratic romance that consists of several interlaced adventures.[47] Chaucer seems to have felt that a main weakness of such romances was the elaborate *entrelacement* of plots. So he disposes of the element of plot in his brief tale by confining it almost entirely to the prospective summary that concludes its Pars Secunda. What he offers us more positively is a poet's creative response to the elements of romance that most fascinated him. He encapsulates these elements into two scenes: the one predominantly masculine and public; the other entirely feminine and intimate. The two panels of this diptych are linked, as it were, by the incomplete interlace pattern represented in the concluding prospectus.

The initial account of Cambuskan's birthday feast will remind many English readers, not so much of episodes from the composite romances, as of the opening scene of *Sir Gawain and the Green Knight*. However, the knight who suddenly rides into the midst of the banqueters and their minstrelsy is no 'hostile challenger'[48] endowed with magical powers, but a bearer of magical gifts that are immediately visible — and none more so than that which bears the ambassador himself. To offer one's mount as a gift is the height of courtesy — especially when it is one that combines the virtues of a flying machine with those of a *wagon lit* (126), and yet looks 'so horsly, and so quyk of ye' (194). Indeed, the knight's deportment causes the narrator to compare him with Gawain himself 'with his olde courteisye' as if 'he were comen ayeyn out of Fairye' (95-6). The allusion adds to the exotic excitement of the oriental 'faraway' the nostalgic appeal of the Arthurian 'long ago'. This nostalgia is later enhanced when the narrator asks, rhetorically, if there is anyone who could describe the signs of amorous intrigue, displayed during the ensuing ball, and answers: 'No man but Launcelot, and he is deed' (287).

The Squire particularly admires the way in which the foreign knight, when he addresses the courtiers, suits the action to the word:

> Accordant to his wordes was his cheere,
> As techeth art of speche hem that it leere.
>
> (103-4)

He has evidently himself mastered the 'art of speche'[49] fairly recently, and exults (a little self-consciously) in his manipulation of the ornaments of style. This is evident in his frequent astrological indications of the time of day, his imaginative *prosopopoeia* of Sleep (347-56), his modesty formulas or 'topics', his use of *occupatio* (refusal to describe or narrate), his use of *rime riche* (on 'fern', 255-6), and his amusing pun on the word 'stile' itself (105-6). One of the commonest rhetorical devices was the use of *exempla* to point a moral or adorn a tale. A flying horse almost inevitably elicits reference to Pegasus, and an artificial steed an allusion to the wooden horse of Troy. In this tale Chaucer exploits such 'stock responses', however, to produce a satirical effect by placing them in the mouths of the many-headed multitude who 'gauren on' the marvellous gifts and speculate knowingly about their mode of operation. Chaucer has the same amused contempt for the opinion of crowds as Shakespeare does.

Canacee seems to be the Squire's ideal of a young girl. She is still under the tutelage of her 'maistresse' — the official term for a woman of gentle birth who supervised the education of a princess.[50] After a polite turn around the dance floor with the fascinating stranger, Canacee obtains permission to retire to bed early. She is concerned, not only to secure her 'beauty sleep' (365-7), but — to the annoyance of her 'maistresse' — to rise early in order to test the powers of her magic ring, which enables her to converse with birds. Although she is too young to experience love herself, she possesses the 'gentil herte' that feels 'pitee' for the sufferings, in love, of a similarly sensitive spirit. This compliment is paid to the princess by the female falcon in the noble *exordium* (479-94) to her narrative, which, in spite of her great personal distress, achieves the eloquent courtesy that can be heard in the opening words of the speeches of some of the most dignified characters in Dante's *Commedia*. Her narrative introduces us to a world of misery and hopelessness of which there was hardly a hint in the tale's glamorous opening scene. Her account of her betrayal by a tercel, who 'semed welle of alle gentillesse', indicates that corruption has now invaded the innocent St Valentine's Day assembly of *The Parlement of Foules*. Even the art of rhetoric, which appeared in so admirable a light in Part One, is perverted by 'this god of loves ypocryte' (514). Whereas the ambassador of the previous scene suited his words to his 'cheere', this tercel painted and combed 'at point-devys / As wel his wordes as his contenaunce', as he tried to 'countrefete the sophymes of his art'. By the end of the tale the Squire shows himself to be the true son of his father. The opening scene may at first look like an escape into exotic fantasy; but, as the narrative finally breaks off, Canacee stands on the threshold of a world of experience hardly less dismaying than that of the Knight's Tale. Indeed, the phrase 'to maken vertu of necessitee', which Theseus had endowed with such hopeful reassurance, is now (593) conscripted merely to express the falcon's hopeless resignation to her enforced parting.

Neither the noun, 'gentillesse', nor the adjective, 'gentil', occurs in

Chaucer's 'own' tale of Sir Thopas. The nearest approach is achieved in the epithet 'gent' (VII, 715) — a word applied only to women elsewhere in the poet's works, and so eminently appropriate to this precious, bourgeois knight-errant.[51] Here is Chaucer's response to the popular romances of his day, especially those of the East Midland 'school' that employ tail-rhyme stanzas.[52] A fair crop of them exists in the earlier fourteenth-century Auchinleck MS (of which Chaucer may have seen a copy), and their quality can also be judged from the work of his Kentish contemporary, Thomas Chestre, the author of *Sir Launfal* and possibly also of the romance that immediately follows it in MS BL Cotton Caligula A II, *Libaeus Desconus* (The Fair Unknown),[53] to whom there is a specific reference at VII, 900.

Chaucer was not the first English poet to amuse himself at the expense of tail-rhyme. Before the form was used for narrative, it had been employed in some of the lyrics in MS BL Harley 2253. The one which bears the editorial title, 'The Fair Maid of Ribblesdale',[54] is an exuberant parody of the type of effusion in which the enthusiastic lover catalogues his lady's charms from top to toe. Like *Sir Thopas,* it laughs at the hackneyed phrases and asseverations that are often employed, especially to give the short tail-lines something to do.[55] The shortcomings of this metre are, however, far more evident when it is used for narrative: the tail-lines are apt to impede the logical 'process' of narration. As Trounce puts it, 'the tail-line was apt to get in the way'.[56] Chaucer manages his freshly acquired idiom and metre with the studied gaucherie of a circus rider who has newly broken in a steed, long since put out to grass. In fact, he changes horses several times, as a variety of tail-rhyme stanzas are employed, including one that has gone lame in one leg as the result of the introduction of a 'bob' (VII, 793, 803, 813, 823 and 887).

Scholars have supplied, and continue to provide, detailed annotations that enhance our appreciation of the burlesque of the worn-out poetical vocabulary, the meaningless tags, the forced rhymes, the incorrect verbal forms.[57] The conscientious student will pursue all the adduced parallels back to their sources in a diversity of romances;[58] but in the course of his quest the humour of Chaucer's jokes is apt to evaporate. He might do better (in the first instance, at least) to read complete just one or two tail-rhyme romances (e.g. those mentioned above) and thereby be enabled to experience for himself the joy of watching many of Chaucer's satirical barbs strike home. But he would also recognize how unfair much of the satire is; some of the popular romances are not as absurd as *Sir Thopas* suggests. I make one specific comparison to illustrate this point. *Sir Launfal* is a 'Breton lai' whose hero acquires a fairy mistress, 'Dame Tryamour'. Through no fault of his own, he has been reduced to poverty and shame. When he has sunk to the nadir of his fortunes, he rides away from civilization, lets his wretched horse graze, and lies down to rest under a tree at 'underntyde' [mid-morning]. Out of the 'holtes hore' [grey woods] come 'gentyll maydenes two' (230 ff.) with brown eyes. They invite him to speak with their mistress, Tryamour, who offers him, not only her love, but also the gifts of inexhaustible wealth and invulnerability. The Flemish 'knight', Sir Thopas — evidently (like Don Quixote) an avid reader of romances — is determined (as the result of a dream) that he shall acquire a fairy mistress. So he sets out 'an elf-queene for t'espye' (VII, 799). He is not a sufficiently attentive reader to have noticed that fairies are not to be commanded thus, and that voyeurs of their activities are apt to come to grief. Moreover, his resolve to acquire an 'elf-queene' as his 'lemman', because no mortal woman is 'worthy' to be his 'make', involves a boorish inversion of the proper sentiment for the truly chivalrous gentleman who suffers from 'love-longynge'.

It is also possible to gloss the contrived inanities of *Sir Thopas* by contrasting them with the calculated felicities of a genuinely superior romance. For example, many readers of *Sir Gawain and the Green Knight*[59] have observed that, when the strange knight (who seems half giant — 'half etayn' [140]) rides into Arthur's hall, the poet looks him up and down for a whole stanza before revealing, in the very last line, the most immediately startling fact about him: he was bright green all over (150). The ridiculous counterpart to this strategy is employed when Sir Thopas encounters a giant whose name — 'sire Olifaunt' [Elephant] — indicates that this poet does not believe in half measures. Having boasted to the giant that he will engage him on the morrow 'whan I have myn armoure', the hero retreats, helped on his way by the stones the giant casts at him 'out of a fel staf-slynge' (David and Goliath inverted). Two stanzas later the poet tells how Thopas arrives home, orders his merry men to provide entertainment, and only then happens to mention that the giant has 'hevedes three' [three heads] (VII, 842). Not only is this information delayed for five stanzas from the giant's first appearance; but it is even held back until after a new 'Fit' has begun.

This fact is not obvious from current editions of Chaucer, which divide the poem into two Fits — the second not beginning until line 891. But some authoritative MSS indicate — as J.A. Burrow has shown[60] — a division into three Fits, the second commencing at 833. Burrow also observes the remarkable fact that the number of stanzas in each Fit is precisely half that of its predecessor. So, by the time the Host interrupts Chaucer in mid-stanza at 919, this nugatory narrative is well on the way to dwindling into complete non-entity. It is ironical that this *aventure*, that lacks 'process', direction or shape, is thus endowed with the most perfect mathematical form of any of the tales.

*Sir Thopas* is an *aventure* without direction. But it seems that Chaucer's creative imagination was not much taken by *aventures* of knights errant, however purposefully directed. We have observed how in the Squire's Tale he set aside the entanglements of *aventure* and concentrated on the scenes from romance fiction that especially attracted him. When anyone who is familiar with the corpus of medieval European fiction hears of 'storial thyng that toucheth gentillesse', he is likely to think first of all about the Arthurian romances, with their large cast of celebrated names. But the only Arthurian story Chaucer tells is the comic Wife of Bath's Tale, in which all the characters are anonymous apart from the king himself; and he is mentioned only fleetingly.[61] When Chaucer narrates a tragic story of 'gentil' lovers, he does not choose to write about Launcelot and Guinevere or Tristan and Isolde, but Troilus and Criseyde. When he writes a story about friends whom circumstances convert temporarily into foes, he does not write of Ywain and Gawain, but of Palamon and Arcite. One reason for this may be quite simply that the Arthurian romances were readily accessible to many of his readers in French, so he decided to concentrate on making available Italian works, such as the 'love of Palamon and Arcite', whose 'story is knowen lite'.[62] But the explanation may go deeper than that. Even sophisticated writers of Arthurian romances who take an intelligent interest in motivation, such as Chrétien de Troyes and Thomas (author of the finest French romance about Tristan), delight in describing fights, not only between knights, but also with giants and dragons. At the end of *Troilus*, Chaucer finds it necessary to apologize for having failed to describe in detail 'the armes of this ilke worthi man' (V, 1766): he is much more interested to write 'of his love' than 'of his batailles endite'. In *The Parlement of Foules* 'batayle' is rejected as the solution to the *demande d'amour*.[63] When a similar situation arises in the Knight's Tale, the plot requires Chaucer to make a spectacle of the tournament,[64] but mainly in order to enhance the irony of the fact that it is not the outcome of this 'batayle' that provides the solution to the lovers' strife. Moreover, in adapting *Il Teseida*, he omits the account of Theseus's military campaigns altogether. He is less concerned with the events of the martial calendar than about the phenomenon of Mars himself and all the unglamorous aspects of human existence that it represents. His Theseus is the responsible 'governour', who is no longer preoccupied with the *aventures* of love and war that characterize the essentially youthful society of Arthurian romance. But his experienced Duke still retains the 'gentil herte' that is moved spontaneously by 'pitee'.

# CHAPTER 3
# The Miller's Tale and Other Tales of 'Harlotrie'

Chaucer's burlesque, in the Tale of Sir Thopas, taps the dregs of the barrel which historians of medieval literature have labelled 'Romance'. But Chaucer's compilation had demonstrated long since that there are other casks to be broached, brimful of 'strong wyn, reed as blood'. The first of them is opened almost immediately after the Knight's Tale is concluded. The 'cherl' who opens it is represented as being quite literally drunk. His inebriation may, nevertheless, have symbolic import, since the Miller's Tale is, in fact, narrated with masterly control. The drunkenness is perhaps meant to imply the compiler's rashness in daring to serve up a fabliau in succession to the Knight's Tale.

When the Host delivers his opinion of Sir Thopas, its narrator protests pathetically that 'it is the beste rym I kan' (VII, 928). Very different is the spirit that pervades the Miller's Prologue. All the pilgrims — but especially the 'gentils' — pronounce the Knight's Tale to be 'a noble storie' (I, 3109-13). The Host invites the Monk to narrate something that will 'quite' the Knight's Tale, *if that ye konne*'. But the Miller insists on relieving his superior of that duty. He ushers in his tale with what is virtually a literary Prologue, but one in which the customary, polite conventions of the *exordium* are inverted. This appears in his 'chere' even before we hear his 'wordes':

> He nolde avalen neither hood ne hat,
> Ne abyde no man for his curteisie,
> But in Pilates voys he gan to crie,
> And swoor ...
>
> (3122-5)

His *fortissimo* outburst, in the tones of a 'ham' actor, perverts the customary protestations of the speaker's inadequacy for his task ('modesty *topoi*') into a series of '*im*modesty *topoi*' — there is no question of his requiting the Knight '*if that ye konne*'. He asserts:

> 'I kan a noble tale for the nones,
> With which I wol now quite the Knyghtes tale.'
>
> (3126-7)

With a single stroke he reduces the knight's 'noble storie' (cf. I, 3111) to the status of a plain tale and will presently elevate his own 'noble tale' into 'a legende and a lyf'. When the Host lets the drunken

Robyn have the stage, the latter resumes in the peremptory manner
ridiculed in the Tale of Sir Thopas (cf. VII, 891-3):

> 'Now herkneth,' quod the Millere, 'alle and some!
> But first . . . '

$$(3136\text{-}7)$$

The unexpected adversative introduces a mischievous parody of
another 'topic of the *exordium*': the *captatio benevolentiae* — the
formal attempt to acquire the favourable disposition of the audience:[1]

> 'But first I make a protestacioun
> That I am dronke, I knowe it by my soun;
> And therfore if that I mysspeke or seye,
> Wyte it the ale of Southwerk, I you preye.'

$$(3137\text{-}40)$$

Such an apology may suffice for the consumption of the pilgrim
audience (except for the Host of The Tabard), but the author feels
that it will not satisfy his readers, so he concludes the Miller's
Prologue with his own extended, and somewhat disingenuous,
*apologia* for relating tales of 'harlotrie'. This apology culminates in
an even bolder perversion of the *captatio benevolentiae* formula. He
has offered them a varied selection of tales: 'Blameth nat me, if that
*ye* chese amys' (I, 3181). The literary sophistication that lies just
beneath the surface of the Miller's Prologue should alert us to expect
something more from the ensuing Tale[2] than a bawdy anecdote or a
run-of-the-mill fabliau.[3]

Various details of the Miller's professed capping of the Knight's
Tale have often been noticed. Whereas the virgin Emelye is wooed by
the two rival knights, the married Alysoun is courted by the young
university clerk and the young parish clerk. The famous portrait of
Alysoun (I, 3233 ff.) 'improves upon' that of Emelye (I, 1033 ff.). There
are verbal echoes that range from the Miller's use of the image of 'the
oxen in my plogh' in his Prologue (I, 3159 — cf. the Knight's use of it
at I, 887 during the preliminaries to his tale) to the appropriation and
trivialization (at I, 3204) of the memorable line from Arcite's dying
speech: 'Allone, withouten any compaignye' (I, 2779).[4]

Another feature that the two tales have in common is their use of
astrology. But the Miller's Tale makes no mention of the planets or
of the pagan gods associated with them; nor, on the other hand, does
it employ astrology in the merely decorative way that the Squire's
Tale does, to indicate times and seasons. Nicholas, the clerk in the
Miller's Tale, goes up to Oxford to take an Arts degree but makes
just one of the Seven Liberal Arts his particular hobby: 'Al his

fantasye/Was turned for to lerne astrologye' (I, 3191). In place of the Knight's Tale's listing of the names of the planets and their properties, we have an inventory of the amateur astrologer's books and instruments, with plenty of technical terms for the sake of verisimilitude. Moreover, Nicholas's interest is in a limited branch of his subject, in what we nowadays call Meteorology; he had the reputation of being able to tell 'whan that men sholde have droghte or elles shoures' (I, 3196). In this tale, rain is rain: there is no mention here of Venus's tears falling upon the scene of action (as in the Knight's Tale [I, 2663-6] or again in Chaucer's poem, *Envoy to Scogan* [8-12]). So are there any gods in the Miller's Tale?

The question may at first seem inept as well as superfluous. Since the tale is set in contemporary Oxford, one would hardly expect the pagan gods of antiquity to appear. Certainly, the institutions of Christianity are much in evidence; but the depth and seriousness of their impact is another matter. Alysoun dutifully goes to her parish church on a feast day 'Cristes owene werkes for to wirche' (I, 3308). But, when she arrives, what she finds is the parish clerk, 'this joly Absolon', who casts 'many a lovely look' on the 'wyves' of the parish (and especially upon herself), whom he also perfumes with clouds of incense, as befits the true objects of his devotions. We might just as well be in the pagan temple of the first scene in *Troilus and Criseyde* where 'many a lusty knyght' and 'many a lady fressh' are assembled 'to herknen of Palladion the servyse' (I, 164), as the young squires in Troilus's retinue parade up and down 'byholding ay the ladies of the town', sighing, as they allow their eyes to 'baiten' on the young women in the congregation. So much for the parish church! Oseney Abbey, just outside the city walls, is introduced into the Miller's Tale as a source of secular employment for Alysoun's husband, the carpenter (as if it were merely the fourteenth-century equivalent of modern Cowley); the bell that summons the friars to Lauds, in their chancel near the carpenter's house, is used to mark the termination of the erotic play between Alysoun and Nicholas, which began soon after the sounding of curfew. Characters invoke St Thomas of Kent and St Frideswide; but these saints were the special objects of a local cult[5] — they almost have the tutelary function of pagan *genii loci*. When the insulted Absolon swears to have vengeance or to let 'Sathanas' have his soul, he might as well be a pagan invoking the divinities of Styx. The carpenter's knowledge of Scripture is decidedly vague: when Nicholas asks him whether he has ever heard the story of Noah's flood, he replies: 'Yis'. . . 'ful yoore ago' (I, 3537). Moreover, Nicholas's ensuing words show that he takes it for granted that John the carpenter will know the story only in the uncanonical form that he has picked up from watching the Mystery

Play of the Deluge.[6] Admittedly John has the manual worker's instinctive scepticism about intellectuals who dabble in 'astromye' (as he calls it) and who try to uncover 'Goddes pryvetee', declaring:

> 'Ye, blessed be alwey a lewed man
> That noght but oonly his bileve kan!'
>
> (I, 3455-6)

But his 'lewedness' surpassses his simple faith, as can be seen a few lines later when he pronounces the 'nyght-spel' on the four sides of the house and the exterior of the threshold. When really alarmed, he does not call in one of the neighbouring friars to perform the exorcisms for which they were evidently famous (cf. III, 864-81). He reverts to his own 'folk-remedy', a jumbled and superstitious incantation (I, 3483-6). So I repeat the question: are there any gods in the Miller's Tale?

A fabliau is hardly the context where one expects to find pagan gods; yet Pluto and Proserpina are among the dramatis personae of the Merchant's Tale. This Pluto, however, behaves quite differently from the sinister figure who, at Saturn's request, sent the fiend that causes Arcite's horse to shy, and so brings about its rider's death. He is more like a mischievous Oberon, especially in so far as he is engaged in a running battle with his Queen. If the couple resemble any of the divinities in the Knight's Tale, it is rather Mars and Venus who squabble over their rival protégés — except that, in the Merchant's Tale, their patronage is concerned with perpetuating the war of the sexes. These deities are an embodiment and manifestation of a spirit that pervades this most singular of Chaucer's fabliaux.

In the Miller's Tale it is the principal characters themselves who exhibit the autonomy and blithe irresponsibility of gods. Although Nicholas and Alysoun are citizens of fourteenth-century Oxford, they in no way suffer from the moral and social inhibitions imposed by medieval christendom. They exercise their sexual and other physiological functions with the energy of the heroes and goddesses of pagan mythology, and behave almost with the irresponsible abandon of the deities described by Marlowe:

> There might you see the gods in sundry shapes
> Committing heady riots, incest, rapes.
>
> (*Hero and Leander*, First Sestiad, 143-4[7])

That Chaucer was well acquainted with this aspect of the gods' behaviour is attested by the Prohemium to Book III of *Troilus and Criseyde*. Even Absolon, after he has been cured of his taste for 'paramours', is almost god-like in the single-minded, red-hot

intensity with which he pursues his vengeance. Not only are these
characters liberated from the restraints of Christian morality, but
also from rational, enlightened notions of human justice, of the kind
embodied in Theseus. This type of fabliau has close affinities with the
comedy of the ancient world, not merely on account of its unabashed
display of the phallus (or adjacent parts), but because of the way in
which those who prosper in its world are the tricksters who can most
successfully exploit their bestial cunning.[8] The cardinal sin is not one
of the Deadly Seven, but folly and gullibility.

In siding with youth, virility, extravagance, vitality, sharpness
of wits and shameless deception, the ethos that prevails in the
playground of the Miller's Tale is similar to that which conditions
life within the park of Deduit (Mirth) in the *Roman de la Rose*.
Readers who are familiar only with the earlier portion of that poem
— the part composed by Guillaume de Lorris — may be surprised by
this comparison. The slapstick 'realism' of Chaucer's tale seems far
removed in spirit from the graceful allegory of Guillaume's narrative.
But Chaucer was no less familiar with Jean de Meun's continuation;
and he would probably have regarded the poem as a homogeneous
entity. Delicate the initial allegory may be, but its ultimate goal (not
reached for several thousand lines)[9] is a gross allegory of phallic
penetration — an allegory of the kind that is designed to reveal more
than it conceals. The route to this desired consummation leads
through worldly wisdom, trickery and hypocrisy; and we encounter
various personifications of these qualities (admittedly, alongside
other more noble and dignified personages, such as Reason and
Nature). Deduit's park is surrounded with high embattled walls to
preserve this playground for those who, privileged like the gods, are
properly equipped to devote their leisured lives to erotic pursuits.
Woe betide any unauthorized person who is caught trespassing in
this exclusive domain! Indeed, on the exterior wall of the park are
depicted, as a warning to such unsuitable postulants, personifications
of the qualities that disqualify a man from passing the wicket-gate,
guarded by Oisif (Idleness): among them is Old Age.[10] The *senex
amans* is a stock figure in fabliaux, and his raison d'être is that he
shall be cuckolded. The ethos that is presupposed by the world of the
Miller's Tale is naturally disposed to expel John the Carpenter from
the park of delight as a foreign body. His sin is not only that he is old,
but also that he is credulous and gullible.

In so far as the tale is presented realistically (and that implies a
very considerable distance), the situation it presents may seem to be
precisely the opposite of what I have just described. The proprietor
of the domain is not Deduit, but John the 'riche gnof' [churl], who
admits into his enclave Alysoun as spouse and Nicholas as lodger.

The jealous husband keeps his wife 'narwe in cage'; he has constructed the perfect defensive system against the conventional, ostentatious, serenading young lover, embodied in this tale in the person of Absolon. Certainly, this youth never penetrates the narrow orifice afforded by the 'shot-window' of the bower. But John's precautions are superfluous, since Alysoun has not the slightest interest in this perfumed velvet-coat. So, when the serenader practises his art one moonlight night outside the matrimonial 'bower', Alysoun can react with unfeigned scorn and righteous indignation, as her husband asks:

> 'What! Alison! herestow nat Absolon,
> That chaunteth thus under oure boures wal?'
> And she answerde hir housbonde therwithal,
> 'Yis, God woot, John, I heere it every deel.'
>
> (I, 3366-9)

No wonder we are told: 'This passeth forth; what wol ye bet than weel?'

John's failure to perceive that the real danger lurks inside the cage is so patently absurd as to render it impossible for us to take seriously any of the tale's elaborate intrigue. Nicholas's stratagem for 'bedding' his landlord's wife is the kind of fantasy that might take root in the fertile brain of a none-too-moral student, lying on his bed one idle afternoon. As a piece of practical intrigue this hoax, concerning the second coming — contrary to the express promise of God (Gen. 9, 11-17) — of 'Noes flood', is utterly superfluous. Alysoun is all too willing to commit adultery with him and opportunities for performing the deed are readily available, without any need for resorting to such a stratagem: we are informed that the carpenter's work for Oseney Abbey obliged him sometimes to stop overnight at the Abbey's grange (I, 3664-8). It is true that, when John makes his arrangements for the coming of 'Nowelis flood' (as he calls it), these include the despatching to London of his two servants, Robyn and Gill (whose lives Nicholas says he is unable to save). But it is never suggested in the tale that the presence of the servants in the house is a serious impediment to the adulterers' concubinage: the only obstacle is the presence of the husband in the bed. The burgeoning detail of the hoax is indulged in by Nicholas in the spirit of pure play; and this bestows on him something of the quality of god-like freedom, and upon the tale as a whole a sense of child-like innocence — in spite of its being a tale of adultery.

This quality of playfulness can be best appreciated if we compare the Miller's Tale with Chaucer's slickly paced version of the traditional story of 'the lover's gift regained': the Shipman's Tale. In this narrative of the cuckolding and financial deception of a husband, every move in the intrigue is absolutely necessary. The Miller's Tale differs from it not only because of the superfluousness of Nicholas's intrigue, but also because the action admits an element of chance — the comic counterpart, as it were, of the unpredictable Saturn in the Knight's Tale. This element enters into the secondary plot of the Miller's Tale, concerning the misdirected kiss, and also operates in the way in which this action is related to the main plot. The misdirecting of the kiss is deliberately engineered by Alysoun; but the misdirection of Absolon's revenge is the chance result of Nicholas's overweening desire to have his share of the insulting fun. Furthermore, the scalded clerk's cry for 'Water' suddenly brings us back to the main plot, which has remained suspended in our memory along with the carpenter, suspended in his tub among the rafters. The ambivalent effect of this cry is, on the level of plot structure, the counterpart of a pun in the realm of syntactic structures.

Some commentators have argued that there is a certain morality in the Miller's Tale in so far as characters are punished. But I see no evidence that the punishment fits the crime. Perhaps John deserved to be cuckolded on account of his failure to perceive Alysoun's true character; but he certainly did not deserve the fall which breaks his arm, nor the final imputation of madness. Indeed, the disproportionately great 'punishment' is the comic counterpart to the terrible consequences suffered by tragic heroes, which are out of all proportion to their shortcomings. Nicholas is punished for taking the joke against Absolon upon himself, but he is never punished for his adultery. Alysoun gets off scot free! The only character who can be said to be 'educated' by events is Absolon, who is cured of his obsession with paramours and discovers that vengeance tastes sweeter than love. Hardly a moral lesson! There is no more 'poetic justice' in this tale than in the Shipman's, where the victim is its only 'decent' character. But there is far more sheer joy in the working out of the Miller's plot, which gives the tale its quality of childlike playfulness, as well as that technicolour brilliance (noted by several critics) which indeed contrasts with the grey efficiency of the plotting of the Shipman's Tale.

Because fabliaux were swift-moving and brief, they usually relied upon narrative and dialogue to make their effects. The Miller's and Reeve's Tales are unusual, even among Chaucer's own essays in the genre, in using substantial descriptions to introduce their dramatis personae. These descriptions are no less remarkable than those which constitute the General Prologue to *The Canterbury Tales* and, like them, are carefully interrelated and designed to complement one another. The description that has received the most detailed attention is the portrait of Alysoun (I, 3233-70). Commentators have compared it, on the one hand, to the portrait of Emelye in the Knight's Tale and, on the other, to formal *descriptiones* of ladies, composed according to the precepts of the twelfth-century *Artes Poeticae*. These 'Arts of Poetry' were a medieval counterpart to the classicial treatises on Rhetoric by Aristotle, Cicero and Quintilian. Their authors, such as Geoffrey of Vinsauf and Matthew of Vendôme, purported to teach, by example as well as by precept, the art of poetic composition — other rhetorical 'Arts' dealt with the composition of sermons (*Artes Praedicandi*) and of formal epistles (*Artes Dictaminis*). Their paradigm for writing the description of a beautiful lady is particularly well illustrated in Chaucer's full-length portrait of Blanche, the 'good fair white', in *The Book of the Duchess*.[11] It is the 'Miller' himself who encourages the comparison of the portrait of Alysoun with that of Emelye; it is the poet's procedures which make a comparison with the *Artes Poeticae* almost inevitable.

The imagery in which Alysoun is portrayed has been described as 'placing' her in her environment (within the market town that Oxford was in Chaucer's day). But, in fact, it does so only by implication, whereas that in the portrait of Emelye does so quite explicitly. Emelye enters the garden on a May morning and is immediately described as being herself 'fressher than the May with floures newe' (I, 1037). She 'gadereth floures, party white and rede' (I, 1053), and her complexion is compared to the lily and the rose. Decorum required that 'ladies' should be associated with what we would nowadays purchase from a 'high class' florist, whereas a 'popelote' or 'wenche' such as Alysoun (I, 3254) is naturally spoken of in terms of the wild 'prymerole' (I, 3268). The final observation about Emelye is that 'as an aungel hevenysshly she soong', whereas Alysoun's 'song . . . was as loude and yerne / As any swalwe sittynge on a berne'. As a 'class indicator', the perch is here as important as the bird. We are far removed from the palace garden, or even the garth of the local manor house, where the voice of the turtle (symbol of the faithful lover)[12] would be heard in the dovecote. Nevertheless, the Miller does momentarily associate Alysoun with her 'betters'. The description concludes:

> She was a prymerole, a piggesnye,
> For any lord to leggen in his bedde,
> Or yet for any good yeman to wedde.

(I, 3268-70)

He seems to visualize the husband of a fourteenth-century Duchess Emelye catching Alysoun behind the estate barn, pinching her cheek, calling her his 'piggesnye' — and proceeding to exercise his *droit de seigneur*.

'Rhetorical' descriptions of beautiful ladies involve fairly formal methods of procedure and quite rigid aesthetic canons. They are usually divided into the *effictio* (description of outward appearance), followed by the *notatio* (account of character and accomplishments). Chaucer does indeed make this division in the description of Blanche (*The Book of the Duchess*, 855-960 [*effictio*]; 961-1033 [*notatio*]). But the division is more readily discernible in the much shorter description of Virginia, the fourteen-year-old heroine of the Physician's Tale, where the transition is made quite explicitly in the course of a single couplet:

> And if that excellent was hire beautee,
> A thousand foold moore vertuous was she.
>
> (VI, 39-40)

It may also be seen at a glance in the final description of the heroine in *Troilus and Criseyde* (V, 806-26), where the *effictio* occupies the first two stanzas, the *notatio* being confined to the third. The procedure within the *effictio* often consists of a *gradatim* descent from hair to toes — though this method is by no means invariably adopted. It is employed in the description of Blanche, but it is not followed in the other two descriptions I have just mentioned. As for the aesthetic canon: the ideally beautiful lady had golden hair, eyes that are described as 'grey' in Middle English literature, and a complexion that is a blend of white and red (usually conveyed by means of the simile of lilies and roses).

These conventions of the *descriptio pulchritudinis feminae* will be familiar to most readers of Chaucer. There are, however, two others that are rather less well known, though hardly less important. The first is the reference to the goddess, Nature, which often appears in *effictiones*, where the lady is said to be her masterpiece of creation. This is most obvious in the account of Virginia, where Nature is introduced in person and makes a speech to this effect (VI, 11-29).[13] The other is a procedure that was advocated particularly by the rhetorician, Matthew of Vendôme, who argued that the writer should fasten upon some epithet that isolates the essential quality of the person to be described, and should reiterate it throughout the description.[14] So a description may ring the changes upon a number of synonymous or closely related adjectives. This is particularly well illustrated in the *notatio* concerning Virginia (VI, 40-71), where the basic quality is her chastity, and so all the epithets embody the idea of restraint, temperance and moderation.

It is all too easy to argue that the portrait of Alysoun is blissfully liberated from such a rigid corset of conventions, and so reveals the girl with a freshness and naturalness not to be found in those other examples. If this observation is meant to imply that 'nature' has somehow replaced artifice, then the remark is clearly facile. There is certainly no formal division into *effictio* and *notatio*: Alysoun's character is implied in the *effictio* itself. But there is method in the way in which this is accomplished. Her tastes may be inferred from the cut of her clothes and the size of her ornaments. These details (like all the others) are dispersed in an apparently haphazard way throughout the description; but they are the result of careful schematization. Similarly, in order to suggest the predominance of her 'animal spirits' (in the modern rather than the medieval sense), Chaucer makes a careful selection of images: the lithe weasel and the unrestrained swallow form a contrast with the strokable sheep ('wether'), the dependent kid or calf, and the wincing colt (an anticipation of the image used to describe her reaction at I, 3282 ff. to Nicholas's uninhibited advances). Her sensuous appeal is conveyed by a series of vegetable images (things good to eat and drink) and the sparkle of the solitary mineral image of the newly minted coin. There are images to appeal to every one of the Five Senses: sight (the 'newe pere-jonette tree' and the 'noble yforged newe'); sound (the swallow); touch (the soft wool of the 'wether'); taste and smell (the sweet drinks and the 'hoord of apples leyd in hey or heeth'). This procedure could be analysed as an imaginative development of Matthew of Vendôme's precept — itself ultimately derived from Horace's advice (*De Arte Poetica*, II, 120 ff.) about maintaining consistency in characterization.

When the anonymous composer of the lyric (in MS.BL Harley 2253), addressed to another Alysoun, departs from the paradigm of ideal feminine beauty, he substitutes black eyes for the approved 'grey'.[15] But Chaucer does not mention the colour of his Alysoun's eyes at all — or that of her hair or of her complexion. He regards her eye, not merely as something to be looked at, but as something that looks at you: 'She hadde a likerous ye.' It has often been remarked that the colour scheme that predominates in the description overall forms a pattern of white and black, which certainly befits this neat, long-limbed and well-washed (cf. I, 3310-11) eighteen-year-old. Although the *effictio* ends with 'hir shoes . . . laced on hir legges hye', the descending order of description is not generally maintained. A 'descent' of a different kind does occur, however. At I, 3264 she stands erect, 'long as a mast, and upright as a bolt', only to be laid low in the final couplet, where she could be described as 'bolt upright' only in the idiomatic sense of 'flat on her back' (cf. I, 4266 and VII, 316).

Chaucer was neither the only, nor even the first, English poet to compose his own playful variations upon the *descriptio* of ladies. I have just referred to elements of description in the Harley lyric about Alysoun. In Chapter 2 I mentioned another poem which appears in the same MS: 'The Fair Maid of Ribblesdale', written in tail-rhyme.[16] The girl described in this piece is as untamed as Chaucer's Alysoun, for the poet declares that he is in pursuit of 'wilde wymmen' as he rides through the vale of the Ribble. Just as Alysoun is fit 'for any lord to leggen in his bedde', so this creature is 'in boure best with bolde' (line 6). Its sophisticated humour is achieved largely at the expense of the all-inclusive descending catalogue of the lady's physical charms. It is one of the few *effictiones* that actually mentions the girl's toe. But only because her girdle hangs down that far. It is, of course, the environs of the girdle that is the ultimate goal of the poem's 'process'. Comparison with Chaucer's description of Alysoun reveals how oddly unerotic Chaucer's portrait is: there is no listing of what are nowadays vulgarly called 'vital statistics'. Alysoun is a confection, put together from ingredients supplied mostly by her natural environment. It is in this homely sense that she is Nature's masterpiece. In this 'wyf' is to be found what the Miller had called 'Goddes foyson' [abundance, plenty] (I, 3165).

If I were to organize an exhibition of English *descriptiones pulchritudinis feminae*, I would hang the portrait of Alysoun between that of 'The Fair Maid of Ribblesdale' and that of Hero, from the beginning of Marlowe's *Hero and Leander*.[17] Here it is Universal Nature, from the stars down to the 'blushing coral' (line 32), that contributes to the eclectic *effictio* (as in Alain de Lille's portrait of the goddess Natura in his *De Planctu Naturae*).[18] But, although Hero is a priestess ('Venus' nun', 45), her behaviour is not far removed from that of any 'wench'. The figure is perhaps a little over-dressed in exotic imagery, coy conceits and the arch use of pseudo-mythology. Whereas comparison with the Harley lyric brings out the unerotic character of Chaucer's description, comparison with Marlowe emphasizes its unexotic quality, and draws our attention to the way in which Chaucer can make poetry out of the humble, unremarkable objects of everyday life. (Incidentally, another reason for urging the reader to compare for himself the Marlowe passage is that *Hero and Leander* is the first narrative poem since Chaucer's time to use the metre we call 'heroic couplet' with comparable felicity — although it is now adapted to accommodate words of very different shapes and sounds.)[19]

But it is time to terminate the loan of Chaucer's black-and-white sketch to this imaginary exhibition and to return it to its proper location, where it forms part of a triptych. This is not the first such triptych that Chaucer had designed. I have already mentioned the formal description of the heroine in *Troilus and Criseyde* (V, 806 ff.). It occurs at the point where she is about to desert Troilus for Diomede, and so her portrait appears flanked by those of her future and her former lover. Alysoun's portrait stands between those of her successful and her would-be young lover, though they are not immediately juxtaposed, being separated by passages of narrative. They are, nevertheless, clearly meant to complement one another.

All the features of the formal *descriptio* of female beauty that are absent from the portrait of Alysoun are, ironically, transferred to that of Absolon (I, 3312-51). Commentators have noticed how his effeminacy is implied by his name and his coiffure;[20] and to that we may add the detail of 'his eyen *greye* as goos', his liking for perfume and, perhaps, the high register of his singing voice. The description also maintains the strict division between the *effictio* and the *notatio* that follows it at 3325 ff. The description of his person descends from his golden hair, with a sudden drop to his ornately carved shoes, from where the picture of his dress ascends. The formal method of procedure certainly accords with the conventional character of this would-be fashionable youth, who experiences 'love-longynge', lies awake all night, and woos his inamorata by moonlight serenades and presents of (among other things) 'wafres, pipyng hoot out of the gleede'. Characteristically, however, he destroys the romantic impression by also offering her cash and by employing intermediaries of doubtful respectability.[21]

Hand in hand with his flamboyant appearance goes his ostentatious behaviour. The *notatio* informs us how, in his free time, he diverted his musical talents, that earned him his stipend as parish clerk, to entertaining the company in taverns, especially in those where there was a vivacious barmaid. We are later informed that sometimes, in order to impress Alysoun with 'his lightnesse and maistrye, / He pleyeth Herodes upon a scaffold hye' (I, 3383-4). The part of Herod, in the mystery play of *The Slaughter of the Innocents*,[22] must have been one of those most coveted by the amateur actor. But, as Hamlet's phrase 'it out-Herods Herod' (III, ii 16) implies, it was a ranting part that demanded a firm *basso profondo*; the register of Absolon's voice must have made him sound ridiculous in the role. On the other hand, there is a violent and ruthless streak in Absolon which shows itself later, in the way in which he intends to revenge himself upon the tenderest parts of his former beloved. The earliest hint that this apparently squeamish individual was not quite what he seemed occurs in the *notatio*, where we are made to understand that he worked as a barber (presumably to supplement his parish clerk's stipend — or possibly to be rewarded with a free 'styling'). The medieval barber's shop was a surgery as well as a salon. In order to work in its perfumed atmosphere Absolon was obliged to 'laten blood', as well as to 'clippe and shave'.

Personal appearance is the subject of almost the whole of the portrait of Alysoun, because that is what makes her interesting to others: it is the subject of much of the description of Absolon, because it is the thing that most interests this narcissistic being. In the description of 'hende [smooth] Nicholas' (as he is almost invariably called),[23] it occupies only a single line: 'And lyk a mayden meke for to see' (I, 3202). The point of the line is to warn us against appearances; for, under this innocent façade, he was 'sleigh and ful privee', as befits one who practises 'deerne love' — not in the traditionally romantic sense of nourishing a secret passion for the unobtainable beloved, but in the sense of one who is expert in conducting clandestine love affairs.[24] When Absolon later goes a-wooing he chews 'lycorys' and other spices to sweeten his breath (I, 3690-3); but Nicholas evidently has no need to resort to such artificial sweeteners, for he is 'hymself as sweete as is the roote / Of lycorys, or any cetewale' (I, 3206-7). Instead of listing his attire, the description dwells upon Nicholas's bed-sitter. Although he is introduced as the traditional 'poure scoler',[25] the very fact that he could afford a room 'allone, withouten any compaignye', suggests that he was better off than most students — then and now. The same impression is given by the mention of books and the itemizing of his expensive astrological equipment. So the *descriptio* aptly concludes with the couplet:

> And thus this sweete clerk his tyme spente
> After his freendes fyndyng and his rente.
>
> (I, 3219-20)

He evidently had rich relatives and enjoyed a private income. The idealized Clerk of Oxenford, in the General Prologue, spent '*al* that he myghte of his freendes hente' (I, 299) on books and on learning. He would rather have 'at his beddes heed' commentaries on Aristotle than rich clothes 'or fithele, or gay sautrie' (I, 293-6). Nicholas's books and scientific implements are also to be found 'on shelves couched at his beddes heed'. But Chaucer adds:

> And al above ther lay a gay sautrie,
> On which he made a-nyghtes melodie

> So swetely that all the chambre rong . . .
>
> (I, 3213-15)

Music is an art practised by both of Alysoun's lovers; and there is a significant contrast in the way in which they practise it. The exhibitionist Absolon plays and sings only when there is an audience to be impressed, whereas Nicholas is content to make music in the privacy of his own room. The genuineness of the latter's interest in the art is further suggested by the naming of the titles of the pieces he performs: '*Angelus ad virginem*' and 'the Kynges Noote'. The inclusion in his repertory of a song concerning the Annunciation (cf. Luke, 1, 26-38) should not mislead us into detecting a religious streak in this 'sweete clerk'. The song was a popular 'hit' at the time, valued more for its melody than its sentiment.[26] The contrast between the two musicians is further enhanced by the way in which Absolon uses his 'gyterne' to accompany his serenade outside Alysoun's bower, whereas Nicholas needs no such instrument to win the girl: it is only after he has obtained a kiss that, by way of celebration, he

> . . . taketh his sawtrie,
> And pleyeth faste, and maketh melodie.
>
> (I, 3305-6)

This literal 'melodie' serves as an earnest of the metaphorical one that is later to be played out between the lovers in the carpenter's bed: 'Ther was the revel and the melodye' (I, 3652).

As the action develops, another contrast between the artistic abilities of the two youths becomes apparent; namely, their use of the drama as a means of furthering their amorous designs. Whereas Absolon exhibits himself in the role of Herod, Nicholas exercises his wonted 'privetee' in his exploitation of the Mystery Play of the Deluge, remaining behind the scenes as author and producer until it is time for him to climb one of the ladders to a secret 'scaffold', and then to descend, as inconspicuously as possible, from this elevated level of make-believe to the crude reality of cuckolding the husband in his own nest.

Nicholas's play-acting emerges from one contrived silence, as he wakes from his pretended trance with the disjointed cry 'Allas! / Shal al the world be lost eftsoones now?' (I, 3488-9); and it concludes in another silence after the three actors have in turn repeated 'clom' [mum!] (I, 3638-9) from their separate tubs and in their different vocal registers. Between these silences comes the most sustained passage of talk in the tale, in which the clerk persuades his impressionable landlord to take precautions against the flood whose imminent onset he predicts. It can hardly be termed a 'dialogue', since it is almost monopolized by the inventive clerk's insistent tones. We do not know whether Rhetoric was one of the subjects he had studied in his Oxford Arts curriculum, but his eloquence is worthy of one of those 'clerkes' who 'ben ful subtile and ful queynte' (I, 3275). These words, however, are not applied to this particular performance; they refer to his earlier wooing of Alysoun, which is (ironically) not at all 'subtile', since he adopts the procedure of 'action first, words afterwards'. Similarly, the notions of ingenuity and delicacy are promptly removed from the adjective 'queynte' by its involvement in the obscene *rime riche* at 3275-6. After indecently grabbing at the girl, 'hende' (too free with his hands) Nicholas incongruously utters the language of the lover who is dying of a secret passion: 'Ywis, but if ich have my wille, / For deerne love of thee, lemman, I spille' — where 'deerne love' has reverted to its traditional, romantic connotation, but 'spille' has possibly picked up an obscene, secondary meaning.

Anyone who is familiar with the literature of *fine amor* will be inclined to compare the episode with its archetypal situation in the *Roman de la Rose*, when Bialacoil (the squire who personifies the lady's 'come-hither' aspect) has brought the Lover into the rose garden. Whereas the Lover tells the courteous Bialacoil of his desire to pluck the rose-bud (whose ultimate significance we have already considered), 'hende Nicholas', as it were, grabs at it for himself. When Bialacoil begins a polite refusal, an uncouth churl springs out from behind the rose bush and drives the Lover unceremoniously out of the garden. He is Daunger, who personifies the lady's power to keep the Lover at a distance, or to cut him dead.[27] It therefore behoves Alysoun to summon her Daunger:

> And she sproong as a colt dooth in the trave,
> And with hir heed she wryed faste awey,
> And seyde, 'I wol nat kisse thee, by my fey!
> Why, lat be,' quod she, 'lat be, Nicholas,
> Or I wol crie "out, harrow" and "allas"!
> Do wey youre handes, for youre curteisye!'
>
> (I, 3282-7)

The 'wynsynge' colt is explicitly re-introduced here; but the presence of another animal from the *effictio* is implied in the wriggling, weasel-like rhythms of her reply. The natural inflections of the wench's speech are exactly caught by the poet's positioning of words within his metrical scheme. This is especially true of line 3285, with its internal rhymes that are surpassed in comic effect only by that of the

famous line 3740: '"Tehee!" quod she, and clapte the wyndow to.'
Her threat to give tongue to the hackneyed cries of the distressed
heroine shows her resistance to be merely token. At the climax of
the tale, however, both she and Nicholas will utter these same
exclamations in earnest (3825). Her attempt, in her closing words, to
play the great 'daungerous' lady, by appealing to Nicholas 'for youre
curteisye', is undercut by the undignified necessity of ordering him,
in the line's first half, to 'Do wey youre handes'.

The playful unreality of this farcical scene becomes still more
evident if we again make a comparison with the Shipman's Tale,
which contains a somewhat similar situation between VII 92 and 209.
The monk, Daun John, is desirous of seducing the merchant's wife;
she is willing to be seduced for the price of one hundred franks. Just
as Nicholas seizes Alysoun by the 'haunchebones', so Daun John
catches the wife by the 'flankes', embraces and kisses her. But
whereas, in the Miller's Tale, the action precedes the dialogue, in
the Shipman's Tale it is taken only after a hundred lines of studied
innuendo.

The scene opens with the monk pacing the garden and reciting,
from his portable breviary, the daily office. An air of conspiracy is
immediately suggested by the wife's 'walkynge pryvely' into the
garden where he 'walketh softe'. She is accompanied for the sake
of propriety. However, she is not chaperoned by a duenna, as an
unmarried girl would be; her companion is 'a mayde child' who is
still 'under the yerde' and consequently in no position to blab about
what she witnesses. The wife and the monk begin to flash signals at
one another even in the very act of exchanging the time of day. When
he jokes about the way in which her husband's attentions must have
given her a sleepless night, he fears he has gone too far, and his
laughter is followed by a self-conscious blush. The wife is not in the
least abashed, but assures him that, on the contrary, her husband's
performance is woefully inadequate. This assertion is a lie. It may be
that, while his mind is preoccupied with his present business
transaction, the merchant is temporarily 'off colour'. But the
concluding scene of the tale shows that he certainly does not suffer
from impotence. Having hinted that Daun John can supply the
alleged deficiency in her life 'abedde', she eventually indicates that he
might also supply the deficiency that she more genuinely experiences:
namely, that in her purse. This is the area where she finds her
husband truly inadequate: 'But yet me greveth moost his nygardye'
(VII, 172). The connection between the supplying of the two
deficiencies is soon established, but in such a way that the attendant
'mayde child' probably does not comprehend what kind of transaction
is implied by her ambiguous assurance at line 190: 'For at a certeyn

day I wol yow paye.' The connection is finally clinched, in all its
crudity, by means of the blatant rhyme at the conclusion of the
monk's reply:

> 'For I wol brynge yow an hundred frankes.'
> And with that word he caughte hire by the flankes.
>
> (VII, 201-2)

Commentators have remarked how, throughout the tale, the
vocabularies of sexual and commercial intercourse are continually
intermingled, producing several *doubles entendres*.[28] This process
culminates in the wife's banter with her husband about paying her
matrimonial 'debt'. The merchant's wife will readily 'paye' her
husband:

> 'Fro day to day, and if so be I faille,
> I am youre wyf; score it upon my taille . . .'
>
> (VII, 415-16)

Indeed, once the ambivalent procedure has been established, sexual
allusions may be discovered lurking beneath far more innocent-
seeming remarks than that. Consider, for example, the concluding
couplet of the husband's reply, where he is talking about his wife's
financial extravagance:

> 'But, by thy lyf, ne be namoore so large.
> Keep bet my good, this yeve I thee in charge.'
>
> (VII, 431-2)

The irony would have been more obvious to readers in an age when
preachers, asserting the superiority of the celibate life, urged girls to
preserve their maidenhead against thieves, robbers and lechers ('with
theoves, with reveres, with lechurs'), as if it were a 'treasure' or
'gemstone' entrusted to their protection by Christ, the ideal Spouse.
The Franciscan friar, Thomas of Hales (from whose religious love
song, or 'luve-ron', I am quoting),[29] is so literal-minded that he
speaks of the maiden's preserving this precious stone 'under thine
hemme' [under your skirt]. If she preserves this capital asset, she will
gain the bliss of Paradise. So we have religious writers to thank for
popularizing, long before Chaucer's day, the correspondences
between commerce and sex.

Compared with the playground frolics of the Miller's Tale, the
adultery of the Shipman's Tale is hideously adult. The duped
husband is no superstitious artisan, but an astute business man, who
operates in the international market, not only more expertly, but also
more profitably than does the Merchant in the General Prologue.

The carefree clerk of the Miller's Tale has grown into the monk who, being an 'outrider' (like his brother in the General Prologue), is entrusted with the business affairs of his monastery. The wife is not fit to be entrusted with her husband's 'honour', let alone the upbringing of the 'mayde child'. The tale's ultimate irony resides in the fact that it is the monk who is the most worldly of its characters and the one who brings off a smart 'invisible deal', whereas the merchant lives an almost cloistered life, shutting himself up in his counting-house and journeying to Paris and Bruges strictly on official business. At VII, 288 he reminds Daun John that for 'chapmen . . . hir moneie is hir plogh'.[30] Certainly he pursues his commercial vocation with the single-mindedness of one who, having put his hand to the plough, never looks back. It might have been better for him if he had sometimes looked over his shoulder. Or is this tale concerned to press home a cynical moral concerning the happiness of being perpetually well deceived?

Formally, the Shipman's Tale comes closest of any of Chaucer's fabliaux to the traditional French type, in so far as it eschews elaborate descriptions and concentrates on dialogue and rapid narrative. The one which departs furthest from the norm is the Merchant's Tale, even though its plot is concerned (like that of the Miller's Tale) with the deceiving of the stock figure of the *senex amans*. But the old man (unusually for a fabliau) is a knight, and his wife (as she reminds him at IV, 2202) is 'a gentil womman and no wenche'. Moreover, the names of the wedded couple, Januarie and May, suggest the *personae* of an allegory rather than the characters of a fabliau, as do likewise the names of Januarie's counsellors on the advisability of marriage, Justinus and Placebo. The 'debate' between the two advisers occupies a considerable portion of the earlier part of the tale; and its closing pages are interrupted by another between — most unexpectedly — the mythological husband and wife, Pluto and Proserpina. The goddess, however, talks like a spiritual sister of the Wife of Bath, whom Justinus had invoked (at IV, 1685) — in wilful contravention of any attempt to maintain narrative illusion. This facetious citation of Dame Alys as one of the great 'auctoures' on the subject of matrimony is matched by references to acknowledged 'auctoures', such as that to 'he that wroot the Romance of the Rose' (IV, 2032). The self-conscious literary air is further enhanced by the continual use of apostrophes — sometimes addressed to the dramatis personae, but also to Fortune (2057), Ovid (2125), and even to the 'perilous fyr, that in the bedstraw bredeth' (1783). Indeed, this tale is so unlike the other fabliaux that I shall postpone further discussion of it until Chapter 6, which will afford a more appropriate context for its elucidation.

Meanwhile, I shall conclude this discussion of tales of 'harlotrie' by returning to the companion to the Miller's Tale. The Reeve's Tale resembles formally its immediate predecessor in so far as it also employs description as well as dialogue. Description is used to introduce Symkyn and his family, whereas the pair of clerks are introduced by the sound of their Northern accents,[31] as they burst into the miller's fenland domain, intent upon preventing any further thefts of their college's corn-meal, now that he has advanced from stealing 'curteisly' to being 'a theef outrageously'. Posting themselves respectively above and below the machinery, in order to ensure that the corn that is fed into the hopper yields the proper equivalent of meal in the trough, John and Aleyn engage in an obviously rehearsed exchange, feigning an innocent curiosity about the working of the mechanism. In an age when mills, clocks and church organs constituted the latest advances in civilian technology, their curiosity is quite plausible; but it does not fool Symkyn, who is an altogether different proposition from the carpenter in the Miller's Tale. After he has sent them scampering into the fen, in pursuit of their warden's horse which he had released, he contemptuously exlaims: 'Ye, lat the children pleye' (I, 4098). In the early stages of the tale he seems to be a formidable opponent in both cunning and physical resources. Whereas the clerks are armed merely with a 'bokeler' [small shield] and a sword (I, 4019) apiece (which they cast aside helplessly at 4085), the 'perilous' Symkyn carries about his person, concealed in his clothing, a veritable armoury of knives and daggers of distinctive types.

We are given the complete inventory of this panoply in the course of the family portraits with which the tale begins. The fact that they constitute a family unit was long ago noticed: the wife follows her husband to church on a festival day, wearing 'a gyte of reed', and he wears hose made from the same piece of material (3954-5); both Symkyn (3934) and his daughter (3974) have a 'kamus nose' [probably a 'snub' nose]. But the sense of family solidarity is underpinned by a technical procedure, whose effect the reader may feel without consciously recognizing how it is brought off: all the family have to share the same description. In other words, the constituent parts of a formal *descriptio* are distributed — more or less one apiece — among the various members of the family.

In the portrait of Symkyn himself, only two lines are devoted to a mention of his thieving habits, and only two to his personal appearance:

> Round was his face, and camus was his nose;
> As piled as an ape was his skulle.

> (3934-5)

These details are not there merely to tell us what he looked like. We have already observed the reason for mentioning his snub nose. The mention of his bald head is a 'plant' to prepare us for the accident of his wife's misdirected blow (4306) in the bedroom scene, when, in the scant allowance of moonlight that filters in through a chink in the wall, she mistakes her husband's 'pyled skulle' for the white cap worn by his antagonist. The bulk of the description of Symkyn is concerned with his 'array'; but (as we have seen) his hose, his pouch and his belt are listed only as the containers of his arsenal.

Details of character (normally the subject of the *notatio*) are mainly reserved for the account of his wife, concerning whom indeed we hear little else. She is introduced with a fanfare: 'A wyf he hadde, ycomen of noble kyn.' But the trumpets immediately begin to sound wrong notes:

> The person of the toun hir fader was.
> With hire he yaf ful many a panne of bras,
> For that Symkyn sholde in his blood allye.
>
> (3943-5)

The avaricious miller demanded a substantial dowry before he would agree to take the parish priest's illegitimate daughter off his hands. But the snobbish yeoman will admit only to being impressed by her superior education and the fact that, having come straight from a nunnery, she is guaranteed *virgo intacta*:

> For Symkyn wolde no wyf, *as he sayde*,
> But she were wel ynorissed and a mayde,
> To saven his estaat of yomanrye.
>
> (3947-9 — my italics)

However, it is not until 3963 that the narrator refers explicitly to the fact that she was, on account of the circumstances of her birth, somewhat besmirched in reputation — 'somdel smoterlich'. Her psychological reaction to a circumstance that might, in the ethos of the time, have rendered her something of a social outcast, is to forestall such treatment by holding herself aloof from society in contemptuous superiority.

We are not told the wife's name nor, at first, that of her daughter, who is introduced together with the remaining member of the family:

> A doghter hadde they *bitwixe hem two*
> Of twenty yeer, *withouten any mo*,
> Savynge a child that was of half yeer age;
> In cradel it lay and was a propre page.
>
> (3969-72 — my italics)

The italicized phrases are common 'tags'; but, as so often in Chaucer's mature works, they are more than empty line-fillers. In view of the circumstances of the mother's nativity, it is as well to establish the legitimacy of the daughter; and the fact that she is their only daughter is crucial to the plot. The plot requires the baby for the sake of its cradle, which becomes an essential stage property at 4212 ff. We are expected to overlook the implausibility of the fact that the twenty-year-old girl has a baby brother as her only sibling. Whereas we are told nothing about the mother's personal appearance, and only a little about Symkyn's, the description of the daughter is concerned with nothing else:

> This wenche thikke and wel ygrowen was,
> With kamus nose, and eyen greye as glas,
> With buttokes brode, and brestes rounde and hye;
> But right fair was hire heer, I wol nat lye.

(3973-6)

Other commentators have remarked upon this compact study in genetics; features proper to one 'of noble kyn' being intermingled with those inherited from the sturdy yeoman stock of her father. Her grandfather, the parish priest, evidently thinks her sufficiently 'fair' to attract a husband of 'worthy blood of auncetrye' – provided she is pieced with a fat dowry. And Chaucer tells us where the money was to come from — in a passage I have already discussed as an example of his deft manipulation of language and metre.[32]

When I earlier compared the portrait of Alysoun with that of Emelye, I was following a well-established critical precedent. But, since the juxtaposition of the tales of the Miller and Reeve is as deliberate as that of the tales of the Miller and Knight, it is no less appropriate to compare the burgeoning description of the Miller's eighteen-year-old heroine with the succinct account of the girl in the Reeve's Tale, who is still unmarried at twenty. Whereas the animal imagery animates the portrait of Alysoun, and her positive and resourceful nature is suggested by her tastes in clothes and ornaments, the picture of the Miller's daughter, by concentrating exclusively on the facts of her personal appearance, seems to deny her any character at all. Eighteenth-century gallants referred to young ladies as 'objects': this girl is an 'object' in a more exact sense than their usage would imply. The only occasion when she shows any initiative is when she tells her unexpected lover where he can find the cake which is baked from the meal that her father had stolen from him.

In her mostly passive role she has certain affinities with Emelye. The association is incongruous, but it seems to be a deliberate part of

Chaucer's satirical intent. Her father and grandfather plan her future in the spirit in which royal families negotiate their international matrimonial alliances (the kind of negotiations in which the court had probably employed Chaucer himself). Her father prizes her merely for the price-ticket around her neck. He reveals his attitude quite involuntarily at the moment when he realizes what has befallen his daughter at the hands of one of the Cambridge undergraduates. He begins, as one might expect, with barely coherent exclamations, but the conclusion of his outburst is hardly that of a loving parent. Addressing the clerk, he roars:

> 'Ye, false harlot,' quod the millere, 'hast?
> A, false traitour! false clerk!' quod he,
> 'Thow shalt be deed, by Goddes dignitee!
> Who dorste be so boold to disparage
> My doghter, *that is come of swich lynage?*'
>
> (4268-72 — my italics)

Professor Charles Muscatine was the first commentator to point out that the verb 'disparage' here has a strong flavour of its original meaning: 'to match unequally; to degrade or dishonour by marrying to one of inferior rank'.[33] This leads him to observe that the miller 'is chagrined, not at what has been done to his daughter, but that it has been done by someone of lower class!' — as indicated by the clerk's Northern dialect.[34] We may gratefully acknowledge the force of Professor Muscatine's lexical observation without concurring with the inference he draws from it. For it seems to me that 'disparage' indicates not so much Symkyn's sense of superiority to the clerks as his own social inferiority to those classes who would normally include the term in their vocabulary. Here is another example of the language of court diplomacy being applied to a village community. 'Disparagement' was the subject of one of the clauses of the Petitions of the Barons of 1258. The barons were concerned that women whose marriage was in the gift of the king should not be 'disparaged', and especially that they should not be given to men who were not of the nation of the kingdom of England.[35]

The use of the word 'nation' (*natio*) in this document supplies a clue as to one possible reason why Aleyn and John are made to speak in Northern dialect. Even before the word was regularly applied to nation states, it was a technical term that was used to refer to the way in which, in the great universities of Paris and Bologna, students were grouped together according to their place of origin (e.g. Normans, Tuscans, Lombards). At Oxford the division was simply between North and South.[36] Just before Chaucer was born, The Queen's College was founded at Oxford by the chaplain of Queen Philippa,

Robert of Eglesfield. He was a Cumberland man and special provision was made for students from that county and from Westmorland — for students, in fact, precisely like the Cambridge pair, who came from a village 'fer in the north' (4015 — my italics). The Northern constituency of the college has survived until today. (I recall my first undergraduate term there, when, as a Southerner, I felt myself to be definitely amid the alien corn to such an extent that the only friend I made during the first few weeks was a fellow Southerner: a Hindu from Madras.) In the fourteenth century, both at Oxford and at Cambridge, antagonism between Town and Gown was exacerbated by the exotic origins of many of the students. The proximity of a large concentration of young males was sufficient reason for Symkyn to recruit his one-man militia for the protection of his wife and daughter. The natural xenophobia of the peasant would make the East Anglian yeoman particularly wary of the two Northerners. There is insufficient evidence for supposing (with Muscatine) that he would have regarded them as socially inferior because they did not speak the East Midland dialect.[37] What principally irks Symkyn is that Aleyn is a clerk, who is almost certainly destined for holy orders and must therefore remain celibate, if he is to receive any preferment, since only clergy in minor orders were allowed to marry. There is no prospect even of forcing a 'shotgun wedding' upon him. The verb 'disparage' at 4271 is used in the slightly extended sense of 'to lower the price on the marriage market'. Symkyn would himself not marry any woman 'but she were . . . a mayde' (3948). Now that his daughter is no longer virgo intacta, her value has slumped utterly.

The Reeve's Tale differs from the Miller's, partly in the extent to which enmity between Town and Gown is present, but fundamentally in its attitude towards love. John the carpenter may be a foolish dotard; but he does feel genuine affection for his young wife. The relationship between Alysoun and Nicholas is entirely physical; but their desire is mutual, spontaneous and gratifying to them both. In the Reeve's Tale there is no genuine love of any kind. Symkyn regards his wife as an asset and his daughter as an investment: we never hear him address either of them by name. We learn the daughter's name only when Aleyn addresses her as 'Malyne' in his mock aubade, which he recites as he departs from her bed (I, 4236-9). He has given her the first (and probably the last) experience of 'romance' in her life; and has caused her to transfer her loyalty from her father to himself. But there is nothing romantic in Aleyn's attitude to her, as can be seen from the way in which he afterwards boasts to John — or so he thinks — of the 'noble game' he has played throughout 'this shorte nyght'. Even when he first resolves to sleep with the girl, he does so in a spirit of retribution. The cool brain of the law student sees the escapade as affording due compensation for the loss the father has inflicted upon John and himself (4177-87). John sleeps with the Miller's wife merely in order that he may not be outdone by his companion, and to avoid the stigma of being called a 'daf, a cokenay' when the story of the 'jape' goes the round of the Cambridge colleges.

In this way, there is built into the narrative itself an audience of *clerkes*, that exists independently of the audience of pilgrims to whom the Reeve addresses the tale with which, according to the framing fiction, he intends to 'quyte' the Miller. But the students' enjoyment of the revenge drama of Trumpington Mill has to be postponed until some imaginary future date. Since the Miller's Tale takes place within the city of Oxford, an audience of *clerkes* is able to appear on the scene (I, 3847) to be regaled with Nicholas's version of the night's events, now that his involuntary cry for 'Water' has made public the private performance of the Mystery of the Deluge which this 'derne' operator has devised. When all the townsfolk 'kiken and . . . cape' (3841) into the roof of the carpenter's house, the 'sleigh' Nicholas has no difficulty in attributing the contrived 'fantasye' of his own invention — which began as he himself '*kiked* on the newe moone' (3445) and '*caped* upward into the eir' (3473) — to the alleged lunatic 'fantasye' (3835, 3840) of the carpenter. Throughout the tale, Nicholas has been the solitary ('allone, withouten any compaignye') representative of the 'gown' amid the purlieus of the 'town'. At the critical moment, he can rely upon the collective 'authority' of the university community to uphold his highly glossed version of events as the truth. The academics establish their position by adopting the simple expedient of shouting down the bewildered carpenter's attempts to describe his 'experience'.

Cicero declared that the functions of an orator are threefold: 'to teach, to delight, and to move' (*De Oratore*, 21, 69). The sentiment was especially familiar to medieval writers, for St Augustine, in *De Doctrina Christiana*,[38] applied the dictum to the role of the preacher. The indispensable function for any teller of tales must be to delight (*delectare*). Whatever moral or sociological inflections they may sustain, the tales discussed in the present chapter are concerned with creating mirth, before all other purposes; they take delight in the unfettered joy of narration. But in the Middle Ages — perhaps more conspicuously than in any other period — narrative was liable to be conscripted to serve a didactic end. In the next chapter, I shall consider Chaucer's handling of a species of narrative that was devised precisely for that purpose.

# CHAPTER 4

# 'Ensamples Trewe and Olde':
## From the Monk's Tale to the Pardoner's Tale

I

In Chapter 58 of *Vanity Fair*, Thackeray quotes the complete text of a 'theme', composed at school by Georgy Osborne, and lovingly preserved in the piano-drawer by his mother:

> *On Selfishness.* — Of all the vices which degrade the human character, Selfishness is the most odious and contemptible. An undue love of Self leads to the most monstrous crimes, and occasions the greatest misfortunes both in *States and Families*. As a selfish man will impoverish his family and often bring them to ruin, so a selfish king brings ruin on his people, and often plunges them into war.
>
> Example: The selfishness of Achilles, as remarked by the poet Homer, occasioned a thousand woes to the Greeks ... The selfishness of the late Napoleon Bonaparte occasioned innumerable wars in Europe, and caused him to perish, himself, in a miserable island — that of Saint Helena in the Atlantic Ocean.
>
> We see by these examples that we are not to consult our own interest and ambition, but that we are to consider the interests of others as well as our own.
>
> George S. Osborne.<br>*Athenè House, 24th April, 1827.*

It is interesting to observe that, only one year before Thomas Arnold became headmaster of Rugby, boys were evidently still being formally taught to search in legend and history, both ancient and modern, for *exempla* to support or illustrate a thesis, just as they had been instructed to do in Chaucer's day.

Probably the best-known *exempla* in the *Canterbury Tales* are the two travellers' tales which the Nun's Priest contrives to insert into his recounting of the fable of the cock and fox (VII, 2984-3109). They are employed by Chauntecleer to support his thesis that some dreams are 'Warnynge of thynges that shul after falle' (VII, 3132). Not only are these anecdotes vivid illustrations of the cock's general contention, but they are 'slanted' by him so as to pour scorn upon Pertelote's contemptuous dismissal of the fear that his own dream has engendered in him. She declares that she cannot love a cowardly husband 'that is *agast* of every tool' (2916) and proceeds to state categorically that dreams are empty of significance: 'Nothyng, God woot, but *vanitee* in sweven is' (2922). In Chauntecleer's first *exemplum*, the pilgrim lodged in an ox's stall appears in a dream to his separated companion, and appeals for help to prevent his murder. But the latter, though woken by fear, merely turns over again to sleep: 'Hym thoughte his dreem nas but a *vanitee*' (3011) — the narrator sarcastically crows. The most memorable feature of the other little anecdote — the one about the two intending seafarers — is the ten-line speech assigned to the ill-fated sceptic (3088-97): 'No dreem . . . may so myn herte *agaste*' he begins, and continues:

'For swevenes been but *vanytees* and japes.
Men dreme alday of owles and of apes . . .'

— where, to Chauntecleer's nagging echo of Pertelote's words, Chaucer appears to add his own reminiscence of the words of the equally sceptical Pandarus (*TC*, V, 382).

Chauntecleer attributes these *ensamples* to 'Oon of the gretteste auctour that men rede' (2984), and follows them with six others, derived from a variety of no less authoritative sources: a Legendary, the Bible, Macrobius and classical mythology. But these anecdotes are cited only in summary form. A fourteenth-century Georgy Osborne would have felt at home, not only with the practice of deploying such *ensamples* to support or illustrate an argument, but also with the particular 'auctour' whose sceptical view of dreams Pertelote had cited (2940-1); for the *Disticha* of Dionysius Cato was a prescribed primary school text. Nor would he have been unduly surprised by the association of such solemn stories with the fable of the cock and fox; for Aesop, and his many redactors and imitators, was studied by schoolboys for the sake of the 'moralitee' that his fables inculcated.[1] In a later chapter we shall see that the academic satire of the Nun's Priest's Tale extends far beyond the walls of the grammar school.[2]

Chaucer could easily have expanded the six subsidiary instances into full-scale *exempla* like the story of the man murdered in the oxstall. If he had prefaced such a sequence with a discussion on the significance of dreams, along the lines of the *Proem* to Book One of *The House of Fame*, and had concluded with an inconclusive epilogue, in the manner of the last five lines of *The Parlement of Foules*, he would have compiled a 'litel tretys' worthy to stand beside his two major collections of *exempla*: *The Legend of Good Women* and the Monk's Tale.

In fact, the Nun's Priest's Tale does quite literally stand beside the Monk's Tale — though it is doubtful whether the Monk would have regarded it as a 'worthy' successor to his series of 'tragedyes'. The Monk defines his chosen genre thrice. At the end of the Introduction to his tale, after enduring patiently the Host's tasteless sexual banter, he solemnly provides a miniature *accessus* ['approach'][3] to his own tale — as if he were writing an academic prologue to the work of an established 'auctour'. He refers to both the 'matter' and prosody of 'tragedye', and follows this with a brief *exordium* in which he apologizes for the absence of chronological order in his compilation. Briefer definitions stand at the beginning and end of the tale proper. The definition at the opening of the Tale occupies, nevertheless, the whole of one of the eight-line stanzas which Chaucer employs only here in the Canterbury series. It is from this stanza that the title of the present chapter is taken:-

> I wol biwaille, in manere of tragedie,
> The harm of hem that stoode in heigh degree,
> And fillen so that ther nas no remedie
> To brynge hem out of hir adversitee.
> For certein, whan that Fortune list to flee,
> Ther may no man the cours of hire withholde.
> Lat no man truste on blynd prosperitee;
> Be war by thise ensamples trewe and olde.

(VII, 1991-8)

This conforms to the standard medieval definition of Tragedy, which had also supplied the paradigm for the series of *exempla* in Boccaccio's *De Casibus Virorum Illustrium* ('On the Falls of Famous Men').[4] It has long been recognized that the Nun's Priest's Tale generates some of its satirical power through its continual backward glances at its predecessor. The comic beast-fable is invested with much of the solemn and dismal rhetorical apparatus appropriate for the recital of a tragedy. The narrator never loses an opportunity of introducing references to Fortune — some more apt than others. Not all these references are immediately apparent to the modern reader: as, for example, when Chauntecleer, during his anecdote about the seafarers, describes how '*casuelly* the shippes botme rente' (VII, 3103). Chauntecleer's sequence of eight *exempla* is no doubt inspired by the series of seventeen which the Monk rehearses before he is interrupted by the Knight. One *ensample* — that of Croesus — is common to both series. The recurrence of this story prompts two considerations.

The first is the fairly obvious point that the same narrative material may be directed to more than one end. Such an Aristotelian distinction between material and final causes is characteristic of the medieval analysis of literary compositions: it is inherent in the distinction (that we have already encountered) between *sensus* and *sententia*.[5] The distortions and disparities that exemplification sometimes produces may be briefly illustrated by comparing Chaucer's with Gower's treatment of two pre-existing stories, that of Constance and that of Troilus. Both poets derive the tale of Constance from the same source: the Anglo-Norman chronicle of Nicholas Trevet. Gower keeps more closely to the text of the original than does Chaucer in the Man of Law's Tale. Nevertheless, Chaucer's intention in relating the story is nearer to that of Trevet; it is seen as a tale of constancy in adversity and of the working of Divine Providence. Gower introduces it into the second book of *Confessio Amantis* (587-1598) as one of two principal exemplifications of detraction or back-biting, a sub-division of the sin of Envy. After discussing Detraction in general terms (with the aid of the Bestiary *exemplum* of the 'Scharnebud', a beetle that alights on ordure in preference to flowers), he turns, at 445, specifically to the subject of Detraction 'In loves Court'. Detraction of lovers is hardly the main theme of the story of Constance. It may indeed be detected in the behaviour of the heroine's two successive mothers-in-law, but their hostility to her is occasioned by the fact that she causes their respective sons to be baptized. The most relevant episode is that of the knight who, after his amatory advances have been rejected by Constance, 'Of hire honour . . . hadde Envie' (811), and so falsely accused her of murder. In the course of the fifty or so octosyllabic couplets devoted to this episode, Gower never employs the word 'detraction'. It is only in the Latin gloss (probably by Gower himself) that we find mention of 'verbis detractoriis'.[6]

While we are considering this section of *Confessio Amantis*, it is interesting to observe Gower's other *exemplum* of Detraction: the story of Demetrius and Perseus. Although this story has nothing to do with love, it is rather more sharply focused than is his tale of Constance upon the vice which it ostensibly exemplifies. Even so, its account of the rise and fall of Perseus (the last king of Macedonia), after slandering his brother and edging his father off the throne, would equally well have served Chaucer's Monk as an example of a 'tragedye' induced by Fortune. Indeed, Boethius had cited this episode as a prime example of 'tragedy'[7] — though Chaucer, in his translation of Boethius's *The Consolation of Philosophy*, misunderstands the reference (cf. *Boece*, II, Prosa ii). Gower himself positively encourages such an interpretation of the usurper's career:

For sodeinliche as he aros
So sodeinliche doun he fell.

(*CA*, II, 1758-9)

Again, when the poet describes how Perseus's forces were riding across the frozen Danube to give battle to the Roman consul, Paulus Aemilius, there is a reference to Fortune:

> ... the blinde whiel,
> Which torneth ofte er men be war,
> Thilke ys which that the horsmen bar          [ys = ice]
> Tobrak, so that a gret partie          [Tobrak = broke]
> Was dreint; of the chivalerie          [dreint = drowned]
> The rerewarde it tok aweie,
> Cam non of hem to londe dreie.
>
> (1822-8)

The most memorable episode in this story is that concerning the consul's daughter who, as her father is about to set off to encounter Perseus, announces tearfully 'Perse is ded' — referring to the demise of her pet dog. Her father takes this as a favourable omen. Although no dream is involved, this 'prenostik', involving a 'hound', might well have interested Chauntecleer. It is not only the coincidence of the name that earns the unwitting girl the title of 'my dowhter prophetesse', but also the fact that it is a dog's nature to bark at a man from behind, signifying the way in which Perseus slandered his brother and caused his death. It also signified that the tyrant would die like a dog, starved to death in prison: a fitting end for one who

> ... with his detraccioun
> Bark on his brother so behinde.
>
> (1860-1)

So the story ends as an *ensample* of detraction. But it might just as well have concluded with a moral about 'the unwaar strook' of Fortune or the uncanny operation of omens.

The story of Troilus is referred to four times in *Confessio Amantis*. The most remarkable of these references occurs at V, 7597-602, where the Trojan hero is introduced as an example of sacrilege in love. Because he first loved Criseyde 'In holi place', he was ultimately forsaken for Diomede: 'Such was of love his laste mede.' Evidently he should have been attending to the service instead of gazing at the girls. When Chaucer, some years earlier, dedicated his *Troilus and Criseyde* to 'moral Gower', could he have guessed that this was how his friend would respond to his 'litel ... tragedye'? In the corresponding temple scene in Chaucer's poem (I, 155 ff.) Troilus, though not guilty of sacrilege precisely, does commit the closely related sin of blasphemy. However, his offence is not against the deity in whose honour the service is being celebrated. His sin consists in scorning the youths in his retinue who are sighing after the ladies. So the angered Cupid avenges himself by causing Troilus to be smitten by a single glance from Criseyde, and thus induces the 'proces' that leads to his ultimate 'tragedye'.[8]

This discussion of the multiple and divergent significations of a single story may seem to be impelling us towards the Quicksands of Allegory. Indeed, the pull of the tide is reinforced by the fact that medieval commentators found allegorical meanings, not only in bible stories, but also in classical myths, fables and other writings. For example, the twelfth-century Rhineland recluse, Honorius (usually known as 'Honorius of Autun'), introduces into a sermon an allegorization of the episode of Ulysses and the Sirens.[9] The three Sirens represent Avarice, Vainglory and Wantonness, respectively. They have women's faces because love of women most readily alienates Man from God; they have birds' wings because the desires of the wordly are volatile. Ulysses (Wisdom) sails past them unharmed in the ship of the Church, having bound himself fast to the mast (i.e. the cross). Certain twentieth-century commentators on Chaucer, assuming the cassocks of their medieval counterparts, have even subjected some of the *Canterbury Tales* to similar exposition. One of the most unlikely subjects to have sustained such treatment is the Shipman's Tale.[10] What Chaucer's attitude to such an approach might have been is a question that will be considered when I resume discussion of the Nun's Priest's Tale in my final chapter. For the present I shall stop my ears against the Siren cries of the three 'spiritual senses' of scripture, and other kinds of allegorical interpretation, and assert baldly that, whereas exemplification is a mode of some prominence in *The Canterbury Tales*, allegory is not.[11]

The other consideration prompted by Chaucer's use of the story of Croesus in two successive tales is rather more interesting. One might have expected the satirical Nun's Priest's Tale to reduce to ridicule the solemn Monk's version of the story; but that does not happen. Chauntecleer's exemplary citation certainly wastes no words:

> 'Whoso wol seken actes of sondry remes
> May rede of dremes many a wonder thyng.
> Lo Cresus, which that was of Lyde kyng,
> Mette he nat that he sat upon a tree,
> Which signified he sholde anhanged bee?'

(VII, 3136-40)

But it is a crude over-simplification of the rather subtle 'brief life' that constitutes the Monk's last 'tragedye'. This is itself an abbreviation, concentrating into thirty-four lines the essential features of the version which, in the *Roman de la Rose*, Jean de Meun had introduced as one of his *exempla* of the characteristics of Fortune.[12] It begins with an averted tragedy. Croesus, rich and powerful, is caught by his enemies 'amyddes al his pryde', and led to the fire to be burnt. But rain extinguishes the blaze and he escapes. Instead of regarding this as a warning of the sudden reversals of Fortune, he interprets it (like Macbeth in comparable circumstances) as a sign that he enjoys a charmed life. So he re-opens his campaign, further assured by a dream 'Of which he was so proud and eek so fayn' (VII, 2741), in which he imagines himself on a tree, washed by Jupiter and dried with a towel by Phoebus. After his daughter's unfavourable exposition of this dream is given, the narrative immediately states: 'Anhanged was Cresus, the proude kyng . . .'. So dreams are not straightforward predictions (as Chauntecleer represents them to be), but rather, like oracles (or the witches' prophecies in *Macbeth*), they are what Criseyde calls 'amphibologies' — ambiguities (*TC*, IV, 1406). Similarly, the 'tragedye' does not consist merely of the precipitate tumble from the zenith of Fortune's wheel which medieval definitions of the genre may seem to imply. The finest *exempla* are, indeed, often precisely those which transcend the didactic 'end' that they ostensibly serve.

To put it negatively: the 'tragedye' of Croesus is not the least interesting of the Monk's *exempla*. The fact that (in some of the most authoritative MSS)[13] it is after this anecdote that the tale is interrupted should warn us against taking too seriously the Host's critical comment, addressed to its teller, that 'Youre tale anoyeth [bores] al this compaignye' (VII,2789). Never a reliable literary critic, the somnolent master of ceremonies is here sheltering behind the authority of the Knight who, however, interrupts the Monk, not because he thinks his performance incompetent, but because he maintains that human kind cannot bear too much unrelieved gloom. Certainly, the tale would have become wearisome if it had been allowed to continue any further. But, in fact, it is already complete — as the recapitulation (VII, 2761-6) of the initial definition of 'tragedye' suggests. There is no evidence that Chaucer regarded what he had written as an example of 'drasty rymyng' (cf. VII, 930). The dark monochrome is part of the design; the repeated invocation of the blind goddess Fortune sustains a deliberate monotony, comparable to that of a litany.

Nevertheless, in spite of the general impression of monotony, there is a certain variety in the sequence. Not only do the *exempla* vary in length, but also in their origins. As in Reason's discourse on Fortune in the *Roman de la Rose*, there are both ancient and modern instances; but in the Monk's Tale the former are taken from biblical as well as classical sources. Chaucer's instances range chronologically from Adam to Barnabo Visconti, who was murdered as recently as 1385, but (as already noted) the biographies are not arranged in chronological order. Just as in the Dance of Death persons of different estates and ages of life are seized, so in this sequence Fortune attacks arbitrarily and 'With unwar strook' the prosperous from all Ages of the World.[14]

Not only is the blind goddess no respecter of persons, she is equally no respecter of merit: the good, the evil and the indifferent are assailed with similar force. The series begins with Lucifer, notwithstanding the fact that 'Fortune may noon angel dere' [harm] (because her sphere of influence does not extend above the moon). The fall of the 'brightest of angels alle' from 'heigh degree' into the misery of hell establishes, *a fortiori*, a propensity that is inherent in all those mortals who are highly placed within the sublunary realm where Fortune holds sway. One might have expected the portrait of 'Sathanas' to be the most repulsive in the series; but he is surpassed in loathesomeness by the monstrous Nero, the manner of whose death may strike us as a comparatively mild punishment for one who commits such unnatural atrocities. Nero's end is far less terrible than that of 'Erl Hugelyn of Pyze', imprisoned in a tower and starved to death together with his small sons. Although in Chaucer's source (Dante, *Inferno*, xxxiii), Hugelyn's counterpart, Ugolino, is punished in the frozen waste of Cocytus on account of his treachery, the English poet sees him merely as the victim of 'a fals suggestioun' alleged against him by his rival, Roger, Bishop of Pisa. His suffering, no less than that of his children (2413-14), is attributed purely to the arbitrary conduct of Fortune (2457). The 'tragedye' of Cenobia, Queen of Palmyra, is derived from the accounts of Zenobia in Boccaccio's *De Claris Mulieribus* and in his *De Casibus Virorum Illustrium*. Chaucer presents this warrior queen as a thoroughly admirable (if slightly eccentric) character.[15] When she was eventually persuaded to marry, she would allow her husband to 'doon his fantasye' only for the strict purpose of begetting offspring. Apart from that,

> He gat namoore of hire, for thus she seyde,
> It was to wyves lecherie and shame,
> In oother caas, if that men with hem pleyde.

> (VII, 2292-4)

In this way she bore only two sons, leaving herself free to engage in her warlike pursuits. This 'worshipful . . . creature' is also 'wys therwith, and large with mesure' (i.e. temperately liberal). When she has the leisure she delights to learn foreign languages and study books in order to learn 'How she in vertu myghte hir lyf dispende' (2310). Eventually Fortune turns against her and she is defeated by the Roman emperor, Aurelianus, who makes her walk through his capital at the head of his triumph and causes her to suffer the humiliation of exchanging her sceptre for a distaff. It is worth remarking incidentally that, if any Chaucerian character is a precursor of twentieth-century feminism, it is Cenobia — certainly not Alys of Bath.

The Monk's Tale's indifference to the rewards of vice and virtue, and its persistent recital of gloom, have caused some critics to allege that it is pervaded by a spirit of un-Christian pessimism. That this is not necessarily so will be evident if we consider the context of Chaucer's one other definition of 'tragedye'. This occurs at *Boece*, II, Prosa ii, 70, where the term is glossed: 'Tragedye is to seyn a dite [poem] of a prosperite for a tyme, that endeth in wrecchidnesse'. Fortune is speaking; and, having referred to the fate of Croesus (and Paulus Aemilius's lament for the fall of his captive, Perseus),[16] she exclaims: 'What other thyng bywaylen the cryinges of tragedyes but oonly the dedes of Fortune, that with unwar strook overturneth the realmes of greet nobleye?' Fortune argues that the man who has lost his former wealth and honours cannot justly complain that she has robbed him of them, since he had no inalienable right to them; she merely loaned them to him. It is her nature to be as mutable as the weather; her wheel never stands still; she is indifferent to men's reactions to her treatment of them. If they wish to play her game, they must recognize that they reach the zenith of her wheel only on condition that they think it no injustice when they are plunged into the depths. In a later part of this Second Book of *The Consolation of Philosophy*, Lady Philosophy demonstrates to Boethius that all temporal objects that men most desire (Power, Wealth, Fame), though good in themselves, are only contingent, mutable goods and mere shadows of true felicity, the *summum bonum*, or Sovereign Good, which she proceeds (in Book III) to identify with God.

This is not the place to examine Philosophy's account (in Book IV) of the relationship between Destiny and Divine Providence, or to consider how she addresses herself to the problem of why the virtuous suffer and the wicked prosper in this world. We need proceed no further than the end of Book II (Prosa viii) to encounter her argument that 'contrarious Fortune' is of greater advantage to man than 'Fortune debonayre'. For, whereas the latter distracts him from the 'sovereyne good', the former draws most men to the 'sothfast goodes' (by preventing them from stagnating in states of temporal contentment). So when, in Chaucer's own century, Petrarch compiled his treatise on the same subject, he entitled it *De Remediis Utriusque Fortunae* — i.e. on the remedies against good, as well as bad, fortune.

It has been shown that the Monk's Tale contains a number of parallels to Boethius's *Consolation*,[17] but it is not the narrator's purpose to use his *exempla* to expound the Boethian providential scheme. By choosing to write in the genre of 'tragedye', he deliberately imposes a limited point of view upon himself so that he perceives only that part of the providential pattern that appears as Fortune ('executrice of wyrdes' — as Chaucer calls her [*TC*,III,617]). His moral purpose is simply to warn men against mistaking her loans for the *summum bonum*: 'For whan men trusteth hire, thanne wol she faille [deceive].' We have seen, in Chapter 1, an instance of Fortune and her wheel painted on the walls of a Christian church, and placed opposite the bishop's throne.

The most often discussed of the Monk's 'tragedyes' is that of Hugelyn, mainly because it invites comparison with its source (*Inferno*, xxxiii), the episode that elicits more pity and terror than perhaps any other in Dante's *Divina Commedia*.[18] We have already remarked that Dante presents Ugolino as an *exemplum* of treachery (to the count's native Pisa). But he mentions this fact only after the narrative is complete and the poet, apostrophizing Pisa as New Thebes (for both Dante and Chaucer the archetypal city of horrific crimes), exclaims that, although the count was reputed to have betrayed some of its fortified outposts, this was no reason for putting his children to such torment; their tender years made them innocent:

> Chè se'l conte Ugolino aveva voce
> d'aver tradita te delle castella,
> non dovei tu i figliuoi porre a tal croce.
> Innocenti facea l'età novella,
> novella Tebe . . .

(xxxiii, 85-9)

[What if Count Ugolino had the reputation of betraying your strongholds! You should not have put his children to such torture. Their young age rendered them innocent, O New Thebes . . .]

In the lines that most nearly correspond to these, Chaucer apostrophizes Fortune instead of Pisa, adds a rather obvious pathetic image, and loses the comparison with Thebes, together with the telling word-play on *novella* (young/new):

Allas, Fortune! it was greet crueltee
Swiche briddes for to putte in swich a cage!

(VII, 2413-14)

Dante does not eschew pathos. He enhances it by quietly
memorializing, in the concluding lines (89-90) of the episode, the
names of the children not already identified in the preceding
narrative. His other notable instance of pathos is one that comes
naturally to an Italian speaker; it likewise involves a personal name.
When Ugolino introduces the speech (all of six words!) of his son,
Anselm, he refers to him as 'Anselmuccio mio' (50). The effect is
impossible to reproduce in English, where diminutive suffixes (as in
'Georgy') are apt to make a personal name sound mawkish. The
inevitable translation, 'my little Anselm', sounds unnatural and
patronizing. So Chaucer was probably wise to refrain from naming
the children, and to distinguish them by simply stating the ages of
two of them.

The most obvious difference between the two versions resides in
the fact that it is the shade of Ugolino himself who reveals to Dante
and Virgil the unknowable story of his last days on Earth — as he
diverts his jaws from their eternal gnawing at the back of the head of
the man who had starved him to death. The archbishop, immersed
up to the neck in the frozen Cocytus, listens in silence throughout the
recital which Ugolino begins, for Virgil's benefit, by echoing the
words with which Aeneas (in very different circumstances) com-
menced his narrative of the last days of Troy.[19] When Ugolino begins
his narrative proper (line 22), he is already inside the 'Hunger
Tower', the moonlight filtering in through the 'Breve pertugio' (little
opening). Chaucer's objective narration conveys no sense of
intimating what could not possibly be known to the outside world
and, indeed, begins outside the tower and proceeds to place the
victim, and his three sons within it:

But litel out of Pize stant a tour,
In which tour in prisoun put was he ...

(VII, 2409-10)

This is as matter-of-fact as the opening of the Reeve's Tale:

At Trumpyngtoun, nat fer fro Cantebrigge,
Ther gooth a brook, and over that a brigge,
Upon the whiche brook ther stant a melle ...

(I, 3921-3)

The *exemplum* continues, following the 'natural order' of narrative sequence, down to its concluding tribute to 'the grete poete of Ytaille', to whom the reader is referred, if he would hear the story 'in a lenger wise'.

It has been pointed out that, in spite of Chaucer's remark, the narrative proper of the Ugolino episode is only three lines longer than Chaucer's version.[20] Nevertheless, Dante's version gives the impression of a longer narrative. It is, in fact, the longest episode in the whole of the *Inferno*; but the impression of long duration is an integral part of this particular narrative, since starvation is a long-drawn-out torture. The experience of hunger is intensified by other forms of deprivation, particularly of sound, space and of light, down to the moment when the father gropes sightlessly with his hands over the corpses of his children. The few incidents that interrupt the passage of the silent, empty days are all the more startling for their infrequency: the dream, the nailing up of the prison door, the father's gnawing of his arms for grief, the children's brief utterances and their falling dead, one by one. The sense of slow, inevitable doom is enhanced by Dante's use of his *terza rima*, whereas Chaucer's employment of his eight-line stanza tends to break up the narrative into separate episodes. The fourth of these stanzas is, however, one of the most memorable Chaucer ever wrote. It may be that this 'tragedye' never rises above the level of pathos, but there is nothing sentimental about the speech that the poet invents for the boy, having entered completely into the child's mind:

> His yonge sone, that thre yeer was of age,
> Unto hym seyde, 'Fader, why do ye wepe?
> Whanne wol the gayler bryngen oure potage?
> Is ther no morsel breed that ye do kepe?
> I am so hungry that I may nat slepe.
> Now wolde God that I myghte slepen evere!
> Thanne sholde nat hunger in my wombe crepe;
> There is no thyng, save breed, that me were levere.'
>
> (VII, 2431-8)

The Wordsworth of *Lyrical Ballads* never achieved anything comparable to the artful simplicity of these lines.

## II

It would be unfair to Chaucer to set his version of the Ugolino story beside Dante's in order to assess their overall achievements as writers of *exempla*. Chaucer's own masterpiece in this kind is the extended tale of the three 'riotoures' seeking Death, which the Pardoner employs to reinforce the doctrine of his sermon on the text: 'Radix malorum est Cupiditas' [Avarice is the root of evils]. Its narration exhibits a mastery of timing and pacing, of the use of sound and of silence, as well as the deployment of significant detail, which Chaucer may possibly have assimilated from his reading of Dante. Yet the tale is so unlike anything that Dante could ever have written that a meaningful comparison would be impossible to devise. Another advantage of this *exemplum* over any of those in the Monk's Tale results from its relationship to its context. Again, this is as subtle as any that Dante produced; yet its effect is quite unlike anything in the *Commedia*. For Chaucer here demonstrates how a work of fiction may, as soon as it is conscripted to act as an *exemplum*, become liable to serve an immoral end, however moral it may be in itself (i.e. however moral its own *sensus* and its intrinsic *sententia* may be). Indeed, he shows how slippery the concept of the 'end' — what Aristotelians termed the 'Final Cause' — of a work of fiction can be.

The relationship of the Pardoner's Tale to its context has been the subject of a controversy among commentators which has (in my opinion) sometimes led to a distorted view of the *exemplum* itself. So I shall first consider this tale in its own right, before venturing to discuss its effect within its setting. There is, however, one preliminary observation that must be made about the relationship between the *exemplum* and the sermon. Chaucer gives merely an impression of the Pardoner's sermon. Its discursive portion has nothing to say about its *theme* of avarice, but is entirely preoccupied with denouncing the sins of the tavern — drunkenness, swearing and gambling (VI, 463-660) — all three of which are destined to play an essential, though subsidiary, part in the *exemplum*. It is as if the discourse grew out of the narrative in which it culminates (VI, 661-895).[21]

The tale of the three rioters seeking Death has often been admired for its dramatic irony,[22] its concentration, and the sense of awe that it engenders: indeed, it has more than once been described as one of the best short stories in English. I shall argue that its concentration and uncanny power are the result of three things in particular: a threefold economy, a double perspective, and a unifying irony.

It is generally agreed that much of the tale's fascination is due to the figure of the 'oold man and a povre' who directs the three rioters to the treasure. Yet there has been considerable disagreement about the identity and the significance of this character. However, John M. Steadman has offered an explanation of his function which is based more firmly upon Chaucer's text than are most of the other interpretations.[23] According to Professor Steadman the old man is not a sinister or a supernatural figure: he is neither the Wandering Jew nor Death in disguise. Moreover, although one of his functions is to act as a *memento mori*, he is not a personification of Elde, one of the traditional messengers of Death. On the other hand, Professor Steadman will not follow W.J.B. Owen to the position of extreme naturalism and argue that he 'is an old man and nothing more'.[24] Whereas Owen maintains that the old man invents the story about Death being under the tree as a convenient means of getting rid of the drunkards who offer him violence, Steadman argues that, like the hermit in some of the tale's analogues, the old man really has seen the treasure and, in his wisdom, has passed it by because he 'knows the causal relations between cupidity and death'.[25] Steadman regards the old man as a generalized 'notion of aged humanity' and aptly remarks that Chaucer's 'attempt to delineate the general through the particular brings him close to the frontiers of allegory, but he does not actually cross.'[26] The way in which this generalized figure hovers near the frontiers of naturalism and of other modes of presentation is one of the factors that produce the double perspective which I shall discuss later.

There is a false start to the story at VI, 463, which is separated from the beginning of the tale proper at 661 by the 'digression' (i.e. the discursive part of the sermon) on the sins of the tavern. What I have to say about this digression is so obvious that it would be hardly worth mentioning, were it not for the fact that it seems to have escaped the notice of several scholars who have written about this tale and who have offered some extravagant and cumbersome explanations of the presence of this passage.[27] The digression is, of course, entirely relevant to the *sentence* of the *exemplum* which is interrupted.[28] Although Avarice is the radical sin that is illustrated in the tale, the three sins that are denounced in the digression all contribute to the bringing about of the tale's catastrophe. If the rioters had not been drunk, they would not have set out upon their quest to 'sleen this false traytour Deeth' in the first place. If they had not been so profligate with their oaths, they might have taken more seriously their covenant of brotherhood and might have paid more attention to the solemn, admonitory imprecations of the old man. 'Hasardrye' is obviously related to Avarice, but it is perhaps worth remarking that the habitual desire of each of the revellers to play for the highest possible stakes causes him to plot against one or both of his 'brothers' and so is directly responsible for inducing the internecine catastrophe.

Once the tale proper has begun there is no further interruption: the action moves forward with a relentless logic to what, when it is reached, appears to be the inevitable conclusion — given the rioters' characters and the circumstances in which they find themselves. This rapid, irresistible progression is reinforced by Chaucer's economy in narrative technique. Not only is there an absence of digression, but an economy in three things principally: in characterization, in description and in narrative itself. I shall consider each of these three in turn.

One of Chaucer's happiest methods of adapting his sources was to pay particular attention to distinctive details of characterization. This can be seen even in such a brief narrative as the Prioress's Tale, where the pathos is considerably enhanced by the way in which the 'litel clergeon' is individualized, mainly through his conversation with his more mundane schoolfellow. In the Pardoner's Tale, however, individualization of character is kept to a minimum. The only character to be described in detail is the old man and, as we have already seen, he is a generalized figure, compounded of 'commonplaces' that were traditionally associated with old age. He is sharply contrasted with the 'riotoures thre', but they are themselves hardly individualized at all: any one of them could have played the part of any other. It might be argued that this is simply because they are presented as a trio of 'sworn brothers', who speak and act in concert — 'we thre been al ones' (696) — until they come upon the gold. It might be pointed out in support of this argument that Aleyn and John, the co-operative pair of clerks in the Reeve's Tale, are far less easy to distinguish than are Nicholas and Absolon, the pair of rivals in the Miller's Tale, whose characters are so carefully contrasted.

The clerks in the Reeve's Tale, however, are distinguished at least by name; whereas in the Pardoner's Tale all the characters, whose voices we hear so clearly, remain anonymous. It is true that this is not the only tale in which the characters are anonymous: there is the Prioress's Tale, for example; but, as we have seen, the 'litel clergeon' in that tale is endowed with a distinct personality of his own. What is so striking about the Pardoner's Tale is the combination of anonymity and impersonality. There is other evidence which suggests that this is deliberate on Chaucer's part. It is uncertain how much importance should be attached to the fact that names are given to the rioters' counterparts in some of the analogues. But it is surely undeniable that it would have been simpler and more convenient for Chaucer if he had referred to the various members of his trio by using personal names, instead of resorting to the slightly clumsy and obtrusively impersonal means of differentiation that we find in the tale: 'the proudeste of the three', 'the worste', 'the yongeste', 'the firste shrewe', 'that oon', 'that oother' . . . What seems to me to clinch the matter is the answer that the servant gives when one of the rioters bids him:

'Go bet . . . and axe redily
What cors is this that passeth heer forby;
*And looke that thou reporte his name weel.*'

(VI, 667-9 — my italics)

But we no more learn the dead man's name than we learn the name
of the servant himself — or, indeed, the names of the rioters, the
taverner, the old man or the apothecary. The servant informs his
master merely: 'He was, pardee, an old felawe of youres.' Three lines
later, however, the intention behind all this contrived anonymity
becomes clearer. The final line of the master's command has alerted
us: we expect to hear a proper name; but the fulfilment of our
expectations is delayed and transferred. Instead of hearing the name
of the stricken man, we hear the name of his assailant: 'Ther cam a
privee theef men clepeth Deeth . . .' This is the only proper name we
hear — apart from the name of God — until we reach the final
episode.

It is perhaps not too fanciful to argue that Death is the only
'character' in the tale who is completely individualized and presented
as a complex personality. We are shown several facets of his
character: his capriciousness; the arbitrary way in which he strikes or
refuses to strike; his stealth and elusiveness; the subtlety and irony of
his way of working. We also encounter some of his 'espye[s]' and
those who are truly 'of his assent': *not* — as one of the rioters and
some modern critics allege — the old man; but plague and heart-
attack, and — more pertinently — Drunkenness, Swearing,
Gambling and, above all, Avarice.

This 'character study' is communicated to the reader through the
dialogue and by means of implication. The only character who is
described in detail is the old man, as we have seen, and that
description is conveyed mainly through dialogue. In several of his
tales Chaucer 'amplifies' his matter by introducing his characters
through more or less formal *effictiones*, but also by giving
descriptions, either concentrated or dispersed, of the setting and
background of the action. In the Pardoner's Tale, however, he is
content with a bare minimum of stage properties, which are
introduced to indicate a change of scene and to provide a concrete
centre around which the characters can group themselves. The
rioters meet the old man 'as they wolde han troden over a stile'. He
tells them that, if they 'turne up this croked wey', they will find
Death under an oak. Nothing is seen of the funeral cortège at the
beginning of the tale; the clinking of the bell is merely heard 'off
stage' — and, incidentally, is all the more alarming for being
introduced in the very next couplet after the one in which we are told

that the rioters were sitting in the tavern 'Longe erst er prime rong of any belle'. When Romeo wishes to buy 'a dram of poison', Shakespeare indulges in an extended description of the apothecary's shop,[29] but we are vouchsafed no description whatever of the establishment that the youngest rioter visits for his more venomous purpose. On the other hand, Chaucer reports in detail the false arguments that the rioter used to persuade the apothecary to sell him the poison, and then, modulating into direct speech, he tells us precisely what the apothecary said in reply:

> 'And thou shalt have
> A thyng that, also God my soule save,
> In al this world ther is no creature,
> That eten or dronken hath of this confiture
> Noght but the montance of a corn of whete,
> That he ne shal his lif anon forlete;
> Ye, sterve he shal, and that in lasse while
> Than thou wolt goon a paas nat but a mile,
> This poysoun is so strong and violent.'
>
> (VI, 859-67)

Chaucer's reporting this conversation in full, while remaining silent about the setting, brings me to the third kind of economy that is noticeable in this tale: what can only be called 'economy of narrative'. It has often been remarked that much of the tale consists of dialogue and that this is mainly responsible for its dramatic quality. But it has another consequence too: the fact that we so seldom hear the narrator speaking in his own voice means that plain narrative, when it does occur, is all the more arresting and telling. Before the full effect of this economy can be properly examined, however, it is necessary to observe just how much information about character, motive and circumstance Chaucer manages to convey through almost completely unannotated dialogue.

The very first exchange sets the pace for the whole tale and subtly introduces two of its most disquieting features. We hear the master's peremptory 'Go bet', but his servant does not obey. There is no need for the serving-boy to leave the tavern in order to satisfy the rioter's enquiry about the meaning of the lich-bell; he knows the answer already: 'It was me toold er ye cam heer two houres' (671). The uneasy sensation of having been anticipated — whether by another character, by events, or by unseen powers — increases as the tale proceeds. The other disturbing feature I have already touched upon: the rioter asks for the dead man's name, but the boy gives him instead the name of his sinister assailant. This is symptomatic of the essential movement of the plot: when the rioters expect to meet

Death, they find the treasure; they find Death, 'hwenne [hie] wene[th] to libben best'[30] [when they have the greatest expections of life].

From the boy's speech it emerges that he conceives of death in the way that his mother had taught him to do, as a 'privee theef' armed with a spear, who strikes men unexpectedly and goes stealthily on his way. Being but a child,[31] he is not so sophisticated as to know about personification and allegory; he accepts as literally true what his mother had told him: 'Thus taughte me my dame; I sey namoore.' The taverner confirms what the boy has said about the activities of Death during the current epidemic of plague. He continues to speak of Death as if it were a real person, following the boy's remark; but he is, presumably, speaking figuratively, whereas the boy was not. Perhaps we are meant to think of him as humouring the boy — with an innkeeper's tact — by continuing to speak in his phrase; to have questioned his conception of Death would, after all, have meant flouting his mother's authority. For the rioters, who are thoroughly drunk by this time (705), the distinction between literal and figurative meanings has become temporarily blurred. Having heard the boy speak of Death as if he were a real person, and then hearing the adult taverner do likewise, they are convinced that he is a palpable public enemy. So they form themselves into a company of 'sworn brothers', like knights errant engaged on a dedicated quest, and resolve to seek out 'this false traytour Deeth' and slay him. The resolution is made to the accompaniment of many great oaths.

When, in the next scene, they meet the old man, they continue to rend 'Cristes blessed body' by their indiscriminate use of oaths. The old man, by contrast, is a courteous figure. He invokes the name of God only three times, and each time the invocation is solemn and deliberate. His last words to the rioters consist of such an invocation:

> 'God save yow, that boghte agayn mankynde,
> And yow amende!' Thus seyde this olde man . . .
>
> (766-7)

But the name of God has become so devalued in their mouths that it rings hollow in their ears. They are so impatient that they can hardly stay to hear the old man's words, let alone to heed them:

> '. . . And yow amende!' Thus seyde this olde man;
> And everich of thise riotoures *ran*
> Til he cam to that tree . . .
>
> (767-9 — my italics)

Within the space of two lines of narrative they have been precipitated into the third scene and transported to the place where the catastrophe is to be played out. After only seven more lines of narrative, dialogue is resumed.

The success of some of the best of Chaucer's shorter tales depends upon the way in which, during the final scene, events move towards their end with an astonishing rapidity and seeming inevitability. But the unimpeded flow of the action at the conclusion of these tales is often made possible only because the author has contrived to introduce into the earlier part of his narrative much of the information and most of the stage 'properties' that are required for the enactment of the dénouement. This kind of anticipation is well illustrated in the Reeve's Tale, where the fact that the miller has a 'piled skulle' is mentioned in the description of that formidable character with which the tale begins.[32] A few lines later Chaucer smuggles in, by means of a parenthesis, a reference to the existence of the baby *and its cradle* at the moment when his principal purpose is to impress upon his audience the fact that — apart from this insignificant infant — the miller's daughter was his only child.[33] The reader will be able to think of other examples without much difficulty. In the Pardoner's Tale Chaucer goes even further: all the technical details of the murders are conveyed to the reader in advance in the course of the dialogue between the two conspirators and in the account of the youngest rioter's visit to the village. So that, when the moment for the catastrophe arrives, there is no need to describe the action in detail; the fate of the three 'sworn brothers' is a foregone conclusion. It follows with an irresistible logic: the rioters are despatched without ceremony in ten lines of summary narrative that are delivered with the coolness and detachment of a mathematician spelling out the *quod erat demonstrandum* at the end of a theorem. The single couplet of misplaced exultation, uttered by one of the homicides, stands out in ironical relief in the middle of this passage where the narrator's own voice has now become dominant:

> What nedeth it to sermone of it moore?
> For right as they hadde cast his deeth bifoore,
> Right so they han hym slayn, and that anon.
> And whan that this was doon, thus spak that oon:
> 'Now lat us sitte and drynke, and make us merie,
> And afterward we wol his body berie.'
> And with that word it happed hym, par cas,
> To take the botel ther the poyson was,
> And drank, and yaf his felawe drynke also,
> For which anon they storven bothe two.

(879-88)

But the theorem has a corollary. Although the narrator refrains from giving a detailed description of the rioters' death, he does not allow us to forget the implications of the apothecary's words that I have already quoted. The apothecary had recommended his 'confiture' to his customer by emphasizing the speediness of its action: it would kill any living thing in less time than it would take you to cover a mile at an ordinary walking pace. From the point of view of the writhing victims, however, twenty minutes is a very long time. Chaucer does not describe their death agony in a series of 'close-ups' as Flaubert does when he recounts the death of Emma Bovary after she has taken poison. He prefers implication to description: he 'distances' the scene and looks at it with the eyes of a coroner reading a pathologist's report that refers him to a standard medical text-book:

> But certes, I suppose that Avycen
> Wroot nevere in no canon, ne in no fen,
> Mo wonder signes of empoisonyng
> Than hadde thise wrecches two, er hir endyng.
>
> (889-92)

The educated contemporary of Chaucer would have recognized more readily than the modern reader just how much the narrator has deliberately left unsaid.

The peculiar strength of this tale derives not only from the kinds of economy and narrative skill that I have examined above, but also from the presence of a double perspective. Looked at in objective sobriety, all the events in the story can be accounted for rationally. We have already considered how the revellers came to set out on their mission to slay Death. The presence of the treasure under the tree may seem extraordinary, but there is no need to resort to supernatural explanations of how it came there. The old man is not portrayed 'naturalistically': his characterization embodies too many of the commonplaces traditionally associated with aged humanity to satisfy the canons of naturalistic representation. But, as we have seen, it does not follow from this that he is, in fact, a supernatural being or an allegorical figure. Finally, the catastrophe can be explained in simple, psychological terms: the rioters bring their deaths upon themselves as the result of their habitual sins.

But we also see the action from another point of view. Much of the dialogue, of which the tale largely consists, is spoken by the revellers while they are drunk. Inebriation has an effect upon them not unlike that which sleep exerts upon the narrator of a medieval 'dream allegory': they are transported 'In aventure ther mervayles meven'[34] [upon adventure, where marvels take place]: we receive through their drunken eyes a glimpse of the world of 'Fayerye'. In that world the frontier between the realm of the marvellous and the realm of everyday experience is opened, so that denizens of the one may mingle freely with inhabitants of the other. It is an eclectic world in which giants and dragons live side by side with gods and demi-gods from various pantheons. Its origins have some associations with the Kingdom of Death (the classical underworld is easily metamorphosed into the fairy kingdom of *Sir Orfeo*); yet it harbours not only the shades of the departed, but also shadowy abstractions, personifications and allegorical figures. Death himself may be encountered walking abroad in this world with many of the attributes of a human being. Conversely, it is always possible that any human being one encounters there may, in fact, be a denizen of the 'other realm', who has slipped across the frontier. When the rioters meet the strange figure 'al forwrapped save [his] face', who seems to be too old to belong rightfully to the land of the living, they are at once suspicious and one of them accuses him of being Death's 'espye' in league with him 'to sleen us yonge folk'. Because Chaucer's presentation of the old man hovers near the frontiers of allegory and personification, the rioter's allegations seem sufficiently plausible to make the reader wonder whether there may not be some substance to them. The fact that this nightmare world is nothing more than a drunken delusion does not diminish the disturbing effect that it has upon the atmosphere of the tale.

When the rioters find the treasure, they experience the sober certainty of waking bliss. The quest that they had embarked upon in their drunkenness is forgotten: the company of 'sworn brothers' is no longer inspired by heroic intentions of ridding the world of a dangerous public enemy. In their sobriety their main source of inspiration is their avarice. As a direct result of their avarice they are destroyed; in their last game of 'hasardrye', Death sweeps the board.

The two points of view from which the action is seen are brought into a single focus by means of an intertwining irony. The irony of the rioters' 'finding Death' only after they have ceased to look for him is not original with Chaucer's version of the tale; but he develops it in a way that would appear to be his own. We have seen how, in the earlier part of the tale, Chaucer builds up the personality of Death, even to the extent of ensuring that he is the only 'character' to be allowed a proper name. We have also noticed how, through the medium of the dialogue, he creates an atmosphere of mystery so that the reader has a sensation of being in the presence of uncanny 'principalities and powers', in spite of the fact that the objective view of the action insists that this is all part of a drunken misapprehension.

The dénouement reveals that 'principalities and powers' are indeed present, but that Death is not the prime mover. In fact, death is seen in the event to be something quite negative; a thing without personality. We do not hear his hollow laughter at his moment of triumph. The spectre of Death vanishes from the rioters' minds as soon as they find the treasure, but one of them attributes their discovery of it to the benignity of another personified power, Fortune (779). She is the deity in whom these 'hasardours' really believe, rather than the God whose name they are continually taking in vain. Later the malignant aspect of Fortune, of which the rioters are oblivious, is suggested by the context in which the phrase 'par cas' occurs at 885. Meanwhile the narrator indicates in passing (at 844) that the real power behind the scenes is neither Fortune nor Death, but 'the feend, oure enemy' who is intent on trapping promising victims by means of their own sins. The rioters are as deluded in the world of sober calculation as they were in their drunken fantasy.

I remarked earlier that, in the last game of 'hasardrye' that the revellers play among themselves, Death steps in and sweeps the board. But Chaucer makes no such explicit comment. It would have been as inappropriate in the context as would any explicit reference to the 'false traytour' or the 'privee theef' with his spear. Nevertheless the naturalistic, objective narrative does happen to show, with tacit irony, how each of the rioters is slain by nothing other than a 'privee theef'[35] and a 'false traytour' — his own 'sworn brother'. When the Pardoner proceeds to his peroration,[36] and points to the *sentence* of his *exemplum*, his theme is not the omnipotence of Death, but the sin of Homicide and the other sins whose 'deadly' consequences are illustrated in the tale.

A further twist that Chaucer gives to the spiral of irony shows that he realized potentialities in the fable that would have appealed to a Greek tragedian; yet, at the same time, he in no way diminishes its propriety within the Christian ethos of his own day. When the rioters are about to set out on their quest, he causes them to boast in their drunkenness: 'Deeth shal be deed.'[37] This piece of hubris will sound to anyone acquainted with the Scriptures like a blasphemously materialistic application of St Paul's promise that 'Death shall be swallowed up in victory'.[38] It is therefore entirely fitting that when Nemesis follows it should afford a disturbingly *literal* illustration of another Pauline text: 'The wages of sin is death.'[39]

## III

Such is the tale that the Pardoner ultimately tells in response to the request of the 'gentils' among the pilgrims for 'som moral thyng' (VI,

325). But the moral tale is narrated at two removes even from this
fictitious audience. It serves as an *exemplum* for the Pardoner's
sermon on the text: 'Radix malorum est Cupiditas.' This sermon
is itself inserted into the Pardoner's so-called 'confession' to the pilgrims, in which he describes how he preaches it to 'lewed' (VI, 392)
village congregations purely in order to further his own avaricious
ends, by persuading them to purchase his indulgences and pay to
reverence his false relics.

The *fortissimo*, histrionic and digressive style of the discursive part
of the sermon contrasts remarkably with the subtlety and concentration of the *ensample*. Although it is a forceful piece of rhetoric, its
shortcomings as a piece of Christian instruction would soon become
evident if we were to consider it in the light of *De Doctrina
Christiana* by that former teacher of rhetoric, St Augustine. But there
is no need to look so far afield.[40] Although the Parson's Tale is not
formally a sermon, it does contain a systematic treatment of sins,
including those attacked by the Pardoner. But, whereas the Pardoner
confines himself to wallowing in the description of vice, the Parson
offers spiritual remedies for each sin by describing the virtues to
which it is opposed. This traditional notion of there being a specific
medicine (*salve*) for each sin may also be found in the latter part of
the section (IV) of *Ancrene Riwle* that deals with temptations.[41]
Although it is dangerous to argue from negative evidence, it is
nevertheless difficult not to suspect that the Pardoner deliberately
avoids referring to such spiritual salves in order that he may
concentrate the minds of his potential clients upon the more tangible
remedies that he offers for sale.

The sermon has much in common with the private sermon on
Wrath which the friar in the Summoner's Tale delivers to the bed-
ridden churl, upon whom he likewise has avaricious designs.[42] The
Pardoner's performance involves a more effective denunciation of his
chosen sins, and his subsidiary *exempla* are better focused than the
friar's exemplary anecdotes. But the main difference lies in the fact
that the Pardoner's discourse concludes with the *exemplum* of the
three rioters. The true irony of his situation depends upon the very
integrity of this tale, so that he can genuinely claim:

> For though myself be a ful vicious man,
> A moral tale yet I yow telle kan.
>
> (VI, 459-60)

He is a supreme story-teller and a superb performer — a fact of
which he is all too narcissistically aware (cf. 398-9). Had he been born
into Shakespeare's London, he might have made an honest fortune

for himself as a professional actor-playwright. As it is, he derives a very considerable income (cf. 389-90) from living by his wits as well as from exploiting his histrionic ability to the point where it becomes hypocrisy. He does not scruple to prostitute his artistic talent by making his tale subservient to his simoniacal 'entente'.[43] Nevertheless, his 'moral tale' retains its intrinsic integrity as a work of art.[44]

His cynicism over-reaches itself when he claims:

> Thus kan I preche agayn that same vice
> Which that I use, and that is avarice.
> But though myself be gilty in that synne,
> Yet kan I maken oother folk to twynne
> From avarice, and soore to repente.
> But that is nat my principal entente.
>
> (VI, 427-32)

Even if this is the effect, the penitential fruits of his preaching gain him no credit with God, Who — according to the 'feend' in the Friar's Tale — will employ even devils as His 'instruments' to bring men to salvation, although that was the opposite of the devils' 'entente'.[45] The Pardoner certainly earns no personal merit in the eyes of the Church. His situation is analogous to that of the priest who celebrates the eucharist while himself in a state of mortal sin. According to orthodox doctrine, he thereby administers the sacrament 'to the salvation of others and to his own damnation'.[46] The Pardoner has, in any case, already revealed himself to be quite ruthless in his attitude towards his clients' spiritual health:

> I rekke nevere, whan that they been beryed,
> Though that hir soules goon a-blakeberyed!
>
> (VI, 405-6)

Moreover, he even pushes them towards their damnation by the uses to which he puts his collection of false relics. His playing upon the credulity of his simple-minded customers is less deplorable than the way in which he exercises his histrionic powers positively to encourage their vicious desires: lechery at 366 ff. and sheer greed[47] at 361-5 and 372-6. Having thus made them pay 'pens, or elles grotes' to use his relics in order to further their pursuit of the World and the Flesh, he employs his preaching routine to persuade them to buy his indulgences in order to take out an insurance policy against their liabilities to the Devil.

Yet the Pardoner is no atheist. In spite of his cynical use of his indulgences (which may, or may not, be 'genuine'), he appears to believe in the phenomenon of divine Pardon. Several commentators have discussed the import of the declaration to the pilgrims, which he makes immediately after he has completed his account of how he deceives the 'lewed' village congregations:

> . . . And lo, sires, thus I preche.
> And Jhesu Crist, that is oure soules leche,
> So graunte yow his pardoun to receyve,
> For that is best; I wol yow nat deceyve.
>
> (VI, 915-18)[48]

Knowing perfectly well that he cannot *hope* to deceive with his quack remedies such an intelligent and canny company as that constituted by the pilgrims, he sees no risk to his trade (practised elsewhere) in mentioning the name of the only genuine Doctor in the business. We have not heard such a sincere admonition since the Old Man's parting words to the 'riotoures':

> 'God save yow, that boghte agayn mankynde,
> And yow amende!'

Perhaps it is a sign that the spark of conscience is not wholly extinguished within the Pardoner, however feeble and moribund it may be. Or has his besetting sin already impelled him so far down the crooked way to spiritual death that he can mouth even these words without being any more affected by them than the 'riotoures' were by the Old Man's admonition?[49]

The pace of the narrative will not allow us to stay for an answer: the Pardoner changes his mood yet again and offers his professional services to the pilgrims themselves. This contrived afterthought can only be meant as a jest: after the way in which he has confessed to being a charlatan, he could hardly hope for a serious sale of his commodities even to the most gullible of audiences. But this raises the question of why he should have decided to expose his unscrupulous activities to his companions on (what he evidently regards as) a holiday outing (cf. I, 680-4). Perhaps I am being obtusely literal-minded in asking such a question? But, in view of the dramatic context Chaucer has created, I think not. It may be due partly to his process of recall. The 'honest thyng' (328) for which he seeks is embedded in the routine that he knows by heart (332). In order to give the company the full demonstration of his histrionic powers, it is necessary for him to explain the circumstances and the motives of his performance. It is, in fact, a misnomer to speak of his 'confession'. For a confession should be made privately to a priest, and in a spirit of contrition, whereas the Pardoner makes public boast of the way in which he operates in order to secure his substantial income (389-90)

— possibly as much as any of the 'professional' men among the pilgrims. He seems concerned to establish his prestige in a fellowship that appears to be dominated by men of the world, several of whom are, in practice, as unscrupulous and as ruthless as he is.

After he has eventually supplied 'som moral thyng' to oblige the 'gentils', the Pardoner seems to remember the Host's original request for 'a myrie tale' (316). The simoniac's mock offer of his wares to the pilgrims may be intended as a response to this demand: the Host is made the particular butt of this outrageous jest. If anyone wished to caricature the basic doctrine of indulgences, and their provision for papering over every sinful hour of one's life with purchased pardons, he could hardly do better than repeat the Pardoner's advertisement to the pilgrims:

> Or elles taketh pardoun as ye wende,
> Al newe and fressh at every miles ende,
> So that ye offren, alwey newe and newe,
> Nobles or pens, whiche that be goode and trewe.
>
> (VI, 927-30)

That does not sound like serious sales talk; nor does his exaggerated account of the possibility of road accidents; and certainly not the chaffing couplet directed at the Host himself:

> I rede that oure Hoost heere shal bigynne,
> For he is moost envoluped in synne.
>
> (VI, 941-2)

The Host certainly regards it as a jest, for he declares at 958-9, 'I wol no lenger *pleye* / With thee, ne with noon oother angry man'. But why had the Pardoner become so angry? It can hardly be because the Host had thwarted any hoped-for sale of his commodities.

The pilgrims might collectively have laughed off the joke against them (cf. 961); but Harry Bailly is not one to bear an insult, however jocular, without exercising his right of reply. We have already encountered an example of the tastelessness of his humour in his rallying of the Monk with his views on celibacy. The 'worthy Monk took al in pacience' (VII, 1965) — as well he might, since the Host's observations are at least a testimonial to the man's virility. The Host's taunt about the Pardoner's personal 'relics' and the appropriate 'reliquary' in which to enshrine them (VI, 952-5) is exceedingly apt; but it hits the man (almost literally) below the belt and upon what is (both physically and metaphorically) the most sensitive spot of this individual, concerning whom the narrator had surmised: 'I trowe he were a geldyng or a mare' (I, 691).[50] The Pardoner's shameless 'confession' had rendered him impervious to any possible attack on his morals; it needed the crude, combative instinct of the Host to sense the true seat of the man's vulnerability. In the act of reconciliation, upon which the Knight insists, the Host too has to sacrifice his dignity up to a point. In view of his remark at 947-50, he must have found it particularly distasteful to bestow upon this *bel amy* (cf. VI, 318) the kiss of amity which the Knight demanded.

The Pardoner's Prologue and Tale probe incisively into serious moral issues concerning the abuse of religion and the possible misuse of the talent to create and perform works of fiction. But the ultimate discomfiture of the Pardoner is brought down to the level of almost farcical savagery that one associates with the dénouement of a fabliau. An inn-keeper's unpolished wit finally reduces to silence the 'noble ecclesiaste' (I, 708), who knew better than most professional preachers how to 'affile his tonge' (I, 712), and how to mesmerize a popular audience by giving them what they wanted:

> Thanne telle I hem ensamples many oon
> Of olde stories longe tyme agoon.
> For lewed peple loven tales olde . . .
>
> (VI, 435-7).

# CHAPTER 5
## *The Quest for Meed*

The drunken rioters in the Pardoner's *exemplum* set out to rid the world of Death, but are diverted from this 'noble' quest when they stumble upon the hoard of florins. The Pardoner himself is intent, from the very beginning of his sermon to the villagers, upon a deliberately venal quest. A similar motive inspires the different quests undertaken by the principal characters in the three tales to be discussed in this chapter — those of the Friar, the Summoner, and the Canon's Yeoman.

Seekers and finders of treasure play their part in several Gospel parables; but the treasure they seek is that which is laid up in heaven (Luke, 12:33). In *Piers Plowman*, Langland introduces the personi-fication, Lady Holychurch, who describes the heavenly reward for the righteous man as the treasure of Truth (God). She distinguishes this treasure from that which is the object of man's inordinate desire for material riches: the treasure of Wrong (the Devil). The Devil is an arch-swindler. With the false lure of his treasure he deceived Judas into betraying his Lord for thirty pieces of silver; and then betrayed him into committing suicide (and so immediately damning himself) when he realized what he had done. So he deceives all 'that trusten on his treasure' (B-text, Passus i, 60 ff.). The lure of such a material reward, out of all proportion to a man's needs or his deserts, exerts so powerful a fascination that Langland later personifies it as the superficially attractive, but basically corrupt, Lady Mede (Meed). Eventually he sets against her the figure of the ideal, righteous man, Piers Plowman, whose actions are motivated by charity instead of cupidity, and who lives the life of Do Well — itself partly personified as Dowel. Piers offers to lead mankind on the quest to Truth. It may prove helpful to retain Langland's scheme at the back of our minds while we follow the activities of some of Chaucer's most venal seekers after meed.

The enmity between the Friar and Summoner, which comes to the surface at the end of the Wife of Bath's Prologue, results in their each telling a tale against a representative of the other's profession. The difference in tone between these linked tales is hardly less striking than that between the Miller's and Reeve's Tales. Whereas the Friar's Tale about the summoner and the devil is suave and condescending, the Summoner's Tale is savage and coarse. The crudity of the latter tale is especially notable in the prologue and epilogue that flank the narrative about the friar and the bed-ridden churl. Yet the

Summoner's Tale is — as we shall see — not without a certain subtlety. Both tales have in common one particular technical detail. Instead of introducing the principal character by means of a static *descriptio* (of the kind used in the Miller's and Reeve's Tales), they expose him, in an 'action picture' of his professional practices, before the narrative proper is reached. The Summoner's Tale begins with a specimen of the friar's preaching in church, whereas the Friar's Tale describes how the summoner operates his network of spies and *agents provocateurs* (III, 1321-75). The account of the archdeacon's administration of discipline within the diocese may remind the modern reader of the organization of the 'party' in a totalitarian state, with the summoner as a lowly placed, but highly corrupt, officer of the political police force. In one respect the situation in the fourteenth century was even more unpleasant than that within a modern totalitarian régime: offenders were summoned to the ecclesiastical court, not merely for ideological impurity (heresy) and for failing to pay the party dues (tithes), but also for private acts of sexual impurity (adultery and fornication). In this tale the church is seen as perverted from its mission of bringing men to salvation, through divine grace and the exercise of charity, into an organization for 'catching out' sinners in order to inflict upon them 'pecunyal peyne' (III, 1314) so that it might fill its coffers and line the pockets of its officials. The summoner in the General Prologue was wont to declare: 'Purs is the ercedekenes helle' (I, 658); and the organization of the diocese, as described at the opening of the Friar's Tale, bears an uncanny resemblance to the organization of Hell as described by the devil to the summoner later in the narrative.

The story is set in that twilight realm, between everyday life and 'the other world', which is also the setting for the Pardoner's *exemplum* of the three rioters seeking Death. There are other features that the two tales have in common. In both tales, the institution of 'sworn brotherhood' is used in an ironical way; both narratives are remarkable for their economy of means, which is largely the result of conveying most of the action through dialogue. Both tales are impelled, quite literally, by movement towards a goal that proves to be other than what the evil-doers had expected. In the Pardoner's Tale this motion is varied: sometimes the rioters walk, sometimes they run, and at others are stationary for a while. In the Friar's Tale the summoner and his new 'friend' are walking continuously toward their goal as they converse, debate and compete with one another.

In the Pardoner's Tale 'the feend, oure enemy' makes a fleeting, invisible entrance (VI, 844-8), when he inspires the youngest rioter with the idea of poisoning his 'brothers'. In the Friar's Tale a 'feend' walks anonymously on to the stage, disguised as a forester, dressed in green. Whereas Christ appointed his disciples to be 'fishers of men', Satan deploys his vassals as hunters of human prey. We nowadays think of huntsmen as being traditionally dressed in 'pink'; but previously their customary colour was green.[1] When the summoner (who dare not mention his own disgusting profession) assumes the title of bailiff, the accommodating, shape-shifting fiend makes himself into his simulacrum, declaring: 'Thou art a bailly, and I am another' (III, 1396); and they become 'sworn brothers'. By III, 1448 the devil considers it is now safe to cast off his own disguise, and by line 1474 to reveal that he sees through his companion's; the summoner seems not to be disconcerted by either revelation. The suave devil answers several of the summoner's questions about the working conditions of Satan's employees until he finally declares that there is no need for his companion to rely upon his description, because the summoner will himself become, as the result of his own 'experience', a greater 'authority' on Hell than ever Virgil or Dante were; he will be qualified to occupy an academic chair in the subject. The obtuse apparitor seems to be flattered rather than unnerved by this assurance.

The proper way to deal with devils is most vividly indicated in the early thirteenth-century legend of *Seinte Marherete*,[2] one of the remarkable group of devotional prose texts in MS Bodley 34. The texts are written in the Herefordshire dialect, and are known collectively as the 'Katherine Group' after St Katherine of Alexandria, one of the three virgin martyrs whose legends the MS contains. While Margaret is in prison, a devil approaches her in the form of a dragon, who proceeds to swallow her; but, when she makes the sign of the cross, he disintegrates. Then she perceives another fiend in the shape of a black man. After struggling with him, she places her foot firmly on his neck and, from this point of vantage, questions him about his mode of operation. He admits that he is the most dangerous fiend after Beelzebub[3] and goes on to describe the technique by which he brings a pure man into contact with a pure woman and insinuates them both into 'that dirty sin' of lechery.[4] He reveals that penance, prayer and confession are the weapons that will avail most effectively against his temptation. He informs Margaret that Satan is their 'keiser and king, icrunet of us alle'[5] [emperor and king, crowned by us all] and that the infernal powers are especially hostile to virgins (like herself), because Christ, their conqueror, was born of a virgin. He has already made it clear[6] that, because of his important position in the organization, he is made to specialize in attacking the righteous. He does not bother with sinners, regarding them as already secure in their damnation.[7]

The fiend who is despatched to fetch down the sinful summoner is of far less consequence. Indeed, his place in the infernal organization is similar to that of the apparitor in the diocesan hierarchy. The legend of St Margaret shows that the only safe position from which to converse with a devil is the one she adopts when she has thrown him to the ground. Moreover, she does not question him about his *modus operandi* out of idle curiosity, in the manner of an academic demonologist. She questions him in the spirit of an intelligence officer interrogating a captured enemy. Theologians denounced presumptuous speculation (*curiositas*) as a vice, just as more popular moralists discouraged the habit of prying into 'Goddes privitee'. The author of *The Cloud of Unknowing* warns continually against 'curiosite'. Understanding of God can be achieved only by 'a devout and a meek, blind stirring of love', not by 'a proude, coryous & an ymaginatif witte'.[8] Langland has a similar attitude. Although *Piers Plowman* never employs the term *curiositas*, this is nevertheless the vice which leads the dreamer astray in his quest for Dowel (B. viii-xi) so that his Will wanders in the 'land of longing' where he is distracted by Fortune's handmaids, 'Lust of the Flesh' and 'Covetise of Eyes' (xi, 7 ff.). If such is the consequence of being curious about theological problems, the summoner is in a more perilous situation, as he is curious about demonological mysteries.

The unwary summoner does not merely indulge his idle curiosity, but engages in a competition with his 'brother' to see who can make the most profitable catch. The episode of the carter shows that the devil is content to play the game according to the rules, whereas the summoner's deployment of lies and threats against the widow shows him to be (quite literally) worse than the fiend, and provokes her into consigning him (together with her pan) to the devil — who duly seizes them as his rightful prize. The summoner is too obtuse to realize that, when a denizen of 'the other world' accosts a human being, he is not seeking his company in order to compare notes or to indulge in friendly rivalry; he has a particular design upon him, whether malignant or benign. Yet, in this respect, he is not so very much more obtuse than the (sympathetically presented) dreamer in *Pearl* who, on encountering the beatified soul of his daughter, asks her to describe her life in the heavenly realm:

> 'I wolde bysech, wythouten debate,
> Ye wolde me say in sobre asente
> What lyf ye lede erly and late.'

> (390-2)[9]

When she informs him that, although she died before she was two years old, she is now a queen in heaven, he demurs. In spite of his promise, he initiates a 'debate' with the maiden on the subject of heavenly rewards, in which he raises logical objections to his interlocutor's assertions, and, in the spirit of scholastic dialectic, tries to 'tie her up in knots'. She has no difficulty in refuting his arguments. Nevertheless, she finds it difficult to make him realize that she has not sought him out to indulge in a competition of wits but that she has been sent to indicate to him the way to his own salvation.[10] This is the obverse of the situation in the Friar's Tale, where the devil tries to conceal from the summoner the purpose of the mission on which his harsh employer has sent him, and positively fosters his 'brother's' competitive spirit so that he may bring damnation upon himself. In both works there is a considerable degree of theological sophistication.

Sophistication is not an obvious quality of the Summoner's Tale. The anecdote, in its Prologue, about the friars' habitat in hell is considerably sharpened as a result of the reference to Dante, as an authority on hell, in the preceding tale (III, 1520). In *Inferno* xxxiv, the worst of all sinners (the three arch-traitors, Judas, Brutus and Cassius) are shown being perpetually gnawed, one in each of Satan's three mouths. The anecdote which Chaucer relates goes beyond Dante by locating the nest of friars in an even more odious part of the devil's anatomy. At the same time, it exhibits a crudity of satire to which Dante never descends. Even coarser is the epilogue or annexe to the tale, in which the squire offers his solution to the problem in 'ars-metrike' (III, 2222), posed by the churl's donation to the friar and his convent. This piece of infantile humour is intended to ridicule the intellectual pretensions of the mendicant orders, which included such formidable minds as those of Aquinas, Roger Bacon, Duns Scotus and William of Occam. In the body of the tale, the friar is too obvious a hypocrite: his losing his temper after preaching to the churl on the subject of wrath is as blatant as his assertion of his abstemious way of life which immediately follows his ordering of the gourmet repast that he describes as 'hoomly suffisaunce' (III, 1843). His somewhat rambling discourse on wrath prolongs itself in a manner similar to that of the Pardoner's sermon on the sins of the tavern. Nevertheless, its length has a twofold justification. First, it is intended to fill up the interval while the huge dinner is being prepared; and it is also designed to build up silent resentment within the churl to such a pressure that it must — quite literally (cf. III, 2149-51) — explode!

In the earlier part of the tale, however, there is a certain subtlety of characterization. The friar is first glimpsed as he preaches in church in order to persuade the congregation to pay his brethren to sing 'trentals' (a series of thirty masses) to speed the souls of their departed relatives through Purgatory. He gives a graphic account of the tortures to which their nearest and dearest are being subjected:

> 'Delivereth out,' quod he, 'anon the soules!
> Ful hard it is with flesshook or with oules
> To been yclawed, or to brenne or bake.
> Now spede yow hastily, for Cristes sake!'

(III, 1729-32)

It is significant that this particular friar conceives of purgatorial tortures in terms of meat-hooks, skewers and ovens; for these would be appropriate instruments of punishment for gluttony, one of his own most conspicuous vices. After listening to this snatch of his pulpit oratory, our ears can hardly catch the Latin words of his hastily muttered concluding prayer:

> And whan this frere had seyd al his entente,
> With *qui cum patre* forth his wey he wente.

(III, 1733-4)

[It is, of course, the Son who, with the Father (*qui cum patre*) and the Holy Spirit, reigns for ever.] This friar's routine is as well established as that of the preaching Pardoner. The phrase *qui cum patre* is the valedictory counterpart to the '*In principio*' with which the pilgrim Friar greets so pleasantly the widow whose mite he is about to charm away from her (I, 252-5). In both cases the proper context (and, consequently, the meaning) of the words has been eroded by the mendicant's grasping haste. By the time the rest of the valedictory formula has been inaudibly muttered, the preaching friar is half way down the aisle: the rhythm of the couplet's second line catches the bustling movement exactly.

Although there are no formal portraits in this tale, one technique associated with the *descriptio* is surreptitiously introduced into the narrative. We have already noted Matthew of Vendôme's precept concerning the repetition of a single epithet that indicates an essential characteristic of the person described.[11] This device can be made more interesting by the use of the rhetorical figure known as *traductio*, whereby the same word is employed in a series of different senses or applications. In the Summoner's Tale the word 'soft' is applied to the friar on three occasions in the earlier part of the main narrative. It is first used adverbially to refer to his unctuous and wheedling tone of voice when he greets the bed-ridden churl in whose house he has previously received lavish hospitality:

> '*Deus hic!*' quod he, 'O Thomas, freend, good day!'
> Seyde this frere, curteisly and softe.
>
> (III, 1770-1)

The Latin tag, which comes forth as soon as he opens his mouth, is characteristic of his affected speech: he later twice employs the French tag '*je vous dy*' (III, 1832 and 1838). His use, in the peasant's cottage, of the language of *courtoisie* is both condescending and flattering. When he greets the peasant's wife ('oure dame'), his 'courtesy' extends to the act of embracing and kissing her. Another indication of his presumptuous familiarity can be heard in his immediate use of the churl's christian name, Thomas, which is promptly reiterated (III, 1770-2). The repetition of the name culminates in line 1832, where it occurs three times, and in conjunction with the French tag.

The second occurrence of the key epithet is again adverbial: this time it is applied to the friar's regard for his flabby and well-cared-for person:

> And fro the bench he droof awey the cat,
> And leyde adoun his potente and his hat,
> And eek his scrippe, and sette him softe adoun.
>
> (III, 1775-7)

The ruthless way in which he dispossesses the cat of its rightful resting-place contrasts markedly with the tender manner in which he seats himself on the usurped bench. The sense of dispossession is underlined by a subtle transference of epithet: 'softe' ought to be an adjective describing the cat, but it has been transferred as an adverb to the action of the animal's human supplanter. Langland introduces into *Piers Plowman* a friar called Sire *Penetrans-domos* (B, xx, 341), whose behaviour reminds his interlocutor of another such, who, entering in the guise of a doctor, 'penetrated' even further than the walls of the house:

> 'I knew swich oon ones, noght eighte wynter passed,
> Coom in thus ycoped at a court there I dwelde,
> And was my lordes leche — and my ladies bothe.
> And at the laste this lymytour, tho my lord was oute,
> He salved so oure wommen til some were with childe.'
>
> (B, xx, 344-348)[12]

The name, at least, would not be inappropriate for the friar in the Summoner's Tale.

The final repetition of the characteristic epithet is so unobtrusive that it operates almost below the threshold of the reader's consciousness. The friar gives the wife his order for dinner:

> 'Now, dame,' quod he, 'now *je vous dy sanz doute*,
> Have I nat of a capon but the lyvere,
> And of youre softe breed nat but a shyvere,
> And after that a rosted pigges heed —
> But that I nolde no beest for me were deed —
> Thanne hadde I with yow hoomly suffisaunce . . .'
>
> (III, 1838-43)

These sporadic insinuations of the word 'softe' help to establish the fact that there is in this friar — as there is in Absolon in the Miller's Tale — a streak of squeamishness. The narrator of the Miller's Tale is quite explicit as to what it is that Absolon is particularly squeamish about (I, 3337-8). Both Absolon and the friar receive their 'reward' from the same physical quarter; the former for his love of 'paramours', the latter for his greed. The enamoured parish clerk never penetrates any further than the hinged window of his beloved's bower. The greedy friar makes himself abundantly at home within the bed-ridden peasant's cottage, and is lured by the cunning churl into putting his hand down the bed and groping around his buttock in order to find the promised 'gift' that he has 'hyd in pryvetee' (III, 2143).

The only remaining tale with a cleric as its villain is that of the Canon's Yeoman.[13] But — as its narrator is rather too careful to point out (VIII, 992-1011) — its satire is not directed against canons as such; it is an exposure of the practice of alchemy. By the time the canon and his yeoman overtake the 'compaignye', the pilgrims have been entertained to a variety of marvels, ranging from a flying horse of brass (in the Squire's Tale) and a magician (in the Franklin's Tale), who claims to denude the coast of rocks, to the three-headed giant in the old 'rym' about Sir Thopas related by the 'elvyssh' Chaucer — not to mention the 'gobet' of Saint Peter's sail, displayed by the Pardoner. So, when the yeoman claims that his master could pave with silver and gold the road between Boughton-under-Blean and Canterbury, the Host remains unimpressed, especially when he remarks the canon's ragged, cheap and dirty vesture. Before the end of the Prologue to the Tale, he has elicited the information that the two of them are obliged to reside in the disreputable 'suburbes' amidst the nooks and blind alleys where thieves maintain their dens. This, however, may not be so much a symptom of their poverty as a necessity of their 'craft': for blacksmiths too were often required to keep their forges away from the centre of the town.[14]

The Tale itself is divided into two quite separate parts; the latter telling the story of a canon — *not* the yeoman's master (or so the narrator insists) — who practises the kind of confidence-trick perpetrated by Subtle and his accomplices in Ben Jonson's *The Alchemist*. Indeed, the words 'subtil' and 'subtilitee' recur throughout the piece. One instance of the canon's 'subtilitee' consists of the way in which he introduces his victim to the exotic vocabulary ('so clergial and so queynte' — 752) of the 'Mystery' and insists upon his participating in the experiments himself. Jonson, of course, delightfully improves upon this by introducing the dupe, Sir Epicure Mammon, as one already 'initiated' who exhibits, with a proprietorial air, his expertise in the craft to the sceptical Surly. More interesting, however, is the shorter first part of the Tale, which continues the Prologue's exposure of the yeoman's own master, now that the latter has fled from the 'compaignye' for shame. Although this canon is not beyond imposing 'illusioun' (VIII, 673) upon many clients, he is essentially what Subtle was before his association with Face and Doll Common: one who has impoverished and hopelessly 'endetted' himself and his collaborators in their futile attempts to bring to a successful 'conclusioun' their obsessive quest for the secret of 'multiplying' and the discovery of the elixir, or 'philosopher's stone'. The canon is driven by the gambler's irresistible demon to the point where, having 'lost his owene good thurgh jupartye' (743), he draws others into the vortex of his own disaster.

At its lowest level, Chaucer's satire on the proto-science of alchemy resembles the schoolboy's jokes about laboratory 'stinks': you can smell the black-faced alchemists a mile off, their 'savour is so rammyssh' that 'For al the world they stynken as a goot' (VIII, 884 ff.). From there it graduates to the kind of ridicule that Swift employs in his account of the Grand Academy of Lagado, where the first researcher (engaged upon a project to extract sunbeams from cucumbers) is of similarly blackened appearance, and the second Projector exudes a comparable odour (*Gulliver's Travels*, III, v). The experiments at Lagado are inspired by the same spirit which Pope satirizes in his glance at the investigations and practical projects of the Royal Society:

> The most recluse, discreetly open'd, find
> Congenial matter in the Cockle-kind;
> The mind, in Metaphysics at a loss,
> May wander in a wilderness of Moss;
> The head that turns at super-lunar things,
> Poiz'd with a tail, may steer on Wilkins' wings.
> *(Dunciad*, IV, 447-52)

What we would regard as Pope's failure to recognize the true

potentiality of 'Natural Philosophy' was only the logical consequence of his belief that 'The proper study of Mankind is Man'.
Chaucer's contemporaries were encouraged to believe that the
proper object of mankind is God. We regard natural science with
approval because it 'works', and because its propositions are
empirically verifiable as well as rationally explicable; and we
consequently place miracles in the same category as magic. In the
Middle Ages a different grouping prevailed. What we call 'science'
was officially regarded, along with magic, as an improper attempt by
Man to control his environment for the gratification of his worldly
appetites, whereas miracles were regarded as a manifestation of
divine grace, designed to strengthen religious faith.

Something of this outlook is implicit in Chaucer's satire on the
'elvysshe' craft (VIII, 751, 842). Not only are there frequent references
to 'feends', but the black-faced alchemists, working at their fur-
naces in their malodorous laboratory, themselves resemble denizens of
hell. Their attempts to 'multiplie'[15] may perhaps be seen as a sacri-
legious parody of the miracle of the Feeding of the Five Thousand.
Similarly, their obsessive and impoverishing quest for the 'philosopher's stone', that will transmute base metals into silver and gold,
is a perversion of the principle that underlies the parable of the pearl
of great price (Matt. 13: 45-46). Just as the alchemists sell the shirts off
their backs to acquire the elixir (cf. VIII, 877-83), so the 'jeweler' —
we are told in *Pearl* — sold all his wares, both woollen and linen
('solde alle hys goud, bothe wolen and lynne' — 731), to purchase the
true pearl of great price, the Kingdom of Heaven. The same poem
indicates that the only way to obtain that pearl is through an interior
transmutation whereby we ourselves become pearls, pleasing to the
Prince of Heaven.[16] As we have already seen, Langland distinguishes
between the treasure of Truth (which is laid up in Heaven as a
reward for the righteous man) and that of Wrong — whose power of
attraction he personifies in the alluring figure of Lady Mede. It is
interesting to observe that he specifically denounces 'Experiments of
Alkemanye', and adds: 'If thow thynke to dowel, deel therwith
nevere' (B. x, 212-13). We remarked how the virtuous life of 'Dowel'
stands at the opposite end of the moral spectrum from Lady Mede.
Langland would certainly have regarded alchemists as typical suitors
of Mede in their search for a gratuitous and 'mesureless' reward out
of all proportion to their genuine needs and deserts.

The climax of the Tale's first part is reached with the vividly
described explosion at VIII, 905 ff. For the yeoman, this event appears
to signify the Real Presence — of the Devil:

> Withouten doute,
> Though that the feend noght in oure sighte hym shewe,

I trowe he with us be, that ilke schrewe!
In helle, where that he lord is and sire,
Nis ther moore wo, ne moore rancour ne ire.
Whan that oure pot is broke, as I have sayd,
Every man chit, and halt hym yvele apayd.

(VIII, 915-21)

The scene of confusion and mutual recrimination that then follows is
the precise opposite of the harmonious relationship that prevails
between the inhabitants of the Kingdom of Heaven, as described, for
example, at *Pearl*, 446-68, where there is neither 'greme ne gryste'
[anger nor resentment] between them, for all are united in the
mystical body of Christ. A further image of hell is hinted at as the
alchemists sift the debris to see if anything of value can be retrieved:

The mullok on an heep ysweped was,
And on the floor ycast a canevas,
And al this mullok in a syve ythrowe,
And sifted, and ypiked many a throwe.

(VIII, 938-41)

One is reminded of the caricature of the covetous man in the early
thirteenth-century Rule for Anchoresses, *Ancrene Riwle*,[17] who,
along with the other Deadly Sins, serves the Devil in his court. He is
the Devil's ash-gatherer, who lies in the ashes and employs himself
busily to heap them into many piles. He blows therein and blinds
himself, and in the muck he traces mathematical symbols ('figures of
augrim') as accountants do. The Devil beholds his play and laughs
till he bursts. The moral to be drawn from this is that 'both gold and
silver, and every earthly possession, is only earth and ashes and
blinds everyone who blows upon them.'

The only experimenter to remain above the hideous quarrel is the
canon himself, who resolves that 'the nexte tyme I wol fonde / To
bryngen oure craft al in another plite' (VIII, 951-2). We may
recognize in his optimistic resolve the dauntless spirit of the genuine
scientist. His disillusioned yeoman, however, regards it as madness
and folly. Chaucer's contemporaries would no doubt regard his
repeated attempts to recuperate his losses of wealth and of time as
equivalent to the frustrated endeavours which the damned in Dante's
*Inferno* are condemned (like Sisyphus) to repeat for all eternity. As
the Yeoman declares: 'For evere we lakken oure conclusioun' (VIII,
672). The obverse to these pursuits is afforded by the famous
autobiographical passage in the final version of *Piers Plowman*. Just
as the alchemists' poverty obliged them to reside in the 'suburbes',

so Long Will's indigence caused him to dwell in a 'cote' [hovel] among the idlers in the disreputable district of Cornhill. But Langland's concern to recover lost time is motivated by the desire of acquiring a profit of another kind. He compares himself to the merchant who has 'lost and lost, and at the last' has chanced to have bought such a bargain that he was the better for evermore. 'The kingdom of Heaven is like treasure hidden in a field', he quotes from Matthew, 13:44 — the chapter which proceeds immediately to recount the parable of the pearl of great price. He then alludes to the parable of the woman who sweeps her house till she finds the lost coin (Luke, 15:8), and continues:

'So hope I to have of Him that is Almighty
A gobet of His grace, and begin a time
That all times of my time to profit shall turn.'
(*Piers Plowman*, C. v, 92-101)[18]

The hidden strength of the Tale's *Prima Pars* subsists largely in the implicit counterpointing of the account of the alchemists' vain quest against that of the true, spiritual journey of the mind to God. Its *Pars Secunda* — the anecdote about the confidence trickster — comes as something of an anti-climax, partly because it is so explicit.[19] Its final warning against alchemy marshals on to the stage a formidable procession of 'auctoures', rising from 'Arnold of the New Town' through 'Plato' to 'Crist' and 'God of hevene'. It does not denounce the science as a false trail, but declares that its secret formula for producing untold material riches is vouchsafed by Christ only to a chosen few; others will merely make God their adversary if they try to discover it. The narrative is characterized by hyperbole. The fraudulent practices of the London canon

. . . wolde infecte al a toun,
Thogh it as greet were as was Nynyvee,
Rome, Alisaundre, Troye, and othere three.
(VIII, 973-5)

He is explicitly called a 'feend' and is said to possess 'an hundred foold moore subtiltee' than the yeoman's own master. He is perpetually reviled by the narrator, and the narrative is continually interrupted by apostrophe and other devices for nudging the reader. The style is reminiscent of that of the self-righteous investigative journalist of the popular press.[20] It in fact derives from that of the popular preacher — a style that Chaucer satirized (as we have already seen) in the Summoner's Tale, when the friar admonishes the churl on the subject of wrath. For an exposure that is so much concerned with 'subtiltee', the treatment is remarkably unsubtle. One longs for the cool dialectic of the Friar's Tale or the undemonstrative innuendo of the Shipman's. The mystique of Alchemy is exploited by the fraudulent London canon as that of Astrology is employed by the immoral Oxford clerk in the Miller's Tale. But the indignant denunciation of the *Pars Secunda* leaves no room for the playful and gratuitous fantasy that transmutes the anecdote of mean cuckoldry and crude retribution into the sublime farce that so unexpectedly emerges 'to quite with the Knightes tale'.

In the course of this chapter we have watched the Friar's summoner move peripatetically towards his just reward, and we have observed the Summoner's predicating friar hurry purposefully out of church, walk along 'hous by hous', and proceed at 'a sturdy paas' (III, 2162) from cottage to court in search of meed, and finally of justice, for himself.[21] The Yeoman's Canon pursued his quest for meed only in a figurative sense, while he remained stationary within his insalubrious stithy. Nevertheless, when the two of them are introduced to us, they are riding in sweating haste in pursuit of the pilgrim company which is already within striking distance of the goal of its quest. When the yeoman claims that his master could pave with gold and silver all the ground 'Til that we come to Caunterbury toun' (VIII, 624), it is the first time that the pilgrims' destination has been mentioned since the Host's address to the pilgrims towards the end of the General Prologue, in which he declares:

'Ye goon to Caunterbury — God yow speede,
The blisful martir quite yow youre meede!'

(I, 769-70)

The Canon soon rides off into the outer darkness beyond the edge of the narrative, leaving the pilgrims to continue their quest,

The hooly blisful martir for to seke,
That hem hath holpen whan that they were seeke.

(I, 17-18)

# CHAPTER 6
# Chaucer's 'Wyves' and the Art of Persuasion

Women are included among the dramatis personae of several of the tales discussed so far, but these narratives have, for the most part, viewed their characters from the outside. We have encountered nothing that approaches Chaucer's representation of Criseyde, which succeeds in being both intimate and mysterious, mimetic and analytic. Indeed, such a complex portrayal is not possible within the limited compass of a tale. There are, nevertheless, a few concentrated representations of 'wyves' to be found among the Canterbury tales, and this chapter is devoted to the four most interesting of them. The tales to be discussed are those which constitute the traditional 'marriage group'. But (as I remarked earlier)[1] I have no intention of reviving Kittredge's theory that they contribute to a debate among the pilgrims on the subject of marriage, initiated by the Wife of Bath and concluded by the Franklin. I adopt this grouping because it aptly illustrates the remarkable variety of ways in which Chaucer attests that *le style c'est la femme*. There is, however, one complicating factor in this stylistic approach. The first of the tales to be discussed is itself narrated by a 'wyf'; and it is also one of the few in the Canterbury series that is permeated by the personality and idiom of its narrator. So it will be necessary to consider the Wife of Bath's prologue before examining her tale.

In the course of the preceding chapters we have listened to several examples of the imaginative way in which Chaucer deploys his command of the art of rhetoric in order to supply various characters with persuasive speeches to enable them to further their designs. These speeches range in dignity and profundity from Theseus's address to the Athenian parliament in the Knight's Tale down to the sales-talk of that 'noble ecclesiaste', the Pardoner, and the fantastic prophecy in the Miller's Tale with which Nicholas induces John, the carpenter, to make hasty preparations against the threatened cataclysm. Chaucer would have had no difficulty in understanding why the ancient Greeks bestowed semi-divine status on Persuasion. He might also have seen special significance in the fact that they deified Persuasion as a goddess: Peitho, daughter of Aphrodite. For some of his most accomplished and instinctive practitioners of the art are to be found among the 'wyves' in the *Canterbury Tales*.

The most formidable of these female persuaders is, paradoxically, the most pacific; namely, Prudence, in the Tale of Melibee, who, by means of her seemingly inexhaustible repertory of proverbs, succeeds in dissuading her husband from taking vengeance against their daughter's assailants. At the other extreme, it is significant that the wife who fares worst of all is precisely the one who is denied the opportunity of uttering a single word. The Manciple's Tale concludes with a sermon on the dangers of an unbridled tongue (IX, 317-end). But its strictures certainly do not apply to Phoebus's wife, whose adultery is betrayed by the blabbing crow. At the moment of the catastrophe, she is an arrow's flight away from her avenging husband. Anyone who recalls the conclusion of the Merchant's Tale may feel prompted to surmise that, if she had been allowed to come within speaking distance, she would have talked herself out of her punitive death. Moreover, the Wife of Bath's Prologue indicates — in what is probably an allusion to this very fable — how she might have accomplished the feat (had she been given the opportunity of exercising her tongue). She could have persuaded her husband that the talking bird was mad — cf. III, 232: 'Bere hym on honde that the cow [chough] is wood.' However, these extreme cases are not the subject of the present chapter.

In three of the four tales that I am about to discuss, the tongue is the woman's principal weapon. Whether it is used dialectically, teasingly, temperately or hypocritically, it is always employed deliberately to achieve a certain end. The exception is the Franklin's Tale; and I shall argue that this fact may in itself guide us towards a juster appreciation of its heroine than that which has been proposed by some recent critics.

## I

Sitting 'easily' upon her 'amblere' (cf. I, 469), no doubt, the Wife of Bath indulges in her 'long preamble of a tale' (III, 831), which itself may seem to 'amble or trotte' (cf. III, 838) at varying *tempi* and in different directions. But, in spite of its air of being a rambling improvisation, this Prologue is in fact a carefully constructed composition. Even that most colloquial of Alys's couplets —

> But now, sire, lat me se, what I shal seyn?
> A ha! by God, I have my tale ageyn
>
> (III, 585-6)

— is simply an idiomatic variation on a literary formula that Chaucer employs when returning from a digression in his best organized tales: 'Now wol I torne ageyn to my sentence.'

It is a further paradox that this most idiosyncratic of Chaucer's monologues is rooted in the procedures of the medieval 'debate' and breathes the spirit of dialectic — if that is not too dignified a term to apply to its continual, comic contentiousness. Dame Alys relishes the interruption by the Pardoner, who is induced to elevate to a chair, as it were, of Applied Matrimonial Studies this female 'authority' who can quote the *Almageste* of 'Ptholomee' at him so aptly, besides threatening him with her 'experiences' 'Of tribulacion in mariage' (173). He concludes by requesting this venerable professor to 'teche us yonge men of youre praktike' (187) — where the word 'praktike' not only refers to Alys's matrimonial 'experience', but alludes (ultimately) to one of Aristotle's technical terms of Ethics: practical, as opposed to speculative, understanding. Similarly, she enjoys settling her score with the Friar who dares to criticize the length of her Prologue. When she describes how she managed to 'get even' with her elderly husbands, she talks in terms of a verbal *disputatio*:

> For, by my trouthe, I quitte hem word for word.
> As helpe me verray God omnipotent,
> Though I right now sholde make my testament,
> I ne owe hem nat a word that it nys quit.
> I broghte it so aboute by my wit
> That they moste yeve it up, as for the beste,
> Or elles hadde we nevere been in reste.
> For thogh he looked as a wood leon,
> Yet sholde he faille of his conclusion.
>
> (III, 422-30)

Finally, the fundamental reason for our protagonist's preference for her fifth husband over his predecessors is that in him she encounters for the first time something like a worthy antagonist. At 822, she applies retrospectively the actual word 'debaat' to their marital intercourse; and we should bear in mind that this term was used, in Chaucer's day, of martial combat as well as of academic debate. As a clerk, invested with the livery of Mercury, Jankin would have enjoyed a far less violent daily dialectic if he had remained faithful to the chaste Philologia,[2] instead of taking to himself a bride who is proud to bear upon her body the stigmata of Mars and 'seinte Venus' (cf. 604-26). As she herself observes:

> The children of Mercurie and of Venus
> Been in hir wirkyng ful contrarius . . . &c.
>
> (III, 697-8 — and ff.)

When no adversary offers himself it is necessary for her to invent one. Throughout the first one hundred and sixty-two lines of her Prologue (i.e. until the Pardoner's interruption) this mere woman takes on single-handed the collective 'authority' of the doctors of the church — a feat which is, in its way, as courageous and as outrageous as that of the twelve-year-old Jesus disputing with the doctors in the Temple (Luke, 2: 42 ff.). She also disposes collectively of her first three husbands, whom she regards as mere ciphers. For this reason, she takes it upon herself to supply, almost ventriloquially, their contribution to the comedy. She had evidently formed in advance her idea of an elderly husband — perhaps from reading the abundant literature concerning the *mal mariée*[3] — and proceeds to recreate her husbands in that prejudiced image. If a literal-minded reader wonders how anybody so young could have come by such wisdom, he may find a clue in the fact that she was still heeding the 'loore' of her 'dame' at the age of forty or more when prospecting for a successor to her fourth husband (575-84). Even if she did not acknowlege openly that her elderly husbands' anti-feminist tirades were purely her own fabrication (379-83), the fact would suggest itself from the style in which they are delivered. Only Dame Alys speaks like this:

> Thou seydest this, that I was lyk a cat;
> For whoso wolde senge a cattes skyn,
> Thanne wolde the cat wel dwellen in his in;
> And if the cattes skyn be slyk and gay,
> She wol nat dwelle in house half a day,
> But forth she wole, er any day be dawed,
> To shewe hir skyn, and goon a-caterwawed.

(III, 348-54)

Having thus established such a competitive standard for her imaginary opponent, she must employ all her wits to surpass herself in her reply. This she succeeds in bringing off triumphantly in a passage such as 431-42, which concludes with her standing on its head the hateful medieval commonplace that the husband should govern his wife just as Reason rules the Passions:

> Oon of us two moste bowen, doutelees;
> And sith a man is moore resonable
> Than womman is, ye moste been suffrable.

(III, 440-2)

It is instructive to observe that George Eliot adopts these lines as the epigraph for Chapter 65 of *Middlemarch* — the chapter in which Rosamond Lydgate finally masters her husband. Any critic who is inclined to take a high moral tone with Chaucer's supreme comic creation — as sublime as Falstaff in her enormity — would do well to compare these two accounts of the art of achieving 'maistrie' in marriage, and to ponder the implications of the comparison.

One reason why Jankin proves to be a worthy antagonist is precisely that he knows instinctively how to 'antagonize' his wife; another is that he has found out that her 'heel of Achilles' is — if I may mix my metaphor — her 'chambre of Venus'. In order to appreciate his tactical advantage, it is first necessary to go back to the opening of the Prologue and her debate with the doctors. Canon lawyers, who disapproved of the re-marriage of widows, were embarrassed by the fact that there is no positive Scriptural authority for its prohibition. So, like Langland's Friars, they 'Glosed the gospel as hem good liked . . . construwed it as thei wolde'[4] by means of their specious gloss on the fact that Christ is recorded as having attended a wedding on only a single occasion (cf. III, 9-13). At III, 26, we applaud as the wife denounces this procedure by its proper name: 'Men may devyne and *glosen*, up and doun.' But our applause is soon followed by a gasp of astonishment. Although Alys begins by setting herself up as a champion of 'experience', she is perfectly willing to play the academic game of 'authorities'. However, like Langland's Mede in her debate with Conscience, her citation of Scriptural authority proves to be wilful and fallacious.[5] Her counter-citation to the theologians' text about the Wedding 'in the Cane of Galilee' (11 — cf. John 2: 1 ff.) is from Genesis 1: 28:

> But wel I woot, expres, withoute lye,
> God bad us for to wexe and multiplye;
> That gentil text kan I wel understonde.

> (III, 27-9)

This childless widow then cheerfully proceeds herself to 'glose' the text so as to justify the practice of 'bigamye' (in the medieval sense of marrying two husbands in succession) — or even 'octogamye'! It is a yet more remarkable volte face which, much later in the Prologue, indicates the power and the nature of Jankin's hold over her. At 509, she admits to being the willing victim of 'glozing' — although the verb is now used in its developed sense of 'to flatter' and its application is — as the rhyme emphasizes — decidedly physical:

> But in oure bed he was so fressh and gay,
> And therwithal so wel koude he me glose,
> Whan that he wolde han my *bele chose*,
> That thogh he hadde me bete on every bon,
> He koude wynne agayn my love anon.

> (508-12)

Another way in which Jankin establishes power over her is by being 'daungerous' (i.e. 'playing hard to get') towards her (514). She accounts for his success in this respect by citing a generalization about women's 'queynte fantasye', which involves one of her characteristically mercantile images (cf. 515-24). But, in fact, he is appropriating, and turning against her, a procedure that she had employed against her elderly husbands (cf. 403-12). It is a similar appropriation that leads to the climax of their 'debaat', with Jankin's lections from his 'book of wikked wyves' (685). In the formal structure of the Prologue this catalogue of *exempla* is the counterpart to the anti-feminist tirades that Alys had earlier placed in the mouths of her elderly husbands. Apart from the splendid anecdote concerning Latumyus and Arrius (757-64), Jankin's performance is far less vivid and cogent than the earlier episode. Alys is herself a far more telling anti-feminist than the 'clerke'. The reason why she is so upset by his lections is merely that it is he who is the lector: she alone is permitted to make anti-feminist jokes.

At this point the 'debaat' degenerates from a contention of tongues to a combat of fists. Yet such a development was potentially a feature of most literary 'debates'. In *The Owl and the Nightingale* the owl early threatens her adversary with violence and, towards the end, the small birds mob the owl;[6] in *Winner and Waster*[7] the embattled supporters of the two debaters are drawn up before the verbal contest begins; in *The Parlement of Foules* trial by armed combat is at one point (533-40) proposed as a possible solution to the hard *demande d'amour*. Eventually the couple 'fille acorded' (812) — not, of course, by submitting their dispute to the judgment of an umpire (as would happen in a literary or academic debate), but 'by us selven two'. One of the less mercenary conditions of this 'accord' — not exactly the 'humble, wys accord' of Dorigen and Arveragus in the Franklin's Tale (cf. V, 789 ff.) — is that the wife should have 'governance' of 'his tonge, and of his hond also' (III, 815). So their 'debaat' (822) — both linguistic and pugilistic — is resolved. Having had the gratification of being declared the winner in the game of Sovereignty (as well as having secured for herself the monopoly of Jankin's Real Estate), she can afford to perform a final volte face by submitting to be 'kinde' and 'trewe' to him for the rest of his life.

## II

An equally unexpected change of mind occurs at the end of the Wife of Bath's Tale when the hag, having heard her husband concede 'maistrie' to her (1236 ff.), 'obeyed hym in every thyng / That myghte doon hym plesance or likyng' (1255-6). This tale is perhaps the supreme example of a wife's tactical use of speech. Formally analysed, the Tale stands in relation to its Prologue much as the concluding *narratio* is related to the main discourse of the popular sermon of the period: it affords an *exemplum* of Alys's *thema*, that what women most desire is 'maistrye'. Many readers, in our own post-Freudian era, have also regarded its magical dénouement as an unconscious ritual act of wish-fulfilment on the part of its aging and most unfairy-like narrator. Certainly, there is a moment in the Prologue that fleetingly reveals her concern about the onslaught of Old Age:

> But, Lord Crist! whan that it remembreth me
> Upon my yowthe, and on my jolitee,
> It tikleth me aboute myn herte roote.
> Unto this day it dooth myn herte boote
> That I have had my world as in my tyme.
> But age, allas! that al wole envenyme,
> Hath me biraft my beautee and my pith.
> Lat go, farewel! the devel go therwith!
> The flour is goon, ther is namoore to telle . . .
>
> (III, 469-77)

If her train of thought had concluded with this rhetorical *conclusio*, the whole passage would indeed have sounded like a poignant elegy for her lost youth and beauty. But the finality of the assertion, 'ther is namoore to telle', is suspect as soon as it is uttered, because what these words conclude is merely the first half of a couplet. Before the rhyme has been supplied for 'telle', the conventional, 'romantic' image of 'the *flower* of youth' has been transmogrified into the edible kind of *flour*; and we are back in the market-place, from where the mercenary Dame Alys fetches so much of her imagery:

> The flour is goon, ther is namoore to telle;
> The bren, as I best kan, now moste I selle;
> But yet to be right myrie wol I fonde.
> Now wol I tellen of my fourthe housbonde.
>
> (III, 477-80)

The Tale is therefore better regarded not so much as a compulsive act of wish-fulfilment as an extension of the Wife's playful response (cf. 192) to the Pardoner's request to her to 'teche us yonge men of youre praktike' (187). What Alys seems to enjoy most in the narrating of the tale is not so much the magical dénouement itself as the lecture by which it is approached; a lecture delivered by her elder, spiritual sister to one of these 'yonge men' who are in need of instruction.

Before the Tale's 'final cause' is ultimately revealed, its immediate 'efficient cause' wantonly pulls her traditional, narrative 'matter' out of its inherited shape[8] and moulds it as an instrument for satisfying her evanescent whims — almost as if it were a sixth husband. She uses it to settle a personal score, to ride several hobby-horses and, above all, to tease. Into the romantic Arthurian *incipit* of her tale, with its apparent nostalgia for the days when 'Al was this land fulfild of fayerye' (III, 859), she insinuates her attack upon friars. The next opportunity for her to indulge in a characteristic *cadenza* is afforded by the series of interviews with women that the condemned rapist conducts in his desperate endeavour to find the solution to the queen's riddle about what it is that women most desire. For the reader, already familiar with Alys's philosophy of matrimony, the answer will be fairly obvious. But this very foreknowledge may itself prevent us from recognizing just how arbitrary the 'correct' solution is; any of the answers ventured by the interviewed ladies is in fact quite as plausible. Indeed, as one realizes this, one is strongly tempted to surmise that the hag (who is privy to the 'correct' answer) may be a disguised young lady-in-waiting of the queen's private chamber, who is determined to secure, by 'foul' means rather than 'fair', the 'lusty bacheler' for herself. Readers who have been schooled by J.R.R. Tolkien will immediately dismiss this surmise, knowing that such a literal-minded approach to fairy stories is improper: in such stories magic must be taken on trust.[9] These replies enable Alys to expatiate further on two topics that she touched upon in the Prologue: a woman's susceptibility to flattery, and her inability to keep a secret. Her third instance of teasing is at the expense of the reader, when she introduces the comic *occupatio* at III, 1073-82, which purports to apologize for neglecting to describe the 'joye' at the wedding banquet when the young knight married the hag:

> Now wolden som men seye, paraventure,
> That for my necligence I do no cure
> To tellen yow the joye and al th'array
> That at the feeste was that ilke day.
> To which thyng shortly answeren I shal:
> I seye ther nas no joye ne feeste at al;
> Ther nas but hevynesse and muche sorwe.
> For prively he wedded hire on the morwe,
> And al day after hidde hym as an owle,
> So wo was hym, his wyf looked so foule.

It is only with the fourth instance of teasing that Dame Alys comes to the point of her Tale, and we encounter the ingeniously tactical exercise of the tongue by one of the dramatis personae. Before the old, poor and low-born hag transforms herself into a young, beautiful and faithful wife, she harangues, from the far corner of the bed, her reluctant young husband on the attractions of old age, poverty and lack of 'gentillesse' (in the sense of 'high birth') (1106-218). In order to appreciate the purport of this long speech, it is first necessary to pursue a little further our investigation of the rhetoric of consolation, begun in Chapter 2.

It was there remarked how readily an element of special pleading enters into examples of the *consolatio mortis*.[10] It becomes most patent when a condemned man is to be persuaded that his death is an advantage to him. Shakespeare furnishes us with an apt example in the speech of the Duke (disguised as a friar) to Claudio in *Measure for Measure* (III, i, 5-41). The speech is an amalgam of commonplaces that even includes the ubiquitous image of the ass bearing ingots (25-8). The Duke, of course, has no intention of letting Claudio die. The role of the hag in the Wife of Bath's Tale is analogous to that of the Duke in this passage: she must persuade her husband that what he regards as worse than death is, on the contrary, a positive advantage to him.

It is surprising that so many commentators have taken this speech in solemn earnest. Perhaps they are daunted by the fact that the hag's argument about the nature of true 'gentillesse' (1109 ff.) occurs elsewhere in serious and very respectable contexts: in Chaucer's Ballade on the subject; Dante's *Convivio* and *De Monarchia*; *The Consolation of Philosophy* itself (III, Prosa vi). It is therefore worth recalling what one of the greatest of English literary critics has to say about the passage. In *The Preface to the Fables*, Dryden remarks:

> *Chaucer* introduces an old Woman of mean Parentage, whom a youthful Knight of Noble Blood was forc'd to marry, and consequently loathed her: The Crone being in bed with him on the wedding Night, and finding his Aversion, endeavours to win his Affection by Reason, and speaks a good Word for her self, (as who could blame her?) in hope to mollifie the sullen Bridegroom. She takes her topiques from the Benefits of Poverty, the Advantages of old Age and Ugliness, the Vanity of Youth, and the silly Pride of Ancestry and Titles without inherent Virtue, which is the true Nobility.[11]

It is interesting that Dryden designates her arguments as 'Topiques'. For, as already noted,[12] once an argument is identified as supplying a 'topic', the possibility arises that its enunciator may not necessarily believe in it himself: he may be employing it as a generally accepted premiss from which he can construct an enthymeme (see above, p.46)

— which may well prove to be a sophism. Surely it is likely that, in this most teasing of Chaucer's tales (after the Nun's Priest's Tale), the 'topiques' are deployed 'in game'. One of the few critics to regard the passage as playful has observed very pertinently:

> It is surely obvious that the first two . . . objections — that she is ugly and old — are the more serious, yet it is the third and least important (though not unimportant) objection [i.e. that she lacks gentle birth] which the hag enlarges on somewhat illogically for over one hundred lines.[13]

Analysed technically, this is a comic development of the ancient procedure in forensic rhetoric whereby an advocate would employ *amplificatio* in order to give prominence to evidence that enhanced his case and *abbreviatio* to gloss over that which told against it.[14] The hag 'amplifies' enormously her reply to the least damaging of the knight's objections in order to dwarf the more pertinent ones concerning her 'filthe' and 'elde'. At the same time, there is a characteristically Chaucerian joke about the limitations of human reason. The hag is sweet reasonableness itself in the one situation where all argument is patently irrelevant. What is more, her prolix 'moral' discourse cheerfully concludes with the non sequitur:

> 'But nathelees, syn I knowe youre delit,
> I shal fulfille youre worldly appetit.'
>
> (1217-18)

The volte face is worthy of Chauntecleer.[15]

The function of the discourse cannot be fully appreciated unless it is viewed in a wider context. In the first part of the tale the knight is manoeuvred into marrying the hag, who has saved his life. The Wife of Bath evidently considers this a more appropriate punishment than death for the rape he has committed — especially as he is a 'lusty bacheler' (883). But it is not enough for him to be legally compelled to marry her. He must voluntarily concede 'maistrie' to his wife; and for this voluntary act he will be rewarded with perpetual bliss. It is essential for his happiness that, when the hag offers her husband the choice at lines 1219-27, he shall leave it to her, recognizing that in her will is his peace. She works for this result by psychological attrition and verbal bombardment[16] so that he is rendered mentally 'punch-drunk' by the end of her relentlessly protracted diatribe on the advantages of his having married someone of low birth. The tone of his reply (1228-35), in which he leaves the choice to her, shows him to be indeed utterly wearied, brow-beaten, and rendered incapable of making any decision.

What Chaucer makes game of in this episode is not so much the particular set of 'topiques' cited by the hag as the general tradition of 'remedies against Fortune', with which all such *solacia* were associated. Petrarch had duly rehearsed these particular 'topiques' in the Second Book of his *De Remediis Utriusque Fortunae*; and it is interesting to observe that when (after 1400) an English translator freely adapted a fragment of that immense 'libellus', the sequence of Dialogues he chose to render was precisely that which included: '*De Deformitate Corporis*' ('Of vnsemeli schap'); '*De Originis Obscuritate*' ('Of Pore Birthe'); '*De Paupertate*' ('Of Pouerte').[17] Chaucer converts to *solas* the basic doctrine of this consolatory tradition which purports to show that (unpleasant) earthly phenomena are other than what they appear to be to our limited human understanding. If the Tale were a moral allegory, the knight would no doubt have embraced the hag in the spirit in which St Francis of Assisi embraced the Lady Poverty:[18] he would discover within her a spiritual and ethical beauty invisible to the outward eye. But the Tale causes things to be 'other than what they appear to be' in a sense that would have horrified Boethius, Petrarch, the saints and the theologians. When the hag transforms herself magically into a being that will gratify *l'homme moyen sensuel*, she virtually stands all the consolatory topics on their heads. This inversion is the Comic Muse's version of the commonplace that underlies so much of the consolatory tradition: 'This world fareth as a Fantasye';[19] and it affords a fitting conclusion to a tale whose narrator had declared: 'Myn entente is nat but for to pleye' (192).

### III

In the Wife of Bath's Tale a woman is obliged to woo her man after their nuptials have been celebrated. It is possible to see the Clerk's Tale as a variation on the same theme; but, whereas the hag overwhelms her husband with words, Griselda is, like the Clerk himself, one who utters 'Noght o word . . . moore than was neede' (I, 304). Similarly, whereas the Wife of Bath's Tale is racy, playfully digressive and self-indulgent, that of the Clerk moves at a deliberate pace and proceeds with the austere concentration demanded by a game of chess.

Before pursuing such a reading further, it is first necessary to glance at the more usual approach to the Tale, which starts from a comparison with its principal source: Petrarch's religiously orientated Latin adaptation (together with its French 'translation') of the final novella in Boccaccio's *Decameron*.[20] Although Chaucer preserves Petrarch's Christian *moralitas* (IV, 1142-8), he will not allow Walter the immunity of a divine tester, but criticizes his treatment of his wife in sharply human terms (e.g. 456-62). Griselda remains an object of wonder. A scattering of biblical references and allusions[21] has encouraged commentators to view her as an embodiment of Christian 'patience', or long-suffering; and the Host's designation of the Tale as a 'legende' — in some MSS[22] — may suggest that she should be regarded as a saint. Unfortunately, the type of saint that she most nearly resembles is one that does not commend itself to modern taste, or to our notions of common humanity. The type has been gently satirized by E.M. Forster in his early novel, *Where Angels Fear to Tread* — in a passage inspired by an authentic medieval work of art.

Much of the action of this novel is set in the imaginary Tuscan hill town, Monteriano — in fact, San Gimignano under a very thin disguise. In the Collegiate Church of Santa Deodata is a series of frescoes depicting the life and death of the patron saint (Forster has in mind the frescoes in the Duomo at San Gimignano concerning Santa Fina). He writes:

> She was a holy maiden of the Dark Ages, the city's patron saint, and sweetness and barbarity mingle strangely in her story. So holy was she that all her life she lay upon her back in the house of her mother, refusing to eat, refusing to play, refusing to work. The devil, envious of such sanctity, tempted her in various ways. He dangled grapes above her, he showed her fascinating toys, he pushed soft pillows beneath her aching head. When all proved vain he tripped up the mother and flung her downstairs before her very eyes. But so holy was the saint that she never picked her mother up, but lay on her back through all, and thus assured her throne in Paradise.
>
> (Chapter VI).

No branch of The Mothers' Union is ever likely to adopt a 'Deodata' as its patron saint. It is even less likely to wish to advocate the canonization of Griselda, when its members read of her 'pacient' response to the supposed killing of her infants. But neither is Chaucer setting her up as a candidate for sainthood. The Clerk's Tale is a secular *exemplum* that explores the possibilities of 'pacience' in a wife, not only 'to the limit' but outrageously beyond the limits of what would be acceptable or desirable 'in real life'. Chaucer applies his religious *moralitas* only 'after the event', just as Henryson, in his *Fables*, appends an allegorical *moralitas* to each of his narratives, which may already have inculcated a somewhat different moral lesson of their own.[23] It may therefore be more rewarding for us to turn our attention away from Saints' Legends, and to view the Tale in the context of another genre where 'sweetness and barbarity mingle strangely': I mean, of course, the secular romance.

Nowhere is such mingling more evident than in the romance of *Amis and Amiloun*[24] which — as the names of its heroes suggest — is concerned with the ideals of friendship. The climax of the action is reached when Amis cuts the throats of his own two children over a basin and uses their collected blood to anoint his best friend — the only possible cure for Amiloun's leprosy (2197 ff.). The children are later discovered alive and well, playing in the nursery where they had been murdered — just as Griselda's son and daughter are, unknown to her, alive in Bologna — where they receive the education away from their parents, which was not so unusual for children of aristocratic families during the Middle Ages.[25]

Both plots are characteristic of a certain type of romance that celebrates, with obsessive determination, a single ideal or virtue to the exclusion of all others. The story of Griselda is less barbaric and less crude than that of *Amis and Amiloun*: the children are not killed; the reader is immediately informed of this fact; but there is no doubt about the extreme suffering of the mother who has promised to obey her husband's every wish without demur. What is remarkable is Griselda's love for the Marquis Walter which survives everything that he does. For it is this love — no less obsessive than Amis's friendship for Amiloun — that is her fundamental motivating force (cf. 507-11, 666-7, 855-61, 972-3, 1090-2); her 'pacience' is the particular manifestation of it that circumstances, together with her husband's temperament and feudal rank, make necessary, if she is to affect him.

The Clerk's Tale may be seen as involving another motif that is common in medieval romance: but, in this instance, the motif is inverted by Chaucer. I mean the situation where a knight woos a proud lady, such as the duchess known as 'La Fiere' in Hue de Rotelande's *Ipomedon*, and is commanded by her to perform various extravagant adventures for her 'worship' before she will return his love. So the hero of the thirteenth-century Anglo-Norman romance, *Gui de Warewic* (Guy of Warwick), falls on his knees before Felice, who is his social superior, and subsequently tries to impress her, not only by maintaining her favour in tournaments, but by undertaking a seven-year quest in Europe and Africa.[26] In *The Book of the Duchess* (1024-32) Chaucer is no less critical of the ladies who test their suitors in this way than he is, in the Clerk's Tale, of Walter's 'tempting' of his wife.

A further inversion of romance convention can be seen in the fact that — to return to our point of departure — Walter has to be wooed after the wedding has been officially celebrated and the nuptials consummated. The marriage of true minds does not occur until after

the mock divorce (cf. 1125-7). This marquis was reluctant to marry
for fear of exchanging his 'liberte' for 'servage' (145-7). By proposing
marriage to a peasant girl, he is able to exact from his prospective
wife an oath of absolute obedience. As soon as she voluntarily gives
her assent: '"This is ynogh, Grisilde myn!" quod he' (365). But he
soon discovers that the one-way obedience that she offers him is not
'ynogh'. He assumes that what is wanting is a sufficiency of
obedience — or evidence of it – on Griselda's part. So he 'tempts' her
by subjecting her to cruel psychological torments and extreme
indignities. But the effect of this 'tempting' is neither to cause her to
rebel nor to reduce her personality to a quintessence of nothingness.
Instead, she acquires a 'pacience' as solid as an animated statue with
finely etched features. Nor is she a dumb heifer, like the motionless
Deodata. She engages in public service: 'The commune profit koude
she redresse' (431), and she issues 'juggementz of so greet *equitee*',
because 'so wyse and rype *wordes* hadde she' (438-9, my italics). Her
restrained speech, when addressing Walter, is an index at once of the
power of her suppressed emotions and of the strength of her self-
possession.

The only occasion when she permits herself to speak to him
eloquently and at length is immediately after he informs her of his
intention to divorce her. The part of this speech (813-89) that has
received most attention[27] is the passage (852-61) (which has no
counterpart in Chaucer's sources) where she ventures to reproach him
for his treatment of her. But the incredibly mild reproach is merely
part of her tactical exordium. It is designed to perform the function
of *captatio benevolentiae*[28] — to play upon Walter's conscience and
pity, only to the extent of disposing him to grant the request that
follows in the main petition of her address. It is characteristic of her
that this petition — admittedly, already in Petrarch — does not
oppose his outrageous proposal, but pursues a purpose that is
limited, practical and modest (in more than one sense). It is also
scrupulously equitable. She restores to Walter everything he had
bestowed upon her since she left her father's house (she had regarded
the children as coming into this category too). Her only request is for
a smock, to protect from the public gaze 'thilke wombe in which
*youre* children leye' (877, my italics). She asks for this garment as a
fair exchange for her maidenhead that she had yielded to him. This
speech is a model of humility and submissiveness, but it also breathes
a spirit of tough-minded independence that is far more impressive
than any complaint about her treatment would have been. At this
moment, above all others, the peasant girl proves by her manner of
speech that she is the genuine aristocrat. By 1044 ff., when he is
about to restore her children to her, Walter appears to have been

convinced of this fact, since he acknowledges the inequity, as well as the iniquity, of his dealings with her:

> And whan this Walter saugh hire pacience,
> Hir glade chiere, and no malice at al,
> And he so ofte had doon to hire offence,
> And she ay sad and constant as a wal,
> Continuynge evere hire innocence overal,
> This sturdy markys gan his herte dresse
> To rewen upon hire wyfly stedfastnesse.

The next stanza begins: '"This is ynogh, Grisilde myn," quod he' (1051). Many of us may feel that Walter is even less entitled to address her in this way now than when he exacted her oath of obedience. But the difference is that he now applies the words 'This is ynogh' to his own actions instead of to her promise. Now he cannot but grant her the full 'fraunchyse' of his love, together with the freedom of her aristocratic status, to which he had previously admitted her only 'tentatively'.

The effectiveness of this tale is, of course, due in no small measure to Chaucer's use of the 'rhyme royal' stanza which he had already employed in *Troilus and Criseyde* to create many slow-moving passages of pathos and reflection. The spell which this particular metre casts upon our ears and our sensibility becomes fully evident only at the moment when it is finally broken. Chaucer first 'distances' the idealized story by lightening the tone in the two final 'rhyme royal' stanzas, with their reference to the Wife of Bath (1163-76). Then in *Lenvoy de Chaucer* the Clerk (in unexpectedly Goliardic mood) launches into his Song without Music ('I wol . . . *Seyn* yow a song to glade yow', 1173-4), a comic palinode composed in six six-line stanzas that employ (with cacophonous and clangorous virtuosity) only three rhyming sounds altogether. The art of verbal riposte, totally alien to Griselda's art of persuasion, is imperatively reasserted:

> Folweth Ekko, that holdeth no silence,
> But evere answereth at the countretaille.
> Beth nat bidaffed for youre innocence,
> But sharply taak on yow the governaille.
> Emprenteth wel this lessoun in youre mynde,
> For commune profit sith it may availle.

> (IV, 1189-94)

The comic insensitivity of the stanza ranges from the demythologizing of the nymph, Echo, into something like what Chaucer elsewhere calls a 'labbyng shrewe' (cf. *CT*, IV, 2428), through the insinuation of the abusively colloquial verb 'bidaffed' [fooled],[29] to the debasement of one of Chaucer's favourite moral collocations — 'commune profit' (already employed seriously at 431)[30] — into a rallying cry for female 'solidarity'. This Battle Hymn for 'archewyves' and their 'sklendre' sisters is one of the noisiest exhortations in Middle English verse; it provides a complete release after the sustained *sotto voce* dynamics of the tale of the wife who conquers by reticence and a strict belief in the principle that *patientes vincunt* — 'they triumph who suffer and endure'.

## IV

The outrageous anecdote that supplies the plot for the Merchant's Tale purports to show that an erring wife will always find a 'suffisant answere' for her husband, even when caught in the act with her lover. Here the wife is required to find two answers: one as soon as Januarie's sight is miraculously restored by Pluto; the other when her husband questions the aptness of her use of the word 'strugle'. May's reply is inspired by Proserpina, a slightly more dignified relative of the fairy in the Wife of Bath's Tale. Like her counterpart, the goddess overwhelms her husband in debate by her manipulation of 'auctoures' and *exempla*, to the point where Pluto is forced to concede: 'I yeve it up' (IV, 2312) — an idiom applied by the Wife of Bath herself to her husbands' enforced concessions (III, 427).

In such a context it would seem to be desirable for the critic to scrutinize almost every sentence that May utters. The task is not as formidable as the Tale's length might suggest; for her first recorded speech occurs at a late stage of the narrative. Earlier we are given her unspoken comments on Januarie's early morning exhibition in bed:

> The slakke skyn aboute his nekke shaketh,
> Whil that he sang, so chaunteth he and craketh.
> But God woot what that May thoughte in hir herte,
> Whan she hym saugh up sittynge in his sherte,
> In his nyght-cappe, and with his nekke lene;
> She preyseth nat his pleyyng worth a bene.

> (IV, 1849-54)

Later she must endure in silence when her husband is woken by his cough, and

> Anon he preyde hire strepen hire al naked;
> He wolde of hire, he seyde, han som plesaunce,
> And seyde hir clothes dide hym encombraunce,

And she obeyeth, be hire lief or looth.
But lest that precious folk be with me wrooth,
How that he wroghte, I dar nat to yow telle;
Or wheither hire thoughte it paradys or helle.

(IV, 1958-64)

The affair with Damyan is conducted first of all with silent exchanges of billets-doux, so private that, on one occasion, she disposes of the fragments down the privy. Later, when Januarie is blind, the intriguers resort to dumb-show. Chaucer's placing of May's first speech is masterly. But, in order to appreciate its effect, it is first necessary to consider certain aspects of his presentation of Januarie.

Chaucer's comedy is unmerciful in its representation of a *senex amans* who regards marriage as the occasion for licensed lust. But the Tale — most unusually for a fabliau — also succeeds in entering into his heart, his imagination (cf. 'fantasye', 1577 and 1610)[31] and even his soul. One of his motives for marrying is religious. Throughout his life he has his body 'folily despended' (1403) 'on wommen, ther as was his appetyt' (1250). He sees marriage partly as an atonement for past licentiousness — though hardly as the Purgatory on Earth that Justinus predicts for him (1670-3).

It is an interesting fact that, of all the 'marriage group' tales, this is the only one that speaks of marriage as a sacrament (1319, 1702). It is the only one that mentions the doctrine that a husband should love his wife as Christ loves His church. In fact, religious references abound in this Tale — sometimes they are cynical, but they are, nevertheless, there (cf. also 1435, 1628, 2171, 2188). Even Januarie's specious argument (1835-41) about a man's not hurting himself with his own knife does at least suggest a consciousness of sin.[32] Another motive for his marrying is the fond hope of begetting children to inherit his property; but the main consideration is that he now believes marriage to be a state of superior bliss, a 'paradys' from which he has always been excluded.

In order that he might realize more effectively the delights of the 'paradise' that has eluded him, he has caused to be constructed a garden 'walled al with stoon' (2029), a veritable *hortus conclusus*, where, in summer, he makes love to his wife. The narrator declares that nobody is able to express its beauty, not even the inventor of the most celebrated medieval garden of love: 'He that wroot the Romance of the Rose' (2032). But the effect of this allusion is double-edged. Whereas Guillaume de Lorris's garden is allegorical, representing a psychological or 'spiritual' phase of experience, Januarie's is a solidly material plesaunce, commissioned to indulge the fancy of a rich man. We may also recall that on the exterior of the wall surrounding Guillaume's park are depicted personifications of various conditions that are permanently excluded from the paradise of *fine amor*. Among them is Old Age.[33] Januarie, who wasted his youth on wanton women, attempts to purchase too late, and with the wrong currency, the earthly paradise he had earlier eschewed.

Within the walls of the garden, however, Januarie's grosser utterances and actions of the bedroom scenes are charmed away, and his romantic 'fantasye' becomes dominant within him. His feelings become articulate in the poetry of his speech at 2138-48, based upon verses from *The Song of Solomon* — with its reference to the 'enclosed garden' or *hortus conclusus* at 2143. It is true that he again takes literally what was often understood in a 'spiritual' sense in the fourteenth century; for biblical exegetes read the passage as if it were Christ's address to his spouse (the soul, or the Church). However, Januarie was by no means alone in 're-secularizing' the obviously erotic language and imagery of this beautiful passage:

> 'Rys up, my wyf, my love, my lady free!
> The turtles voys is herd, my dowve sweete;
> The wynter is goon with alle his reynes weete.
> Com forth now, with thyne eyen columbyn!
> How fairer been thy brestes than is wyn!
> The gardyn is enclosed al aboute;
> Com forth, my white spouse! out of doute
> Thou hast me wounded in myn herte, O wyf!
> No spot of thee ne knew I al my lyf.
> Com forth, and lat us taken oure disport;
> I chees thee for my wyf and my confort.'

The attention of critics has been focused upon the narrator's comment on this speech, which may appear to 'undercut' its poetic effect: 'Swiche olde lewed wordes used he' (2149). But I believe the 'sinking' effect has been exaggerated. The usual meaning of 'lewed' in Middle English is 'lay', hence 'uneducated'. In combination with 'olde' it means something like *démodé*, 'unfashionable'. In Chaucer's social and literary circle, presumably, sophisticated, smart young men no longer worked this particular vein of imagery and diction when wooing their ladies.

It is instructive to compare this speech with another which draws upon passages from the *Song of Solomon*: I mean that uttered by the ridiculous Absolon in the Miller's Tale (I, 3698-707), as he serenades Alysoun through the shot-window of the room where she lies in bed with her successful lover, Nicholas.[34] In this instance the biblical poetry is utterly destroyed because Chaucer makes Absolon cut the ground from under his own feet by inserting into the body of his speech such a line as: 'That for youre love I swete ther I go.' The poetry of Januarie's speech, on the contrary, is allowed to make its full appeal to the reader. When Absolon's 'faire bryd', his 'sweete cynamome', replies, her rasping idiom blasts his fantasy concerning her:

> 'Go fro the wyndow, Jakke fool,' she sayde;
> 'As help me God, it wol nat be "com pa me".
> I love another — and elles I were to blame —
> Wel bet than thee, by Jhesu, Absolon.
> Go forth thy wey, or I wol caste a ston;
> And lat me slepe, a twenty devel wey!'
>
> (I, 3708-13)

These words are what might be termed the 'articulate correlative' to the unspoken insult that she bestows upon him through the shot-window a few lines later.

Januarie's evocation of the *Song of Solomon* does not receive such an immediate reply from the object of his 'fantasye'. He continues with a speech that places him in the most sympathetic light in which he ever appears. He begins:

> 'Now wyf,' quod he, 'heere nys but thou and I,
> That art the creature that I best love . . . '
>
> (IV, 2160-1)

Although these lines are ironical (since Damyan is already concealed in the bush), Januarie's sentiment rings true; the tone is reminiscent of Troilus's words to Criseyde when their love is about to be consummated: 'Now be ye kaught, now is ther but we tweyne' (*TC*, III, 1207). Januarie continues:

> 'For by that Lord that sit in hevene above,
> Levere ich hadde to dyen on a knyf,
> Than thee offende, trewe deere wyf!'
>
> (2162-4)

Here is a decided advance from the licensed lust of the bridal night to something that sounds like genuine love. In the earlier scene he apologised to May because

> 'Allas! I moot trespace
> To yow, my spouse, and yow greetly *offende*,

Er tyme come that I wil doun descende . . .'

(IV, 1828-30, my italics)

His use of the image of the knife also marks a changed attitude since he employed it in that same speech to justify speciously his view (clean contrary to the Church's teaching about marriage) that 'we han leve to pleye us by the lawe' (1841). His expression of love continues:

> 'For Goddes sake, thenk how I thee chees,
> Noght for no coveitise, doutelees,
> But oonly for the love I had to thee.
> And though that I be oold, and may nat see,
> Beth to me trewe, and I wol telle yow why.
> Thre thynges, certes, shal ye wynne therby:
> First, love of Crist, and to youreself honour,
> And al myn heritage, toun and tour . . .'

He is even self-critical:

> 'And though that I be jalous, wyte me noght.
> Ye been so depe enprented in my thoght
> That, whan that I considere youre beautee,
> And therwithal the unlikly elde of me,
> I may nat, certes, though I sholde dye,
> Forbere to been out of youre compaignye
> For verray love; this is withouten doute.
> Now kys me, wyf, and lat us rome aboute.'

It is at this point that we hear 'fresshe' May speak for the first time. Her reply reveals her to be a brazen, assured, fully armed hypocrite; it evaporates the sympathy we felt for her earlier when she suffered in silence the comic horrors of the bedchamber. She first weeps and, when she addresses her husband 'benignely', she is careful to sound a religious note:

> 'I have,' quod she, 'a soule for to kepe
> As wel as ye, and also myn honour,
> And of my wyfhod thilke tendre flour,
> Which that I have assured in youre hond,
> Whan that the preest to yow my body bond . . .'

Standing upon her dignity, she reminds him that: 'I am a gentil womman and no wenche.' Certainly, her idiom is not that of 'So gay a popelote or swich a wenche' (I, 3254) as Alysoun in the Miller's Tale; but her actions have all the vulgarity of a fabliau heroine.

Januarie's later exclamation — 'O stronge *lady* stoore' (IV, 2367, my italics) — is nicely judged. After she has concluded her speech with some feminist reproaches, the narrator continues:

> ... she saugh, wher Damyan
> Sat in the bussh, and coughen she bigan,
> And with hir fynger signes made she
> That Damyan sholde clymbe upon a tree.
>
> (IV, 2207-10)

The speaker of that speech hardly needs the supernatural promptings of a Proserpina to supply her with her 'suffisant answere' when Januarie's sight is restored. She has no difficulty in persuading her husband, who is so susceptible to 'heigh fantasye' (1577), that the reality which he at last beholds is itself a 'fantasye'.

## V

The Merchant's Tale and the Franklin's Tale have certain fairly obvious points of contact. Both narratives are preceded by some theoretical discussion of marriage; in both tales a marriage is attacked by a young squire; a garden provides a significant setting in both narratives; both stories employ magic in a rather sophisticated way. But these similarities merely have the effect of indicating essential differences between the two tales. The most striking difference is in the characters of the respective heroines. Dorigen has not had 'a good press' among recent commentators, some of whom have dismissed her as 'a silly woman'.[35] But I confess that, after the series of poised, self-assured and articulate wives we have been considering, I find her artless spontaneity refreshing.

There are only three occasions when we hear Dorigen speak to anyone. The first is the conversation with Aurelius (V, 979-1005), when she makes her rash promise to give him her love if he will remove all the rocks from the Breton coast. The second consists of the few words that are reported of her exchange with Arveragus (1463-71), when she informs him of her predicament, now that the rocks have disappeared. The third consists of the even fewer words she speaks to Aurelius (1512-13) on her way to the garden to keep her promise. This enumeration may not correspond with the reader's impression of her utterances; for she has, in fact, many more lines assigned to her. At 1342-456 she utters a 'pleynt' which most modern readers indeed find too long for their taste; and at 865-93 she apostrophizes 'Eterne God' in her powerfully eloquent 'complaint' prompted by the sight of the 'grisly rokkes blake' that she regards as a threat to her husband's safety. But, like many soliloquies, these speeches are merely a poetic device for making articulate a character's unspoken thoughts and feelings. It is appropriate that most of Dorigen's lines are of this kind; for her essential life is internal. When she opens her mouth she is apt to lose control over her utterances. Yet, although this initially brings her into a 'trappe' (1341), it is also a powerful contributory cause of her ultimate release.

Because of the importance of her interior life, the most revealing place at which to begin our observation of her character will be that first 'compleynte' (865-93): the one inspired by her fear of the 'grisly feendly rokkes blake' into which all her volatile apprehensions about her absent husband's safety have been concentrated and solidified.[36] She asks why 'swich a parfit wys God and a stable', who had 'a greet chiertee / Toward mankynde' when He created man in His own image, should allow the existence of such objects of mortal danger to him. And she adds:

> 'I woot wel clerkes wol seyn as hem leste,
> By argumentz, that al is for the beste,
> Though I ne kan the causes nat yknowe.'

The 'clerkes' about whose 'argumentz' she is so sceptical are of course the eminently orthodox followers of Boethius who argue that man's view of the world is partial: if he could perceive God's total design, he would realize 'that al is for the beste'; regarded *sub specie aeternitatis*, the phenomena of this world will be recognized for the deceptive appearances that they are, and no longer be taken for ultimate reality. We have already observed how the Comic Muse that inspires the Wife of Bath's Tale playfully turns such consolatory 'topics' upside down; the present context compels us to consider the objections to them in sober earnest.

The very context of Dorigen's 'compleynte' is one of failed consolation. Although the tale is a romance that involves magic, Chaucer encourages us from an early stage to seek for psychological explanations for his heroine's actions.[37] Observe, for example, the technical terms of medieval psychology in the following passage:

> For in this world, certein, ther no wight is
> That he ne dooth or seith somtyme amys.
> Ire, siknesse, or *constellacioun*,
> Wyn, wo, or chaungynge of *complexioun*
> Causeth ful ofte to doon amys or speken.
>
> (779-83, my italics)

It is, of course, 'wo' (grief) that ultimately drives Dorigen to 'amys

. . . speken' at lines 989-98 when she makes 'in pley' (988) her offer
to love Aurelius, if he will perform the (apparently impossible) task
of removing all the rocks from the Breton coast. But its immediate
effect is to induce in her a 'derke fantasye' (844). The primary
contextual meaning of 'fantasye' must be 'obsession'; but, as in the
Merchant's Tale, it can also mean 'illusion'. In order to assuage her
excessive grief, her friends (who are evidently familiar with the
standard repertory of *solacia*) 'prechen hire' (824), maintaining that
'causelees she sleeth hirself', and apply 'every confort possible in this
cas'. Eventually her mind 'Receyved hath . . . / The emprentyng of
hire consolacioun' (833-4) so that the worst of her 'rage' abates. But
the seaside walks that they prescribe for her convalescence merely
aggravate her fears when she sees the black rocks.

Although she is emotionally overwrought, there is no occasion for
us to feel patronizing or condescending towards her 'compleynte' (as
certain critics have done).[38] Her arguments would have been
regarded, in Chaucer's day, as at least intellectually respectable. The
question of how Chaucer's contemporaries would have judged the
theological opinions of a character in a work of fiction set in pagan
times is not quite as straightforward as some 'historical' critics would
have us believe. Nevertheless, there is no harm in conceding that
Dorigen's complaint would have been condemned, not only by the
author of *The Consolation of Philosophy*, but also by the other two
'auctoures' whom Chaucer invokes along with him in the Nun's
Priest's Tale (VII, 3241-2): 'the hooly doctour Augustyn' and
Chaucer's near contemporary, 'Bisshop Bradwardyn'. Bradwardine,
for example, argued that nothing created is, by nature, bad:
everything created, as coming from God, is good.[39] When discussing
the closely related question of how a perfect and omnipotent God
can permit the existence of sin in his creatures, he follows 'the hooly
doctour Augustyn', maintaining that the beauty of the universe is not
to be considered from its individual parts, but, as with a picture, our
judgment must come from its overall aspect. It is interesting to find
that St Augustine (as quoted by Bradwardine) goes on to argue that:
'As the black in a picture is, in relation to the rest of it, a means of
enhancing its beauty, so sin must be regarded as enhancing the good
in the universe.'[40] It is, incidentally, the blackness of the rocks that
makes them particularly abhorrent to Dorigen. In the same context
Bradwardine observes: '. . . in vocibus diuersis unam harmoniam
perfecit'[41] — or, as Alexander Pope was to phrase the idea (in a
passage that derives ultimately from the same tradition of *consolatio*):
'All Discord, Harmony, not understood.'[42]

But Bradwardine finds himself in scrious logical difficulties in
trying to maintain this position.[43] Moreover, the 'modern Pelagians',

against whose influential arguments he directed the *De Causa Dei*, would have appreciated Dorigen's predicament sympathetically. These unnamed opponents almost certainly included Bradwardine's compatriots and near contemporaries, the 'Nominalists', William of Occam and Robert Holcot.

Occamists — according to the traditional interpretation of their position[44] — denied that it was possible to demonstrate rationally the truths of 'natural religion' and maintained that one could not prove the existence of God by means of the traditional 'argument from design'; nor could one make any rational demonstration of His attributes. But Occam and Holcot were both friars and professedly devout Christians. They regarded belief in God as a matter of faith that existed altogether outside the sphere of logical demonstration. This position is not unlike Dorigen's. Having declared her dissatisfaction with 'clerkes' who maintain 'by argumentz, that al is for the beste', she makes an act of pure faith:

> 'But thilke God that made wynd to blowe
> As kepe my lord! this my conclusion.
> To clerkes lete I al disputison . . .'
>
> (V, 888-90)

It is only then, as an afterthought, that she utters the extravagant, but very human, wish that all the rocks 'were sonken into helle for his sake' (i.e. for her husband's safety). Her friends divert her inland to the garden where she meets Aurelius. But the black rocks have not sunk into hell: they have merely sunk into her 'subconscious', from which they arise (an upsurge of her 'derke fantasye') to cause her irrationally to make her offer to Aurelius — another afterthought.

It is now possible to appreciate the irony in the developing situation. When Dorigen quite reasonably rejects the traditional consolation of 'clerkes', concerning the ultimate illusoriness of (unpleasant) worldly phenomena, she is still suffering from a 'fantasye' (obsession) which later causes her to offer to love Aurelius, if he can make 'the coost so clene / Of rokkes that ther nys no stoon *ysene*' (995-6). The desperate young squire seizes upon these words and (unknown to her) causes a 'clerke' — very different from those envisaged by Dorigen! — to juggle with appearance and reality so that, for a week or two, 'it *semed* that alle the rokkes were aweye' (1296). So she is caught in a 'trappe' (1341) constructed out of her own words. The remainder of the tale purports to show that this 'trappe' is itself illusory, and does not justify the self-slaughter to which she is pointed, in her second 'compleynte' (1355 ff.), by the 'auctoures' whose *exempla* she has evidently searched in vain for consolation.

Fortunately, she ignores their unanimous advice and declares her perplexity to her husband. In order to appreciate properly the dénouement that then follows, it is first necessary to consider her original compact with Arveragus and also to examine the behaviour of Aurelius.

The 'humble, wys accord' between the married partners has been the subject of much comment. G.L. Kittredge considered that it conformed to Chaucer's own notion of an ideal marital relationship — which it may well do — and also that it supplied the happy conclusion to the 'marriage debate' between the pilgrims.[45] Some more recent commentators have, on the contrary, argued that Chaucer's contemporaries would have regarded the arrangement as absurd, because it contravened the Church's teaching that a husband should govern his wife as the head rules the body or Reason the Passions[46] — but we have already noticed how Chaucer makes the Wife of Bath playfully stand that commonplace on its head. Both comments seem to me to be beside the point. The primary reason for the compact's taking the form that it does is because it is a necessary datum for the particular story that Chaucer tells: it sets the rules according to which the 'game' is to be played. The 'accord' cannot be regarded as a solution of any problem or issue, because the action has not yet begun.

What the narrator emphasizes is that *neither* party is the other's 'thral' or serf (V, 769-70). On the other hand, the 'libertee' of line 768 is not identical with licence. The partners enjoy both the equality and the obligations of friends. But friendship is understood as a state of voluntary, mutual obedience: 'Freendes everych oother moot obeye, / If they wol longe holden compaignye' (762-3). When, at 1463, Dorigen reveals her predicament to her husband, she, in effect, voluntarily places herself under his jurisdiction, because she regards herself as the offending party who has forfeited her *libertee*. It also proves to be just as well that they both agree to respect social convention to the extent of allowing that Arveragus shall have 'the *name* of soveraynetee . . . for shame of his degree' (751-2), since this enables Dorigen to inform Aurelius convincingly at 1512-13 that she has come to the garden to keep her 'trouthe' with him 'as myn housbonde *bad*' [commanded]. More important than this external arrangement, however, is the internal quality of their 'accord' that depends upon mutual love and trust: they observe the conditions 'the which that lawe of love acordeth to' (798). The only law that will hold their essential marriage together is that of love; the marriage will survive only so long as that persists. They will not rely upon legal sanctions — onc spouse's legal 'rights' of possession over the other — to protect their relationship. Their marriage survives the crisis because their love is genuine.

Arveragus's action in sending his wife to keep her tryst secretly with Aurelius causes the narrator some embarrassment. He is forced on to the defensive:

> Paraventure an heep of yow, ywis,
> Wol holden hym a lewed man in this
> That he wol putte his wyf in jupartie.
> Herkneth the tale er ye upon hire crie.
> She may have bettre fortune than yow semeth;
> And whan that ye han herd the tale, demeth.
>
> (V, 1493-8 — not in the Hengwrt MS)

What is striking about this piece of special pleading is the fact that it attempts no moral justification (or psychological explanation) of Arveragus's action; his behaviour is defended simply by an anticipation of the plot's happy ending. For the truth is that Arveragus (unlike Dorigen and Aurelius) is, for the most part, a 'function of the plot'. The attempt, at 1472-9, to provide him with a principle of action seems to me unconvincing — although his complex emotional reaction to the situation almost succeeds in persuading me that he is 'real'.

However, this shortcoming (if that is what it is) does not affect, in any very important way, either the 'process' or the *sentence* of Chaucer's Breton lai.[47] Obviously, 'in real life', no loving husband would take such a risk with his wife (put her 'in jupartie'). He could easily maintain Arveragus's principle that 'trouthe is the hyeste thyng that man may kepe' (1479) by upholding the legal and moral superiority of the marriage vow, in order to over-rule any obligation his wife had (unintentionally) incurred to a third party. That is almost certainly how a medieval canon lawyer would have ruled in such a case. The author of a naturalistic novel might — before following some such reasonable escape route — have allowed himself a paragraph of speculation about the possible effect upon the lover, if the husband had indeed despatched his wife to keep her 'trouthe' with him. But in a romance, set in a remote period when mores were not quite the same as those of the author's own times, conditional surmises can become actual experiments. Dorigen's plight is engineered partly by magic — an unexpected outrage against the laws of nature. Her release can be initiated only by something equally wonderful: Arveragus's action is an 'outrage' against the expected behaviour of an offended husband. But her plight is also due to her own unpremeditated speech; and it is another unpremeditated speech of hers that ultimately effects her release.

Arveragus's act of 'gentillesse' would have elicited no response if the same quality were not seated deep down within Aurelius's nature; but, for the moment, it has become overlaid by the fantasy that the squire has cherished concerning Dorigen. In terms of modern, Jungian psychology, Aurelius is an extreme case of one who has 'projected' his own *anima* on to the lady. In terms of medieval psychological theory, he is an acute sufferer from what, in the Knight's Tale, is diagnosed as 'the loveris maladye / Of Hereos' (I, 1373-4) — that 'Heroic Love' that Robert Burton later diagnosed as a disease of the soul in his *Anatomy of Melancholy*. Again, as in the Clerk's Tale, there is in the Franklin's Tale an inversion of a motif that is sometimes found in medieval romance. Here it is the situation where a lady marries a lord whom she loves according to her bond, no more nor less, until the day arrives when she meets (or re-encounters) her destined 'soul-mate' and their consequent passion consumes, and even destroys them. The most famous examples in medieval romance are the stories of Tristan and Iseult and Lancelot and Guinevere.[48] The conflict in these circumstances is between the 'legalistic' ties of marriage and the 'genuine' bond of *fine amor*. Aurelius, as it were, fancies in all seriousness 'that I am trewe Tristam the secounde'.[49] An obsessed lover cannot believe that 'his' lady loves another. Certainly Aurelius cannot believe that Dorigen loves Arveragus; after all, he is only her husband! But he is made to realize that he stands outside the charmed circle of mutual love. As the narrator asks near the beginning of the Tale:

> Who koude telle, but he hadde wedded be,
> The joye, the ese, and the prosperitee
> That is bitwixe an housbonde and his wyf?
>
> (V, 803-5)

One of several ironies in the Franklin's Tale is that the bond of *fine amor* is felt between the married couple and that it is the lover who attempts to impose a legalistic attachment upon the wife — although Aurelius tries to deny that he is doing anything of the kind:

> 'Nat that I chalange any thyng of right
> Of yow, my sovereyn lady, but youre grace . . .'
>
> (V, 1324-5)

'Grace,' in this context, is a term of *fine amor*; but 'chalange' is a technical term of law.[50]

What moves Aurelius 'in his herte' — the phrase occurs twice (1515 and 1520) — to appreciate the true situation is the manner of Dorigen's brief reply at 1512-13, when he asks her 'whiderward she wente':

And she answerde, half as she were mad,
'Unto the gardyn, as myn housbonde bad,
My trouthe for to holde, allas! allas!'

This distracted, only half-articulate, outburst reveals the true state of her heart far more effectively than any studied speech or eloquent plea would have done. It is the genuine distress that it expresses, no less than Arveragus's act of 'gentillesse' towards the squire, that moves Aurelius to declare:

'I have wel levere evere to suffre wo
Than I departe the love bitwix yow two.'

# CHAPTER 7

# Gems of Chastity

Children are among the least fortunate of mortals in the *Tales*. Four of them have speaking parts; and, of these, there is only one who is not murdered. Even this child — the serving-boy in the Pardoner's Tale — is introduced somewhat ominously to warn against the activities of the 'privee theef, men clepeth Deeth'. As for the others: the seven-year-old schoolboy in the Prioress's Tale has his throat cut by Jews, the three-year-old son of Hugelyn in the Monk's Tale is starved to death along with his father and brothers, the fourteen-year-old Virginia in the Physician's Tale is decapitated by her father in order to save her from a fate worse than death. I have already discussed the story of Hugelyn; this chapter is concerned with the stories of the other two innocent victims, but more especially with the Prioress's Tale.

The obvious companion piece to the Prioress's Tale is that told by her own companion, the Second Nun. Apart from the Man of Law's Tale concerning Custance (which hovers between the genres of saint's legend and romance), these are the only tales of 'hoolynesse' in the compilation. They are both examples of 'affective piety' — attempts to edify the hearer by appealing to the emotions rather than to the intellect.[1] The Second Nun's Tale is indeed a saint's legend; the Prioress's Tale belongs to another well-established genre, the 'Miracle of the Virgin'. The Legend of St Cecilia was written before the compilation of the *Tales* and later incorporated as the Second Nun's Tale (see Chapter 2). It is not, in my opinion, one of Chaucer's more successful poems. Nor do I regard the Physician's Tale as particularly successful. But this tale, set in the legendary period of Roman history, will serve as a foil to set off some of the more positive qualities of the Prioress's Tale.

The Prioress prefaces her narrative with an Invocation to Mary, composed in an elevated style that draws upon Dante for much of its sentiment and diction. Nevertheless, its dominant note is one of humility. It begins by citing the Psalm verse, 'Out of the mouths of babes and sucklings hast Thou perfected praise, O Lord', and concludes with the speaker's likening herself to an infant — in the etymological sense of 'a child . . . That kan unnethes any word expresse'. So she beseeches Mary: 'Gydeth my song that I shal of yow seye' (VII, 487). The designation 'song' is appropriate enough for this brief and pathetic narrative, as there is an almost lyrical quality about its use of the 'rhyme royal' stanza. Moreover, this 'song' is a

song about a song: the Marian antiphon 'Alma Redemptoris Mater',
which the schoolboy determines to master because it is 'maked in
reverence / Of Cristes mooder' (VII, 537-8 — my italics) and sings it
'wel and boldely' on his way to and from school.[2] Unfortunately, his
route traverses the Jewish quarter, and Satan (we are told) incited the
Jews to feel resentment against the singing, within their territory, of
something whose 'sentence / . . . is agayn youre lawes reverence'
(563-4 — my italics). So they hire a cut-throat to murder the child
and dispose of his corpse in a privy 'Where as thise Jewes purgen hire
entraille'. It is in this unsavoury environment that the miracle occurs.
The child's whereabouts is revealed by his continuing to sing the
Marian antiphon, even though 'with throte ykorven [he] lay
upright':

> He Alma redemptoris gan to synge
> So loude that al the place gan to rynge.
>
>                                        (VII, 612-13)

Nor is this repulsive place his final auditorium. For the Prioress (cf.
'quod she' at VII, 581) has already affirmed that this 'martir,
sowded to virginitee' has now joined a choir where he may sing in
perpetuity:

> Now maystow syngen, folwynge evere in oon
> The white Lamb celestial — quod she —
> Of which the grete evaungelist, Seint John,
> In Pathmos wroot, which seith that they that goon
> Biforn this Lamb, and synge a song al newe . . .
>
>                                        (VII, 580-4)

This example of 'affective piety' certainly moves the pilgrim
audience (VII, 691). But the first reaction of a twentieth-century
reader may well be to regard it as sentimental, mawkish, superstitious, credulous and — in view of its attitude towards the Jews —
bigoted.[3] His second reaction may be to wonder whether Chaucer is
not being ironical; whether he is not satirizing effusions of 'affective
piety' of the kind that might well appeal to the 'conscience and
tendre herte' of the Prioress of the General Prologue — the murdered
'clergeon' now being substituted for the hurt animals. Still another
reaction may be experienced when one remembers that the author of
'Lucy Gray', and principal contributor to Lyrical Ballads, was
moved to modernize Chaucer's 'song'. Wordsworth's prefatory
remark about the 'fierce bigotry of the Prioress' is often remembered.
But we should also recall the way in which his sentence continues:

The fierce bigotry of the Prioress forms a fine background for her tender-hearted sympathies with the Mother and Child; and the mode in which the story is told amply atones for the extravagance of the miracle.

The mode in which the story is told is indeed remarkable. Whatever may be urged against it, the Prioress's Tale remains one of the most memorable of the Canterbury series.

That is more than can be said for Chaucer's other story of child murder, the Physician's Tale. In fact, this tale, derived ultimately from Livy's history of Rome, has a much more interesting plot than that of the miracle of the Virgin. Virginius had brought up his only child in accordance with the austere and decent standards of conduct so much admired in the early republicans by later generations of moralists. Her beauty was noticed by the corrupt and lecherous justice, Appius, who contrives, by abusing his judicial power and by an outrageous perversion of the law, to obtain the girl as his ward. Her father, in order to save his beloved daughter from becoming the slave to Appius's lust, kills her. The dilemma in which Virginius finds himself is even more acute than that of Isabella in *Measure for Measure*: it is 'tragic' by any definition of the term. Yet the Physician's Tale never realizes its tragic potentiality. How is it that it fails to come to life, whereas the Prioress's Tale is so vivid?

Before pursuing further this critical question, it is necessary to consider a difference between medieval and modern attitudes towards children that affects our appreciation of both tales. Child murder is not the only feature that the narratives have in common. The phrase 'gemme of chastitee' is applied to both child victims. Virginius addresses his daughter with this phrase as he is about to kill her (VI, 223). The 'clergeon' is so described at VII, 609, where he is also called 'this emeraude/And eek of martirdom the ruby bright'. Such a way of regarding children may strike us as rather precious. It also occurs in *Pearl*, where the dominant image, when applied to the child who died before she was two years old, includes chastity among its multiple significations. It is largely on account of his chastity that the image of the pearl is associated with the hero of another poem in the same MS: *Sir Gawain and the Green Knight*. During the dénouement Bertilak says that, just as a pearl is of greater value than the white pea, so is Gawain worth more than other knights:

'As perle bi the quite pese is of prys more,
So is Gawayn, in god fayth, bi other gay knyghtes.'

(2364-5)

The commendation is well deserved, since the hero has thrice resisted

pressing temptations to commit adultery. But it may seem to us that a
baby and a boy of seven hardly deserve to be praised for what they
cannot possibly have earned. The medieval attitude was different: its
rationale is set out in the course of the debate in *Pearl*. The dreamer
objects to the maiden's being made a queen in heaven, when she died
so young that she was incapable of either pleasing God or praying to
Him, being ignorant even of the Paternoster and Creed, the very
rudiments of religious instruction. He asks:

> 'What more honour moghte he acheve
> That hade endured in worlde stronge,
> And lyved in penaunce hys lyves longe,
> Wyth bodyly bale hym blysse to byye?'

(475-8)

The maiden argues that, on the contrary, the longer one lives on
Earth, the more opportunity one has for committing sin. Admittedly,
it is possible for the sinner to repent and to be restored to a state of
Grace through God's mercy. But the innocent child, who has never
fallen out of the state of Grace bestowed in baptism, is guaranteed
salvation (665-8, 684). Chastity, like innocence, was a quality that
God prized for its own sake, whether one had striven for it or not.

The 'litel clergeon', having only just attained his first climacteric,
was still officially 'within degree of innocence'.[4] So, on the several
occasions when the Prioress calls him an 'innocent', the term has
something of a technical sense. He is also associated with the Holy
Innocents, the children of two years and under, whom Herod
ordered to be slain (Matt. 2: 16-18).[5] At VII, 574, the Jews are
apostrophized as 'cursed folk of Herodes al newe', and at 627 the
child's mother is called 'This newe Rachel' — where she is compared,
by implication, with the mothers of the Innocents (cf. Matt. 2:18).
We have remarked how, after death, he joins the choir of (male)
Virgins, who follow the Lamb (Rev. 14: 3-4). It was believed that
the Holy Innocents too formed part of that procession. Whereas the
Gospel for the Mass for Holy Innocents' Day (28 December) consists of the passage from Matthew that describes their massacre, the
Epistle consists of the account of the procession from Revelation.
The Holy Innocents were regarded as having been baptized in their
own blood, and were celebrated as the first Christian martyrs, even
though they did not seek martyrdom. On the same principle, the 'litel
clergeon' is not only a 'gemme of chastitee' but also 'of martirdom
the ruby bright'. The child in *Pearl*, though no martyr, is also
associated with the children 'a bimatu et infra' ['of two years and
under'] whom Herod ordered to be slain. The association is made by

implication when the dreamer says to the maiden 'Thou lyfed not two yer in oure thede [country]' (483); it is also implied by including her in the procession of the hundred and forty-four thousand Virgins who follow the Lamb (though here the virgins are female, unlike those in Revelation).

Virginia, that other 'gemme of chastitee', is in a somewhat different position, not only because she is a pagan, but also because she has already attained her second climacteric. She is old enough to have taken deliberate measures to maintain her chastity:

> And *of hir owene vertu, unconstreyned,*
> She hath ful ofte tyme syk hire feyned,
> For that she wolde fleen the compaignye
> Where likly was to treten of folye,
> As is at feestes, revels, and at daunces,
> That been occasions of daliaunces.
>
> (VI, 61-6 — my italics)

She is prepared to tell a 'white lie' in order to be virtuous. Christians are, of course, required not only to resist temptation, but to avoid 'the occasion of sin'. The behaviour of this pagan girl would have won the approval of any medieval (or Victorian) father.[6] She has none of the forwardness that modern teenagers are supposed to delight in. Though she was as 'wis as Pallas', she never spoke out of turn. Nor did she employ 'countrefeted termes ... to seme wys' (51-2) — in other words, she used no 'wise-cracks' or vogue expressions in order to appear a sophisticated little madam. In commenting (rather ponderously) on the vices she shuns, the narrator never forgets that she is still a child:

> Swich thynges maken children for to be
> To soone rype and boold, as men may se,
> Which is ful perilous, and hath been yoore.
> For al to soone may she lerne loore
> Of bouldnesse, whan she woxen is a wyf.
>
> (VI, 67-71)

(i.e. '... when she has grown up to be a woman'). These remarks lead on naturally to the two apostrophes, to governesses and parents respectively. 'Maistresses' of lords' daughters are reminded of their solemn responsibility for their charges. Indeed, their accountability is seen as similar to that of baptismal sponsors:[7]

> Looke wel that ye unto no vice assente,
> Lest ye be dampned for youre wikke entente.
>
> (VI, 87-8)

The apostrophe concludes:

> Of alle tresons sovereyn pestilence
> Is whan a wight bitrayseth innocence.

(VI, 91-2)

The story that follows, however, is not about Innocence betrayed by
a tutor, but — even worse — by a judge. We are told that Virginia
'So kepte hirself hir neded no maistresse' (106). Nevertheless, the
tone of the passage shows that she is thought of as still being virtually
'within degree of innocence' — no less than the child in *Pearl* or the
'litel clergeon'.

It was not unprecedented for a girl of such an age to be regarded in
this way in fourteenth-century England. In Chapter 2, I referred to
letters of Edward III concerning the death of his fifteen-year-old
daughter, Joan. In them, the King gives thanks that God has snatched
his daughter away from the miseries of this deceitful world, when
'puram et immaculatam, in annis Innocentiae suae' (pure and
spotless, *in the years of her innocence*). He has deigned to call her to
Heaven, where, joined to the Heavenly Spouse, 'in Choro Virginum
perpetuo regnatura' (she will reign for ever in the choir of Virgins).[8]
These are the very sentiments expressed in *Pearl* and the Prioress's
Tale. Unfortunately, Virginia, as a pagan, can fall back only upon the
rather negative *solacium*: 'Blissed be God, that I shal dye a mayde!'
(248).

To return to 'the mode in which the story is told'; that of the
Physician's Tale is deliberately sententious. Of the tales that employ
formal rhetoric with serious intent, the Physician's has the highest
proportion of 'amplification' to narrative. Virginia is introduced by
means of a formal *descriptio*; and we have already remarked how it
is rigidly divided into *effictio* and *notatio*.[9] Moreover, we observed
that this *effictio* expands the customary allusion to Nature into a
prosopopoeia, in which the goddess steps on to the stage and
pronounces her own panegyric of the girl's physical beauty. The
proper function of 'amplification' is to make a narrative more
significant, or to 'slant' it in a particular direction, rather than merely
to fill out its bulk. Such is indeed the purpose of Nature's oration
here. She first makes the standard boast that her creations are
superior to anything that even the finest human artists can produce.
But the idea is expressed in a particularly telling way:

> 'Thus kan I forme and peynte a creature,
> Whan that me list; who kan me countrefete?
> Pigmalion noght, though he ay forge and bete,
> Or grave, or peynte; for I dar wel seyn,

Apelles, Zanzis, sholde werche in veyn
Outher to grave, or peynte, or forge, or bete,
If they presumed me to countrefete.'

(VI, 12-18)

The repetition of the slow procession of mostly monosyllabic verbs
conveys a vivid impression of the artists laboriously plodding in an
attempt to catch up with the demiurge whose creations they vainly
try to imitate.

In the second part of her speech Nature declares herself to be the
'vicaire general' to God, the 'formere principal',[10] and she says of
Virginia: 'I made hire to the worshipe of my lord' (26). The effect of
this passage is to cause the lustful designs of Appius to appear, not
only humanly atrocious, but as an act of sacrilege against God's
prized creation. It is therefore appropriate that it should be 'the
feend' (130) who suggests to the wicked judge the legal trick by
which he may gain the wardship of the girl.

The portrait of Virginia's beauty (30-8) is a not very imaginative
exercise in periphrasis, and the succeeding *notatio* is (as we have
seen)[11] largely a study in writing variations on a basic epithet. At VI,
72, the sententious conclusion of the *descriptio* leads into the two
admonitory apostrophes, each supported by its own *exemplum*.
'Maistresses' are informed that they have been engaged for one of
two reasons: either because they are virtuous, or for the opposite
reason — that they are all too familiar with 'the olde daunce' (79).
Chaucer applies this phrase also to the Wife of Bath and her
knowledge of amorous dalliance (I, 476). The momentary bringing
together of these two disparate worlds is the first hint of a threat to
Virginia's sheltered upbringing. Chaucer is probably here thinking of
the duenna in the *Roman de la Rose* (called 'Vekke' in the ME
translation) — which is, in fact, his most immediate source for the
story of Appius and Virginia. The 'Vekke' is appointed as Bialacoil's
gaoler after the lover's first, unsuccessful attempt to obtain the rose-
bud. She is appointed precisely because she knows the tricks of the
trade. As Chaucer's *exemplum* observes, former poachers often
make the best game-keepers:

A theef of venysoun, that hath forlaft
His likerousnesse, and al his olde craft,
Kan kepe a forest best of any man.

(VI, 83-5)

(There is hardly any need to draw attention to the sexual overtones
of both vocabulary and imagery in these lines.) In Jean de Meun's

poem the 'Vekke' notoriously betrays her trust;[12] so it is as well that Virginia 'so kepte hirself' that she needed no such keeper. The threat to innocence is increased in the image that supports the apostrophe to the parents of less privileged children. The apostrophe itself merely gives the conventional — and irrelevant — medieval admonition of 'spare the rod, and spoil the child'. But the supporting *exemplum* envisages the wolf worrying the charges of a 'shepherde softe and necligent'.

The narrator self-consciously concludes this apostrophe with the comment:

> Suffiseth oon ensample now as heere,
> For I moot turne agayn to my matere.
>
> (VI, 103-4)

It does indeed look as if the narrative is about to be resumed, but it is a false dawn: what is resumed is the *notatio*, which even includes a formal personification of Envy. The narrator calls this personification a 'descripcioun', and attributes it to an anonymous 'doctour' (who has been identified as St Augustine).[13]

When the story eventually gets under way at VI, 118, its narration is not particularly well managed. The manner in which Appius brushes aside Virginius's plea is too blatant to be credible; and the speed with which 'a thousand peple in thraste' to denounce the notoriously (cf. VI, 262-6) corrupt judge, after Virginia has been decapitated, merely makes the reader wonder why they had not acted earlier. The scene between father and daughter certainly has some moments of pathos. But why does Virginius address her as 'endere of my lyf' (218)? When the dying Arcite addresses this conventional, amatory phrase to Emelye (I, 2776) it has a poignantly literal meaning; but it is inept to put it into Virginius's mouth when it is he who is about to end his daughter's life. In his *Ars Versificatoria*, Matthew of Vendôme had recommended five possible ways of ending a poem. One was 'per recapitulationem sententiae' — a summary of the work's moral 'sentence'.[14] The tale concludes with ten lines of sententious epilogue, whose import is neatly encapsulated in the chiasmic final line: 'Forsaketh synne, er synne yow forsake.' But this moral is both misplaced and tactless; for it seems to imply that the reader will have identified himself with the villain of the story! Perhaps the explanation for its presence is to be found in the tale's immediate source. In the *Roman de la Rose*, Jean de Meun introduces the story as an *exemplum* into a discussion about corrupt judges.[15] Chaucer has shifted the interest of the story from Appius to Virginia, but has nevertheless concluded with a *sentence* that would have been more appropriate in his source. A slightly more apt moral is afterwards extracted by the Host, who is deeply roused by the tale (VI, 287-300). The moral focus of the tale itself remains blurred; and, despite certain local felicities, the whole suffers too obviously from having been subjected to the 'process' of applied 'amplification'.[16]

It would be untrue to say that there is no rhetoric in the Prioress's Tale; but rhetorical devices do not obtrude themselves as they do in the Physician's. The 'clergeon' may be destined for sainthood; but he is not introduced by way of an idealized description; instead, he is shown in his first term at school. The first two stanzas tell us, with the factual precision and economy of a well-organized fabliau, all that we need to know about the location of the school. Almost immediately a slight discrepancy between the 'tale' and its 'teller' is noticeable. The Prioress's tone is sentimental as well as devout. She refers to the boy as 'litel child', 'litel sone' and 'litel clergeon' — where the substantive is itself already a diminutive form. This even colours his environment: he attends 'a litel scole', where he learns from 'his litel book'. The Prioress is immediately reminded of 'Seint Nicholas' (514), to whose legend she had already alluded in her Prologue, when she described how infants 'on the brest soukynge' had praised the Virgin (VII, 458-9). At 538, she continues to groom the boy for sainthood by calling him 'this innocent', thereby invoking the various, highly charged connotations of that term which we have already considered.

The discrepancy resides in the fact that the small boy himself is no sentimentalist; nor is there any evidence of his displaying abnormal piety. In fact, the Christian school is 'litel' in quite an objective sense, since more than one class has evidently to be accommodated in a single room. It is this arrangement that enables the boy to overhear the children in the higher class sing *Alma Redemptoris Mater*. He has its first verse by rote before he knows that it is addressed to Mary. Evidently he is first attracted by the tune and by the same impulse which caused my seven-year-old daughter to find her elder sister's prescribed piano pieces more interesting than her own. He is no Peter Pan, and has no wish to remain for ever in the infants' class with his 'litel book'; he wants to be doing what the bigger boys are doing. He beseeches an older boy to translate the song for him 'Ful often tyme upon his knowes bare' (529). This may sound exaggerated to us. But 'on his bare knees' was a stock phrase; and the action itself would not be thought unusual in an age when formal gestures were common, and when, for example, servants might be expected to kneel to offer a cup to their master.[17] Schoolboys are notorious sticklers for 'class'-distinctions. The reason for the older boy's initial reluctance to grant this request is soon apparent. He declares: 'This song, *I have herd seye*, / Was maked of our blisful Lady free' (my italics). And he concludes with the archetypal schoolboy confession: 'I lerne song, I kan but small grammere' (i.e. 'Latin') — incomparably less than the 'small Latin' with which Ben Jonson credited Shakespeare.

As soon as he hears what the song is about, the younger boy's eagerness to learn it all is redoubled. But even this is not necessarily a symptom of unusual piety. We have already been informed that it was his own widowed mother who taught him to reverence the image of the Virgin when he passed a wayside shrine (505). His desire to master the antiphon 'er Cristemasse be went' may be as much motivated by a desire to please his own mother as Christ's. In the mind of a seven-year-old the distinction would, in any case, be somewhat blurred: the latter would be seen by him as just a sublimation of the former. His singing of the anthem aloud in the street is an entirely unselfconscious act: he was unaware that it would offend the Jews. Nor was he aware that it would one day disconcert the Philistines. No doubt most passers-by in a modern English street would be embarrassed if they encountered a child singing 'wel and boldely' a hymn he had just learnt at school; in Italy, on the other hand, it would seem perfectly natural. There is no evidence that the 'clergeon' sought martyrdom deliberately, as did that other seven-year-old who sings a snatch of church music as he is about to be killed: the Saint Kenelm of the *South English Legendary*.[18] The boy king is warned of his death in a dream, which his nurse correctly interprets for him. Nevertheless, he allows his treacherous 'maister', Askebert, to conduct him alone to the Forest of Clent. When Askebert makes his first attempt to slay him, the boy calmly informs him that he is wasting his time, since his martyrdom is ordained to take place in another spot. When they reach the destined place, he asks his 'maister', Askebert, 'wel mildeliche', why he does not 'get on with it at once',[19] and sings from the *Te Deum* the appropriate verse: 'The faire compaygnie of martyrs, Louerd, herieth [Thee].' Chaucer was familiar with the legend. In the Nun's Priest's Tale, Chauntecleer cites it as an *exemplum* to support his argument about the prophetic nature of dreams. He remarks of Kenelm:

> . . . but he nas but seven yeer oold,
> And therfore litel tale hath he toold
> Of any dreem, so hooly was his herte.

> (VII, 3117-19)

There is no suggestion that the 'litel clergeon' wishes likewise to join prematurely 'the glorious army of martyrs'. Nevertheless, this lack of conscious intent would not (as we have seen) have prevented him, any more than the Holy Innocents, from entering that company.

If the Prioress seems a little too 'enthusiastic' in her representation of the 'innocent', what shall we think of her attitude towards the Jews?[20] Stories about the ritual murder of Christian boys by Jews were common enough at the time.[21] Is Chaucer implicitly criticizing the intelligence of this nun for accepting such a tale credulously and uncritically? At least the tale's 'fierce bigotry' could not have done any immediate harm, as Edward I had imposed his 'final solution' to 'the Jewish problem' as long ago as 1290, when all Jews were expelled from England (and were not officially permitted to return until the time of Cromwell). The opening stanza places the action in remote 'Asye', but the final stanza brings it home by invoking the boy, Hugh of Lincoln, 'slayn also / With cursed Jewes . . . but a litel while ago'. In fact, the event was supposed to have taken place in 1255. It is unlikely, however, that the narrator's prime intention here was to be inflammatory. It was customary for a pious work to conclude with a prayer, and especially an invocation to an appropriate saint. Hugh of Lincoln was the obvious choice from among the 'innocents'.

Nevertheless, it is impossible to overlook the epithet 'cursed', which is here applied to the Jews not for the first time in the tale. Nor can one disregard the description of Satan prefatory to his incitement of the Jews to conspire against the singer of (what was for them) blasphemy:

> Our firste foo, the serpent Sathanas,
> That hath in Jues herte his waspes nest,
> Up swal, and seide, 'O Hebrayk peple, allas! . . .'
>
> (VII, 558-60)

Is the mixed metaphor meant to betray the confusion of an over-emotional narrator? It might be thought that the narrator dwells with too obvious satisfaction upon the punishment of the perpetrators of the murder (628-34). But at least the punishment is just. The stanza concludes by declaring that the Provost 'heng hem by the lawe'; and the narrator comments 'Yvele shal have that yvele wol deserve'. The Jews are punished according to the Mosaic law which they would themselves recognize. It also happened to be, in effect, the civil law of the Middle Ages. Christians would have been treated in the same way. The treatment of the perpetrators of this hideous child-murder is similar to that of those accused of murdering the traveller, in the anecdote inserted into the Nun's Priest's Tale (cf. VII, 3058-62).

Finally, we return to 'this newe Rachel' at the end of the preceding stanza. The liturgical reason for bestowing this title upon the child's mother has already been considered. Nevertheless, it may seem tactless, in the context, to associate her with the wife of Jacob (also called 'Israel') and mother of the Jewish race. Against this, however, should be remembered the fact that, in Chaucer's day, Rachel was regarded as a 'type' of that later Jewess, the Virgin Mary.[22] It is also easy to forget that the Holy Innocents were Jews. It is important to notice that the hostility towards the Jews in this tale is religious rather than racial. In the Asian city, where the action is set, the villains might just as well have been Muslims. The attitude of the Jews towards the 'clergeon' and his song is not unlike that of the Sultana towards Custance and her 'font-ful water' in the Man of Law's Tale (II, 357). It is impossible that our reading of this tale should be unaffected by our memory of the Nazis' murder of six million children, women and men, because they were born of Jewish stock. The memory of that unspeakable atrocity should prevent us from feeling self-righteous and smug when reading a story of 'medieval barbarity'. But the nearest modern analogy to the situation in the tale strikes much nearer home than the Third Reich. If a Roman Catholic boy were to walk through a Protestant area of Belfast singing a Marian antiphon, it is not impossible that members of some extreme Protestant organization might behave as the Jews do in the tale; and the same might equally well happen — *mutatis mutandis* — to a Protestant child. The 'conscience and tendre herte' of a devout nun, on hearing of such an atrocity, might well react in the way that the sensibility of the Prioress does. Certainly the narrator of this tale is partisan; but she belongs to the same party as Chaucer, who also had a special devotion to the Virgin. The 'mode in which the story is told' enables us to enter into the mind of a teller who is sincerely affected by a work of 'affective piety'. At the same time (as so often happens when reading Chaucer), we are left wondering whether the apparent inconsistencies in the tale may not have been 'planted' in order to encourage us to take a detached, critical view of the narrative and the genre to which it belongs.

# CHAPTER 8

# 'Taketh the Moralite, Goode Men'

If the 'litel clergeon' of the Prioress's Tale had lived to pursue the curriculum of a grammar school, he would sooner or later have encountered the Fables of Aesop, or one of his redactors. As I have already remarked,[1] every schoolboy would have expected a fable to yield a moral. Chaucer plays upon such an expectation, in an oblique and sophisticated way, in the two tales that are the subject of this final chapter: those of the Manciple and of the Nun's Priest. The latter has been regarded, almost universally, as the masterpiece among Chaucer's comic tales, and a fresh exploration of its elusive and allusive texture will provide a fitting end to this study of the major tales.

The Manciple's Tale concludes with over forty lines of moralizing, attributed to the narrator's mother, about the advisability of controlling one's tongue and of refraining from tale-bearing, even if the tidings are true (IX, 317-62). The harangue ends, as it began, with the advice: 'Kepe wel thy tonge, and thenk upon the crowe' — alluding to the fable (ultimately from Ovid's *Metamorphoses*) on which the Manciple bases his tale. The Nun's Priest likewise concludes his beast-fable with a passage of moralizing which, though far less extensive, is no less emphatic:

> But ye that holden this tale a folye,
> As of a fox, or of a cok and hen,
> Taketh the moralite, goode men.
> For seint Paul seith that al that writen is,
> To oure doctrine it is ywrite, ywis . . .
>
> (VII, 3438-42)

St Paul's statement, at Romans 15: 4, was often cited to justify the composition of secular fiction and especially the narration of fables. The saint's words were also often associated with the advice to the reader which immediately follows: 'Taketh the fruyt, and lat the chaf be stille.' This exhortation has encouraged some modern commentators to look for allegorical significance in the narrative. The favourite interpretation seems to be that which regards the tale as an analogue to the story of the Fall of Man[2] — a reading which leans very heavily upon the passing mention of Adam at VII, 3258, who is introduced as an *exemplum* to support the facetious aside about the folly of trusting 'Wommennes conseils'. On the other hand, a commentator, whose sensibility is more in tune with the spirit of this little comic masterpiece, has observed that 'the fruit of the Nun's

Priest's Tale is its chaff';[3] and several recent commentators have argued that the moralizing in the Manciple's Tale is likewise part of the author's oblique strategy.[4]

In both tales the moralizing is part of the general rhetorical inflation of the inherited 'fable'. Indeed, the proportion of 'amplification' in these tales rivals that to be found in the Physician's Tale. But, whereas in the story of Virginia it is employed in solemn earnest, in these tales it is exploited with considerable sophistication. The Nun's Priest's Tale has long been recognized as one of Chaucer's most brilliant performances.[5] But it is not merely a piece of literary virtuosity. The critic who was moved by the nature of its learned allusions to exclaim that it was 'as full of reading as an egg is full of meat, whipped into the lightest of omelettes' errs in the direction of hedonism almost as far as the earnest allegorists do in the direction of naïve edification.[6] In spite of its satire on sententiousness, it contains some serious and penetrating analysis of the human condition. It maintains a nice balance between 'earnest' and 'game'. No such claims can be made for the Manciple's Tale. Nevertheless, as another critic remarks: 'The interest of the . . . [tale] lies not in the story itself (which is poor), but in the way the Manciple reveals himself.'[7] In order to recognize this fact, the tale must be considered in relation to its Prologue. Furthermore, in order to appreciate the full effect of this Prologue, that occurs in what we know as Fragment IX, we must first glance again at another such introduction that comes near the beginning of the compilation.

After the Knight's Tale is concluded, the drunken Miller prevents the Monk from complying with the Host's invitation to tell the next tale. The tale which Robyn insists on telling proves to be so offensive to the Reeve that he promptly retaliates with his story concerning a dishonest miller. At the beginning of Fragment IX there is something like an inversion of that situation. The Host seeks to divert the company by unkindly demanding a tale from the thoroughly inebriated Cook; but the Manciple good-naturedly offers to relieve him of his obligation. At least, the Manciple begins by making his offer in a generous and courteous spirit (IX, 25-9), but soon yields to an instinctive urge to take his toll from the man he has put under an obligation. Declaring that it is not in his nature to flatter ('Of me, certeyn, thou shalt nat been yglosed'), he proceeds to heap insults upon the incapable Cook:

> 'See how he ganeth, lo! this dronken wight,
> As though he wolde swolwe us anonright.
> Hoold cloos thy mouth, man, by thy fader kyn!
> The devel of helle sette his foot therin!
> Thy cursed breeth infecte wole us alle.'
>
> (IX, 35-9)

One is reminded of the description of the Miller's mouth in the General Prologue:

> His mouth as greet was as a greet forneys.
> He was a janglere and a goliardeys,
> And that was moost of synne and harlotries.
>
> (I, 559-61)

'Synne and harlotries' is precisely what emerged from the Cook's mouth when, at the end of Fragment I, he broached his tale of Perkyn Revelour, which breaks off at the mention of a wife who kept a shop as a 'front' behind which she 'swyved for hir sustenance'.[8] In response to the Manciple's taunts, the Cook can do no more than glower at him. But the Host warns the Manciple that, although drink renders the Cook incapable of retaliating at present, he may, on another occasion, take the opportunity of criticizing his dishonest methods of accountancy. The Manciple is genuinely alarmed by this possibility for, as the General Prologue has revealed, the Host's comments have come near the mark. So, in order to prevent the Cook's 'doing a Reẽve's Tale upon him', he makes an overture by offering him a drink of wine from the gourd which he carries — acting, presumably, on the principle of 'the hair of the dog that bit you'. The Cook gladly accepts, and the Host speaks in praise of Bacchus as the bringer of peace — a sentiment very appropriate for an inn-keeper.

The Prologue reveals the Manciple as a coarse-grained fellow, who takes delight in criticizing others, but whose situation in life has obliged him to cultivate a courteous manner, to be used when necessary, and to develop techniques for ingratiating himself in order to avert exposure of the unprofessional conduct that enabled him to cheat the learned and nimble-witted lawyers who were his employers. One scholar has pointed out that employees in positions similar to that of the Manciple were regularly advised to bridle the tongue, to cultivate discretion and to avoid tale-bearing. This, the critic remarks, helps to account for the Manciple's 'manner of speaking', which causes him (both in his Prologue and in the Tale) to retract the carping criticisms that come so readily to his tongue. It also accounts, of course, for his choosing to tell the tale of how the crow was punished by its master, Phebus, for faithfully reporting to him (with evident relish) the fact that he had witnessed Phebus's wife committing adultery.[9]

Even before he has informed us that Phebus's wife took as a lover a man greatly inferior to her 'gentil' and usually considerate husband, the Manciple has cynically declared such a propensity to be natural

to women (IX, 160 ff.). This assertion is supported by three *exempla*.
The first is that of the bird, kept in a golden cage, and fostered
'tendrely' on the most exquisite fare, but who naturally desires to
escape to a 'forest . . . rude and coold' and to feed on worms 'and
swich wrecchednesse'. The second concerns the pet cat who will
gladly spurn his silken couch and milk-saucer in order to catch a
mouse. The third declares that a she-wolf will always prefer for a
mate 'the lewedeste wolf that she may fynde'. One cannot but feel
that the Manciple is, at the same time, unconsciously revealing, by
way of this imagery, his own nature. His social status obliges him to
inhabit a golden cage of discretion, restraint and courtesy; but his
predilection is for the coarse and gross. Indeed, having indulged in
this generalization about women's appetites, he immediately retracts
it by declaring:

> Alle thise ensamples speke I by thise men
> That been untrewe, and nothyng by wommen.
> For men han evere a likerous appetit
> On lower thyng to parfourne hir delit . . .
>
> (IX, 187-90)

Such a disingenuous disclaimer is a familiar Chaucerian 'ploy'. When
the narrator of the Nun's Priest's Tale makes his disparaging remark
about 'Wommennes conseil', he is quick to add:

> But for I noot to whom it myght displese,
> If I conseil of wommen wolde blame,
> Passe over, for I seyde it in my game.
> Rede auctours . . .
>
> (VII, 3260-3)

These lines may be seen as the one place, in this most Chaucerian of
tales, where the Nun's Priest emerges as a character in his own
right.[10] As one of three priests attendant upon the Prioress, he
occupies a not particularly distinguished position in her entourage.
He retracts his anti-feminist sentiment lest he appear insubordinate.
It is a gesture that the Manciple would understand.

An even closer parallel to the Manciple's aside occurs in a passage
of *Troilus and Criseyde* which is commented on in Chapter 2.[11] At
V, 1772-85 the narrator turns to the ladies in his audience and
begs them 'be nat wroth with me' because 'Criseyde was untrewe'.
Her guilt, he says, may be found in books by other authors; he would
rather have written about 'Penelopeës trouthe and good Alceste'.
Then, performing an even more astonishing volte face than the
Manciple, he claims that his chief concern is 'for wommen that

bitraised be' and that his moral conclusion is 'Beth war of men'. The final book of *Troilus* has an obvious affinity with the Manciple's story of how a wife cuckolded her husband with

> A man of litel reputacioun,
> Nat worth to Phebus in comparisoun.
>
> (IX, 199-200)

Even in the act of 'falsyng' Troilus with Diomede, Criseyde is aware of the incomparable superiority of her discarded lover:

> 'For I have falsed oon the gentileste
> That evere was, and oon the worthieste!'
>
> (*TC*, V, 1056-7)

The sympathetic narrator of this poem is so discreet that he can hardly bring himself to acknowledge that Criseyde loved Diomede: 'Men seyn — I not — that she yaf hym hire herte' (*TC*, V, 1050). If the Manciple had narrated these events in the idiom that comes most naturally to him, he would no doubt have said: 'Anon they wroghten al hire lust volage' — as he does of Phebus's wife and her 'lemman' at IX, 239. His instinctive idiom resembles that of Shakespeare's Thersites. His assumed courtesy obliges him to apologize for uttering the word 'lemman' (IX, 205 ff.). But he does not retract it. The man of humble birth now expresses openly his opinion of the philanderings of the upper classes. If a man of 'gentil' birth keeps a mistress, she is called 'his lady, as in love', whereas a poor man's mistress is called 'his wenche or his lemman'. But it makes no difference in practice; 'Men leyn that oon as lowe as lith that oother.' The Manciple becomes so carried away by the theme of the injustice of class distinctions that he cites, as a supporting *exemplum*, an anecdote concerning Alexander (IX, 223-34) which has nothing whatever to do with sexual relationships.

He brings himself back to his narrative from this digression by declaring that he is not 'textueel' ['bookish']: 'I wol noght telle of textes never a deel.' He repeats this disclaimer at the conclusion of his narrative, when he explicitly offers the fable of the crow as an 'ensample' of the danger of an unbridled tongue. He finds himself quoting the appropriate proverb by 'Daun Salomon' and referring to the testimony of 'wise clerkes' (314). But this 'lewed man' whose 'wit' surpasses 'The wisdom of an heep of lerned men' (i.e. the lawyers who employed him — cf. I, 574-5) is again anxious to dissociate himself from his 'betters'; and so he attributes his education to the proverbs his mother taught him. It was not unusual to cite a parent as a source of proverbial wisdom.[12] Although the mother herself cites Solomon, the Psalter, and 'Senekke' (345), she is, as a source of proverbial wisdom, only a 'lewed' counterpart to Melibee's learned wife, Prudence. This layman, who has made a comfortable living for himself by outwitting the graduates whom he serves, concludes by rejoicing in the fact that the university that prepared him for life was, quite literally, his *alma mater*.

The relationship between the university and the universe is a main preoccupation of the Nun's Priest's Tale. This is the most 'textueel' of the *Tales*; and it can be fully appreciated only by a reader who is himself prepared to be 'textueel'. At the same time, it is precisely the erudite expositor who is likely to be the most vulnerable of its readers.[13]

Within every critic there is a commentator and an interpreter. The Nun's Priest's Tale flatters both: the commentator has found in its detailed allusions and encyclopedic range of reference a delightful challenge to his erudition; the interpreter, seizing upon the allegorical possibilities of a beast-fable, exercises his ingenuity in demonstrating that the tale is something other than what it purports to be.[14] But this most insidious of comic tales has ambushes prepared for both parties. Although Chaucer does not anticipate Swift's practice of inserting 'spoof' references,[15] the zealous commentator is easily tempted by 'fascination' and 'false fire' — *ignis fatuus* — to explore by-ways that lead nowhere. The interpreter, on the other hand, must be perpetually on his guard in a tale that — most obviously in the discussion of Chauntecleer's dream — makes interpretation itself one of the principal targets of its satire. Again, whereas the commentator is in danger of accumulating 'huge heaps of littleness', the chief risk for the interpreter is that he will sacrifice the poem's wealth of detail in order to purchase a unique principle of meaningful organization. Chauntecleer was caught when, in full voice, he closed both his eyes; the critic will be caught in full cry if he closes only one of his: commentator and interpreter must continue to operate in harmony. I shall attempt to illustrate how our appreciation of the tale may be enhanced if we maintain such a stereoscopic view of the text: 'so moote I brouke wel myne eyen tweye!' (VII, 3300). I offer only a little fresh seasoning to the banquet of erudition and I make no claim to have discovered a definitive interpretation.

The encyclopedic range of reference, the way in which so much of the syllabus of a fourteenth-century university is enclosed within the narrow and humble compass of the chicken run, suggests that, if the fable's hero represents mankind, then he is seen in particular as *homo sapiens*. I adopt the anachronism advisedly: there is more than a hint or two that the author of this tale was, in certain respects, a Darwinian by prolepsis. He writes as one who is tired of hearing the medieval commonplace that Man (*animal rationale*) possesses intelligence in common with the angels and that his reason is what distinguishes him from the beasts. The writer's instinctive reaction to such a platitude is to let a beast stand for his intellectual: to present Man with 'his Animal Faculties perpetually a-cock-Horse and Rational' (to borrow a memorable phrase from Swift's 'A Meditation upon a Broomstick'). It is true that Chaucer had once before used a bird to satirize an academic. But the soaring eagle in *The House of Fame* is able to scale the heavens, whereas Chauntecleer normally flies no higher than his perch. When he eventually flies up into a tree, the action seems no less miraculous than the sudden presence of mind that enables him to escape from the fox's jaws.

The reputation of cockerels in medieval mythology is ambivalent. On the one hand the cockerel was the alert time-keeper and rouser of men: Honorius of Autun regarded the weather-cock as a symbol of the preacher;[16] and Chauntecleer certainly exhibits the preacher's fluency. On the other hand, the strutting cock was a symbol of vanity and, as in all ages, was regarded as one of the stupidest of creatures. Nor are Chaucer's intellectuals invariably wise; and it is instructive to compare Chauntecleer with some of his other clerks. He is the very opposite of the sober and celibate Clerk of Oxenford, of whom it is said: 'Noght o word spak he moore than was neede' (I, 304); for this cockerel is a 'performer', intellectually as well as vocally. In his ability to argue a case by means of an inexhaustible repertory of *exempla* he resembles the Wife of Bath's fifth husband — although he differs from him in that he is nobody's fifth husband, but (on the contrary) is the possessor of seven 'wyves'. Like Nicholas in the Miller's Tale, he has a naturally winning way with women and exploits his academic training elaborately and obsessively in order to secure the enjoyment of one of them physically. In the tale generally there is a disconcerting tendency for the volatile intellect to gravitate towards sex. Nicholas, unlike the idealized Clerk (I, 296), is an accomplished amateur musician (I, 3213-18). But, as a musician, Chauntecleer has more in common with the professional singer in the Miller's Tale, the ostentatious and narcissistic parish clerk, Absolon; both have much of the vanity of a leading tenor. Moreover, both Absolon and Chauntecleer are cured of their folly and rally towards the end of their respective tales.

A convenient, though not a comprehensive, framework for our exploration of the function of the medieval world of learning in the Nun's Priest's Tale is afforded by the scheme of the Seven Liberal Arts — traditionally divided into the *trivium* (grammar, rhetoric, dialectic) and the *quadrivium* (astrology, arithmetic, geometry, and music).[17] I shall argue that Dialectic is the most important for an understanding of Chaucer's intentions; but several of the other Arts are of more than incidental interest. The two strictly mathematical subjects are too abstract to play any part in this mainly literary satire — though I shall not be surprised if someone, cleverer than I, one day discovers a comic 'numerological' key to the tale. So the only parts of the *quadrivium* that appear in this tale are (as in the Miller's Tale) Music and Astrology. At VII, 3293-4, the flattering fox refers to Boethius's theoretical treatise, *De Musica*, in conjunction with 'any that kan synge'. However, it is in the initial description of the hero that the most significant references to Music (in conjunction with Astrology) occur. Modern critics have appreciated the ironical effect of Chaucer's preceding this colourful and grandiloquent panegyric of a cock by the plain and sober account of his owner's frugal way of life. The fourteenth-century reader, trained to cultivate a sense of decorum, would have appreciated the description's humorous inversion of the doctrine of levels of style.[18] The animal hero is made to appear not only incomparably more splendid than the poor widow, but also superior to the most accomplished of educated men.

Because Chauntecleer's singing is of central importance in the fable, Chaucer considers it first, praising it for both its aesthetic and utilitarian attributes. The comparison of his voice to the sound of an organ is — like the comparison of his comb to a crenellated castle wall — felicitously incongruous. The comparison would be less incongruous if Chaucer were referring to the lightweight, high-pitched 'portative' organ of the period. But these instruments seem to have been used mostly for secular occasions or in outdoor processions, whereas Chaucer specifies a pair of organs 'On messe-dayes that in the chirche gon' (VII, 2852). So he is more likely to be thinking of the larger 'positive' organ or even the permanently installed 'great' organ.[19] The point of this simile — like the comparison of his time-keeping with that of 'a clokke or an abbey orlogge' — is to imply that he could produce effortlessly and instinctively results achieved only by the most ingenious devices of human technology. Organs and clocks were constructed by the same craftsmen[20] and were the outstanding mechanical contrivances of the period. *Clokke* was a fairly recent loan-word in English and the thing itself was still an object of wonder. Within only a year or two of the tale's composition there was constructed for Wells Cathedral the famous time-piece (referred to as 'la clokke' in a chapter roll of 1392-93)[21] which even today attracts a 'Greet . . . prees that swarmeth to and fro / To gauren on' the hourly joustings of its automata.[22] But, however diverting the playful automata and astrological dials of fourteenth-century clocks may have been, their basic time-keeping was notoriously imprecise and inaccurate.[23] So the statement that Chauntecleer's crowing was '*wel sikerer* . . . Than is a clokke or an abbey orlogge' is no piece of idle hyperbole.

This slight digression into the mechanical arts brings us to the next of the Liberal Arts in the panegyric: Astrology. How did fourteenth-century man fare when out of sight of his elaborately contrived chronometers? For an answer we need look no further than the Introduction to the Man of Law's Tale, where the Host takes fourteen lines to work out laboriously from celestial observation that the time is 'ten of the clokke' (II, 1-14). Only four lines are needed to describe how the avian computer operates:

> By *nature* he knew ech ascencioun
> Of the equynoxial in thilke toun;
> For whan degrees fiftene weren ascended,
> Thanne crew he, that it myghte nat been amended.
>
> (VII, 2855-8 — my italics)

The precision of the calculation will be appreciated when it is observed that the homely phrase 'in thilke toun' corresponds to the more technical 'as in that latitude' of II, 13. The effect of the whole panegyric will be enhanced if we recall another medieval common-place; namely, that fallen man must endeavour through the arts and sciences to recover laboriously some part of what he possessed '*by nature*' in Eden.

When we next hear Chauntecleer 'calculate' — 'And knew by kynde, and by noon oother loore' (VII, 3196) — astronomical time, he is himself about to fall. By elaborate astrological allusions, Chaucer indicates the time of the catastrophe to be the hour of 'pryme' on 3 May. Later, when the hero is already in his predator's jaws, he adds that it was a Friday — *Veneris Dies*. The upsetting 'influence' of the planet 'geery Venus' is discussed in the Knight's Tale (I, 1534-9), where she also appears as the goddess of the classical pantheon. When the Nun's Priest takes the almost inevitable side-step from the astrological to the mythological, however, she is not apostrophized as 'goddess of love', but as 'goddesse of plesaunce' (3342). The move is symptomatic of the tale's tendency to deviate into sex. Chauntecleer is said to be her 'servant' because he practises coition 'Moore for delit than world to multiplye' (3345). The satirical intent is obvious enough, but it acquires an added piquancy if we recall the solemn debate contrived by Jean de Meun in the latter part of the *Roman de la Rose*. Jean introduces the goddess Nature (the Creator's viceroy in the physical realm) and her priest Genius (the god of reproduction), who condemns sexual love unless it is practised for the sake of 'engendrure' (i.e. 'world to multiplye'). This view of human love is opposed to that of *fine amor* or 'courtly love' that Guillaume de Lorris, in the earlier part of the poem, had presented allegorically as a veritable paradise. Jean ultimately condemned that ideal as a false counterpart to the true celestial paradise, which man can enter only if he performs the divinely sanctioned work of 'engendrure'. So the true servant of Venus will — like Cupid in the Prologue to *The Legend of Good Women* (F., 329-31) — regard Genius's doctrine of love as 'an heresye ayeins [her] lawe': Love is a religion to be pursued as an end in itself; it is not to be reduced to a mundane, utilitarian function, even if divinely sanctioned. But the controversy is reduced to delicious absurdity when applied to the activities of a chicken that result in the production of 'somtyme an ey or tweye' [an occasional egg or two] (2845) for the poor widow's table.

Only once does the tale notably transcend the scheme of the Seven Arts to tug at the skirts of Theology, the Queen of Arts and Sciences: namely, when the narrator considers — or rather, pointedly refuses to consider — the problem of divine foreknowledge and human free will. Before laughing the matter off, he refers the reader to two standard *auctoures* (Augustine and Boethius) and to the work of the latest anti-Pelagian (Bishop Bradwardine). But he also says enough to show that his knowledge of the subject is more than bibliographical — as can be seen from his reference to the Boethian distinction between 'simple' and 'conditional' necessity. Commentators have regarded this passage as the epitome of the tale's tendency to make 'game' of what Chaucer elsewhere treats as 'earnest'. The comment is true enough, provided that it is not taken to imply that Chaucer's 'serious' fictions are ever straightforward exemplifications of Boethian philosophy. The closest parallel to the present passage occurs in Troilus's labyrinthine meditation in the temple (*TC*, IV, 960-1078), where the hero is no more able to find a solution, or 'bulte it to the bren', than is the Nun's Priest here (VII, 3234 ff.); and Chaucer's attitude to Boethius there is no less oblique than it is here. Later I shall observe an even more striking parallel with the fourth book of *Troilus*; but first I must descend to the 'Trivial' Arts.

Even the lowly art of Grammar plays its part in the comedy — though this elementary Art will not strike us as particularly lowly when we recall that what grammar schools taught was Latin. The diminishing number of such schools today will soon make editorial renderings of Chauntecleer's '*Mulier est hominis confusio*' (VII, 3164) something more than an act of supererogation. The necessity of explaining will make the joke seem even less amusing than it does to most Latinate readers today. But, in fact, even the Latinate reader's appreciation of the wit may be enhanced if he is himself prepared to suffer a little explication. What Chaucer gives us is an — admittedly quite blatant — instance of the ease with which, in commentaries of his own day, glossing can degenerate into 'glozing' — both in the sense of 'misinterpretation' and of 'false flattery'. Chauntecleer introduces his own gloss thus:

> 'Madame, the *sentence* of this Latyn is,
> "Womman is mannes joye and al his blis."'
>
> (VII, 3165-6 — my italics)

The word 'sentence' occurs several times in this tale; almost every time it has a different meaning. Here the obvious meaning is 'meaning'. But it should be remembered that a medieval *grammaticus* was accustomed to expound a text with reference to its *littera*, its *sensus*, and its *sententia*.[24] The last of these was concerned with the deeper or inner meaning of the passage and sometimes involved allegory. It is well known how some medieval exegetes — especially friars — were able to discover, in both biblical and secular texts, allegories unsuspected by the innocent modern reader.[25] In classical and medieval treatises on rhetoric, allegory is defined as 'to say one thing, but to mean another'. Irony was often regarded as a subdivision of the trope and represented the extreme application of this principle: 'to say one thing, but to mean its opposite' — which is what Chauntecleer's gloss does.[26] Chaucer would have relished the irony that six hundred years after his birth a coterie of critics would arise, in a continent undiscovered in his day, who would apply these very principles to the interpretation of his own works, and who would be prepared to demonstrate that his poems mean the very opposite of what they purport to say.[27] A favourite text with the modern hermeneutical school of criticism is Romans, 15: 4. Chaucer's citation of it at the tale's end — 'For seint Paul seith that al that writen is, / To oure doctrine it is ywrite, ywis' (3441-2) — may seem like encouragement to those who would have us read the tale as an allegory of the Fall of Man; interpret Chauntecleer and Pertelote as Adam and Eve (what about the other six 'wyves'?); regard the fox as the devil, or the friars, or Nicholas Colfax; understand the poor widow as the Church. But the satire, earlier in the tale, on the vagaries of interpretation will warn a more sensitive reader against the dangers of the allegorical trap.

Even if the place of Rhetoric in this tale were not generally well known, its central position would be obvious from the way in which the present argument continually crosses the frontiers into its province even while purporting to discuss one of the other Liberal Arts. There is no need for me to describe how the tone of mock-tragedy is enhanced by the use of figures, tropes, and devices for 'amplification' that are listed in such a treatise as the *Poetria Nova* by Geoffrey of Vinsauf — Chaucer's 'Gaufred, deere maister soverayn' (3347).[28] It is the continual citing of *exempla* that gives the tale its encyclopedic character: its frequent 'back-to-front' use of them makes it into a distorting *Speculum Minus*[29] of the world of learning. A single instance of this process must suffice here. Chaucer employs the various *morae* ('delays') — as Vinsauf calls them — to control the pace of his comic narrative. As the story reaches its catastrophe these interruptions and digressions become briefer, more frequent, and more exaggerated until, at the moment of the fox-chase, the brake is released and the narrative gallops towards its conclusion. Only two comparisons interrupt this headlong and cacophonous passage; both are more vivid and strike nearer home than do the academic allusions earlier in the tale. The first says of the pursuing peasants that 'They yolleden as feendes doon in helle' (3389); the other compares their noise, and that of the farm animals, to the din made by 'Jakke Straw and his meynee . . . Whan that they wolden any Flemyng kille' (during the Peasants' Revolt of 1381). Yet even here Chaucer may be viewing life through the spectacles of books. There may be a literary joke at the expense of Gower, whom Chaucer had honoured in *Troilus and Criseyde* (V, 1856), but to whom there may be a teasingly uncomplimentary allusion at *CT*, II, 77-89.[30] The description of a farmyard scare in terms of the events of 1381 looks suspiciously like an inversion of Gower's procedure in a notoriously cacophonous passage of Latin verse where he describes the rebellious peasants thus:

> Quidam sternutant asinorum more ferino,
> Mugitus quidam personuere boum;
> Quidam porcorum grunnitus horridiores
> Emittunt, que suo murmure terra tremit.
>                         (*Vox Clamantis*, I, xi, 799-802)[31]

Earlier in Gower's chapter there is some crude, onomastic humour at the expense of the rustics, whereas Chaucer names 'Malkyn, with a distaf in hir hand' together with 'Colle oure dogge, and Talbot and Gerland' (3383-4). Later Gower refers to the peasants in terms of ganders and swarms of wasps, which may have prompted Chaucer's inclusion in the chase of the (entirely superfluous) geese and swarm of bees (3391-2). Dare one also suggest that the sublimely banal references to Fortune in the Nun's Priest's Tale are partly prompted by Gower, with whom such references are almost a mannerism?

This is merely incidental parody. The burlesque of rhetorical techniques and pretentiousness is focused principally upon the tale's hero. As well as being introduced as the subject of an epideictic description, he proves himself to be a master of deliberative oratory in his dazzling performance in the debate about the significance of his dream. But that performance exhibits even more strikingly his expertise in the last, and most revealing, of the Arts to be discussed here: Dialectic.

Ideally Dialectic was concerned with establishing the truth by means of logical argument; but all too often in practice it amounted to little more than a repertory of techniques and 'ploys' for putting down an opponent. In order to win a scholastic disputation two things were necessary before all others: the disputant must have the best 'authorities' at his finger-tips and he must be expert in the art of making apt and telling distinctions.[32] As the authoritative text to support her contention that all dreams are void of significance, Pertelote quotes the maxim, 'Ne do no fors of dremes', from the paltry Dionysius Cato (VII, 2940-1), whose 'Distychs' was used as a First Latin Reader in grammar schools. Chauntecleer counters with 'oone of the gretteste auctour that men rede' (VII, 2984); and one can hardly do better than that — unless one were actually to name the authority by whom one sets such store. However, commentators have noted that the exemplary anecdotes that he recites are to be found in very respectable 'auctoures' and, in any case, Chauntecleer is hardly at a loss for names as he continues with his 'replicacioun' that converts what had begun as a debate into a monologue. Again, whereas Pertelote dismisses all dreams as empty of significance and attributable to psychosomatic causes, Chauntecleer is able — if not exactly careful — to distinguish:

> 'Reed eek of Joseph, and ther shul ye see
> Wher dremes be somtyme — *I sey nat alle* —
> Warnynge of thynges that shul after falle.'
>
> (VII, 3130-2 — my italics)

Whereas Pertelote knows only about the unreliable *somnium naturale* (usually rendered 'swevene' in this particular text), Chauntecleer knows also of the *somnium coeleste* or *visio* (usually rendered here as 'avysioun'). What is more, events prove his diagnosis to be correct — in so far as any interpretation in this tale can be said to be either 'proved' or 'correct'. The col-fox's breaking into the hen-yard is described as having been 'By heigh ymaginacioun forncast' (VII, 3217). 'Heigh ymaginacioun' is a technical term of medieval psychology: it denotes the faculty that enables one to experience a *somnium coeleste* or 'avysioun', as opposed to a natural dream.[33] In sleep, the ordinary imagination was indeed (as Pertelote argues) subject to illusions caused by vapours rising from the stomach (cf. 2923 ff.). But the 'exalted imagination' could, as the result of divine inspiration, experience either a vision of eternal verities or a warning of things that will happen 'in this lif present'. So Chauntecleer's apprehension about his dream seems to be vindicated theoretically as well as in practice. Nevertheless, no sooner does he establish himself as victor in academic debate with his 'wyf' than he finds himself a victim in a more disparate contest of wits — not with a temporary opponent but with his natural 'contrarie' (3280). It is a 'debate' into which he should not even have entered.

The debate between cock and hen assumes such enormous proportions, and is so revealing of Chauntecleer's character, that there is a danger that it will 'up-stage' the inherited fable about the cock and fox, which was (presumably) the tale's initial *raison d'être*. Indeed, Chaucer goes some way towards implying that the essential crux of his mock tragedy lies in the earlier episode. The tale concludes with a proverb, cited antiphonally at VII, 3431-5 by the cock and fox. Such a proverbial ending is a traditional characteristic of fables: for, just as one form of allegory was anciently defined as 'extended metaphor', so the traditional fable may be defined as an expanded proverb.[34] But only a naïve reader will suppose this *moralite* (about the opening and closing of eyes and mouth) to be a revelation of the essential *sentence* of this complex, sophisticated and elusive tale. Certainly it constitutes the *sentence* of the fable that Chaucer inherited. But, seizing upon a reference in one of his sources to the cockerel's dream, he has extended the expanded proverb into something quite unproverbial. In constructing the debate about this dream he bids fair to shift the balance, the tone and the significance of the narrative as a whole. He appears to have brought forward the narrative's centre of gravity from the moment when the fox seizes the cock to the moment when Chauntecleer flies down from the beam and so puts himself in the way of his encounter with his natural predator. The descent from the beam is represented by Chaucer as the fatal, pivotal action in his mock *tragédie manquée*. Its importance is emphasized by the way in which it is looked forward to at 2942, is described when it occurs at 3172, and is looked back upon regretfully at 3231 and again at 3339. This crucial act is the altogether unexpected issue of the debate between cock and hen.

The situation in some respects resembles that to be found in the most critical episode of *Troilus and Criseyde*. I mean the closing scene of Book IV, where Troilus argues energetically in favour of the lovers' eloping to a non-belligerent country, but eventually acquiesces in Criseyde's ill-judged and ill-fated plan for her to depart temporarily to the Greek camp.[35] As soon as she emerges from Troy

she encounters the predatory Diomede. Chauntecleer argues with
equal energy against Pertelote's opinion of his dream, yet concludes
his monologue with an action that implies his tacit acquiescence in
her opinion. As soon as he flies in the face of what his reason
deduced about the admonitory dream, he places himself in the way
of the encounter with his own natural predator. The main difference
between the two situations is that in the 'tragedye' Troilus
reluctantly capitulates out of respect for his lady's wishes and
because she proves to be unpersuadable. In the mock *tragédie
manquée* the hero's volte face is more blatant and outrageous.

The tale eventually reveals that Chauntecleer's energy in arguing
against his 'wyf' is generated by motives less creditable than the
desire to establish the truth by dialectical means. The more obvious
of these motives is his fear of the laxatives she has prescribed: 'I hem
diffye [mistrust], I love hem never a deel!' (3156) — we shall find
this verb used again in a very significant passage. His opinion that
'they been venymous' is well justified: any one of the laxative herbs
prescribed at 2963-6 would have sufficed to remove from his
stomach the consumed 'digestyves / Of wormes' and, consequently,
the excess of choler from which he is alleged to suffer. The whole
pharmacopoeia, swallowed at once, would have killed the wretched
bird. His other — and far more important — motive can be traced
back to an even earlier stage in the narrative; namely, to Pertelote's
immediate reaction to his account of his alarming dream:

> 'Now han ye lost myn herte and al my love.
> I kan nat love a coward, by my feith!'
>
> (2910-11)

His main anxiety is to refute this charge of cowardice in order to
regain her lost love. The rhetorical and dialectical performance that
he stages for her benefit is a substitute courtship ritual. Having
mastered her in academic debate, he feels entitled to master her
sexually. In order to do this, it is necessary for him to fly down from
the safe, but inconveniently narrow, perch into the roomy, but
insecure, hen-yard. His subsequent exhibition of sexual virtuosity so
befuddles and diverts his mind that he entirely forgets the tenor of
the eight *ensamples* that he had cited in his exhibition of academic
prowess. But the essential collapse of his intellect under the pressure
of female charm had already occurred in the final line of his
monologue. He declares that, when he feels Pertelote's 'softe syde',

> 'I am so ful of joye and of solas,
> That I *diffye bothe* sweven *and* dreem.'
>
> (3170-1 — my italics)

He thus wilfully abandons the skilled dialectician's practice of making significant distinctions. His substitution of the more general term 'dreem' for the technical 'avysioun' implies a further suggestion of carelessness and recklessness. The crucial importance of his failure to distinguish is indicated by the fact that this line constitutes the first half of the couplet whose second line describes the fatal action that makes the catastrophe possible:

> And with that word he fley doun fro the beem.
>
> (3172)

There is significant symmetry in the fact that, when Chauntecleer eventually recovers his wits, he flies upwards again — to the safety of a tree.

The much debated question of whether or not Chaucer believed in the significance of dreams is irrelevant in this context. What matters is that, at the conclusion of the debate about dreams, Chauntecleer is in an undiscriminating, reckless, and self-satisfied mood, which renders him particularly vulnerable to the fox's wiles. Daun Russell is not exactly a dialectician; but he had leisure (cf. 3216) to study his intended victim's 'form'. Besides playing upon the histrionic vanity of the performer, he is careful to establish rapport with the academic. Being a swift and single-minded operator, he eschews Chauntecleer's rhetorical prolixity and confines himself to 'dropping the name' of one 'auctour' and with alluding (misleadingly, as it happens) to only a single *exemplum*.[36]

By leaving the Nun's Priest's Tale till last, it has been possible to conclude this critical study with discussion of one of Chaucer's most brilliant and characteristic performances — itself almost an essay on the art of reading, writing and interpreting narrative. We cannot know to whom the Host would have awarded the prize supper, but no doubt many readers would place this tale on their 'short list' as being one 'of best sentence and moost solaas' (cf. I, 798). However, *The Canterbury Tales*, as the compilation has come down to us, does not conclude with a prize-giving, but with an act of penance. The Parson's Tale is assigned to a priest who has no time for verse (either alliterative or metrical — cf. X, 42-4) and who rejects the Host's request for a 'fable' (X, 29-31) — a term which the Parson understands as meaning fiction generally, and not merely the narrative genre to which the present chapter has so far been devoted. The concept of 'moral obliquity' would strike him as a sophistication to be avoided: he is interested in following only the simple and direct path to the 'Jerusalem celestial'. As the pilgrims enter the outskirts of an unnamed village late in the day, he takes as his text, appropriately enough: 'Stondeth upon the weyes, and seeth and axeth of olde pathes . . . which is the goode wey . . . '.

The purpose of the prose manual on Penitence, that is assigned to the Parson, is as practical as that of any modern text-book of morbid anatomy. It incorporates a long diagnostic section on the Seven Deadly Sins and prescribes specific remedies for each in turn. It embodies the standard method that Christians employed to examine their consciences, especially after the Fourth Lateran Council of 1215 decreed that every Christian should go to confession at least once a year.[37] Since the Parson's Tale is followed, in most MSS, by the Retractions, we are presumably meant to imagine that the treatise has moved Chaucer to perform his own act of penitence. This act consists of his revoking 'my translacions and enditynges of worldly vanitees' (X, 1085), including (among other items) *Troilus and Criseyde*, *The Parlement of Foules* and 'the tales of Caunterbury, thilke that sownen into synne' — which implies nearly all the tales that have been discussed in the present study. He thanks God that he has been granted the grace to devote some of his time to writing saints' lives, homilies and books of 'moralitee', which he hopes may be acceptable as 'satisfaction' for his sins. One is reminded of how, a century later, Florentines, moved by the preaching of Savonarola, made public bonfires of their 'vanities' — including works inspired by humanist learning.

We do not know what Chaucer's final intentions were for the arrangement of the *Tales*; but the Parson's Prologue certainly has an air of finality about it. The Host declares that only one tale remains to be told (X, 15-25). The pilgrims think it desirable 'To enden in som vertuous sentence' (63). The Parson, taking up an image introduced by the Host at X, 28, offers to tell his prose 'tale' 'To knytte up al this feeste, and make an ende' (47). Some commentators have seen special significance in the latenesss of the hour (X, 5) and in the reference to the zodiacal sign of Libra (X, 11) — the Scales (of the Last Judgment?). There are, however, some incongruous details in this Prologue. Twice the ensuing 'tale' is described as a 'meditation' (X, 55 & 69). The term had a precise connotation at the time: the Parson's Tale does not answer to its definition. Another problem is caused by the image of *knitting up* 'al this feeste'. The expression may be no more than a periphrasis for 'conclude'. But if it is meant to imply that the ensuing tale will tie up all the threads of 'The Book of the Tales of Canterbury', it is unsatisfactory. Although the Parson's Tale provides some useful glosses on particular passages, it by no means constitutes a *summa* of Chaucer's moral attitudes as revealed in the General Prologue and in the tales themselves.

The narrator of the Nun's Priest's Tale follows his injunction, 'Taketh the moralite, goode men!', by another: 'Taketh the fruyt, and lat the chaf be stille'. I have already commented upon the uncertainty about what the elusive poet means us to understand by the 'fruyt' in this passage. The Parson employs a similar image, when he rejects 'fable':

> 'Why sholde I sowen draf out of my fest,
> Whan I may sowen whete, if that me lest?'
>
> (X, 35-6)

There is no uncertainty about what he values as fruit and repudiates as chaff. No doubt thoughts of the ultimate harvest of souls urged Chaucer, in his Retractions, to draw up a list of the first-fruits of his literary labours that would be acceptable to a higher 'juge and reportour' (cf. I, 814) than the Host of the Tabard Inn. The problem of double standards, that is raised by the sentiment of the Retractions, will, in turn, raise historical and theological questions about morality in 'works of art'. Theoretical discussion of such questions falls outside the scope of the present critical study. All I have claimed to do is to gather, analyse and savour what I regard as the 'fruits' most worth garnering for the sustenance of our imagination, and the delight and instruction of our minds, as we journey along the thoroughfare of 'this lif present'.

# Notes

## NOTES TO CHAPTER 1

1. See R. A. Pratt and K. Young, 'The Framework of the *Canterbury Tales*', in W. F. Bryan and Germaine Dempster (edd.), *Sources and Analogues of Chaucer's Canterbury Tales* (London, 1941), pp. 1-81; Helen Cooper, *The Structure of the Canterbury Tales* (London, 1983), Chs 1 & 2.

2. Most notably G. L. Kittredge, *Chaucer and his Poetry* (Cambridge, Mass., 1915), Lectures 5 & 6; and more recently R. M. Lumiansky, *Of Sondry Folk: The Dramatic Principle in the Canterbury Tales* (Austin, Texas, 1955).

3. R. Baldwin, *The Unity of the Canterbury Tales*, Anglistica, 5 (Copenhagen, 1955).

4. See C. Muscatine, *Chaucer and the French Tradition* (Berkeley and Los Angeles, 1957), pp. 167 ff.

5. R. M. Jordan, *Chaucer and the Shape of Creation* (Cambridge, Mass., 1967). D. R. Howard, *The Idea of the Canterbury Tales* (Berkeley, 1976), p. 190, speaks of the application of the phrase 'Gothic form' to *CT* as a cliché, but still valid.

6. Howard, *op. cit.*, pp. 202 ff.

7. *Ibid.*, pp. 326 ff. On p. 72 Howard acknowledges a prior reference to this idea in D. W. Robertson, Jr., *A Preface to Chaucer* (Princeton, 1962), p. 373.

8. Howard, *op. cit.*, p. 219. On *entrelacement* in romances, see E. Vinaver, *The Rise of Romance* (Oxford, 1971), Ch. 5 .

9. J. B. Allen and T. A. Moritz, *A Distinction of Stories: The Medieval Unity of Chaucer's Fair Chain of Narratives for Canterbury* (Columbus, Ohio, 1981), pp. 18 ff. For the suggestion that a structural model for *CT* may be found in the *Aeneid*, see J. Norton-Smith, *Geoffrey Chaucer* (London, 1974), pp. 88-103.

10. V. A. Kolve, *Chaucer and the Imagery of Narrative: The First Five Canterbury Tales* (London, 1984), pp. 365 ff.

11. This fact is recognized by R. O. Payne, *The Key of Remembrance: A Study of Chaucer's Poetics* (New Haven and London, 1963), pp. 150-1. But I do not agree altogether with Payne's evaluations of tales.

12. On the meaning of *sententia*, see G. Paré *et al.*, *La Renaissance du XII<sup>e</sup> Siècle: Les Ecoles et l'Enseignement* (Paris, Ottawa, 1933), pp. 267-74; the terms are discussed in A. J. Minnis, *Medieval Theory of Authorship: Scholastic literary attitudes in the later Middle Ages* (London, 1984), see under *sensus* and *sententia* in 'Index of Latin terms', p. 316. See also below, Ch. 8, pp.169-70. Also relevant is the distinction between the French terms *matiere* and *san* (or *sens*) as used by Chrétien de Troyes in the Prologue to *Le Chevalier de la Charette [Lancelot]*, ed. M. Roques, *CFMA* (1958), line 26. The notion of *san* is discussed by Vinaver, *The Rise*

*of Romance*, Ch. 2; see esp. p. 23 for his consideration of Chrétien's Prologue. The terms are rendered respectively 'subject matter' and 'treatment' in Chrétien de Troyes: *Arthurian Romances*, trans. by D. D. R. Owen (Everyman's Library, London, 1987), p. 185. But their meaning in this passage is uncertain (see *ibid.*, p. 511).

13. 2nd ed., Oxford, 1957. All quotations from Chaucer in the present study are from this edition, unless otherwise stated. A third edition (General Editor: L. D. Benson) is due for publication shortly — see below (p.202) for details. See below (*ibid.*) also for a complete list of editions of Chaucer that are cited in the present study.

14. National Library of Wales MS. Peniarth 392 D. Cf. *The Canterbury Tales of Geoffrey Chaucer edited from the Hengwrt Manuscript* by N. F. Blake (London, 1980). See also P. G. Ruggiers (ed.), *A Facsimile and Transcription of the Hengwrt Manuscript* (Norman, Oklahoma, 1979). See further below, n. 66.

15. See J. M. Manly and Edith Rickert (edd.), *The Text of the Canterbury Tales*, 8 vols. (Chicago, 1940). There is a list of MSS of the *Tales* in F. N. Robinson (*ed. cit*), 886-7, but for an up-to-date list (which includes dates of MSS) see D. A. Pearsall, *The Canterbury Tales* (London, 1985), Appendix A, pp. 321-5.

16. See N. F. Blake, *The Textual Tradition of The Canterbury Tales* (London, 1985) for the most radical reconsideration of the problem. See also D. A. Pearsall, *The Canterbury Tales* (London, 1985), Chs 1 & 2. For the argument that the order of groups in Ellesmere (and certain other MSS that involve only a minor variation) had Chaucer's own approval, see L. D. Benson in *SAC* 3 (1981), pp. 77-120, esp. p. 81. Professor Benson is the general editor of the forthcoming revision of Robinson's edition.

17. On the notion of the *compilator* and of Chaucer as a compiler, see A. J. Minnis, *Medieval Theory of Authorship*, pp. 191 ff.

18. For ref., see Benson, *art.cit.*, in *SAC*, 3, p. 113, n. 26.

19. On the notorious 'Bradshaw shift' in the ordering of tales, that resulted from supposed topographical misplacing of Rochester and Sittingbourne in Ellesmere and other MSS, see S. B. Greenfield, 'Sittingbourne and the Order of the Canterbury Tales', *MLR*, 48 (1953), pp. 51-2; Helen Cooper, *op.cit.*, pp. 58-9.

20. *Sir Gawain and the Green Knight*, lines 701-2. See nn. on these lines in the ed. by Tolkien & Gordon, rev. N. Davis (Oxford, 1967), p. 98. The oft-repeated assertion that Chaucer was residing at Greenwich at the time is, however, conjectural (on the basis of MS marginal gloss to *Envoy to Scogan*, line 45). For a summary of documentary evidence concerning Chaucer's associations with Kent, see M. M. Crow and Clair C. Olson (edd.), *Chaucer Life-Records* (Oxford, 1966), pp. 512-13.

21. See J. Newman, *West Kent and the Weald* in 'The Buildings of England' series, ed. N. Pevsner (Harmondsworth, 1969), p. 453;

H. Loxton, *Pilgrimage to Canterbury* (Newton Abbot, 1978), pp. 155-6.

22. Cf. I *Henry IV*, l. ii, 120-5, where the conspiring thieves mention Rochester specifically with reference to 'pilgrims going to Canterbury with rich offerings, and traders riding to London with fat purses'.

23. Newman, *op. cit.*, pp. 464, 469. The relevance of this painting to the Monk's Tale is noted by R. A. Pratt (ed.), *Chaucer's Tales of Canterbury* (Boston, 1974), p. 209.

24. Howard, *op. cit.*, pp. 28 ff.

25. C. A. Owen, Jr., *Pilgrimage and Storytelling in the Canterbury Tales: the Dialectic of 'ernest' and 'game'* (Norman, Oklahoma, 1977), Ch. 2.

26. A committed proponent of such a theory might, for example, look further back into Fragment VII to establish associations with the Prioress's 'Miracle of the Virgin' concerning the murder of a Christian boy by Jews. (a) Rochester claimed its own miracle of the Virgin, although it concerned a drowning harper instead of a singing child (Loxton, *op. cit.*, p. 154). (b) The opposition between the Jewish and Christian faiths is represented in the fourteenth-century sculpture surrounding a doorway in the cathedral's SE transept: it contains a conspicuous 'Synogoga et Ecclesia' (Newman, *op. cit.*, p. 460). (c) At VII, 513-15 the Prioress recalls St Nicholas who 'so yong to Crist dide reverence'. The main nave altar (used by the parishioners) was dedicated to that patron of children and scholars. When in 1423 it was eventually superseded by a parish church (built in the cathedral churchyard), that too was dedicated to St Nicholas. (d) A few miles to the S. (on a subsidiary pilgrim route) lay the Cistercian abbey of Boxley. One of its two notorious frauds (exposed at the Reformation) concerned the statue of St Rumbold. It is not the statue, but the saint himself, who concerns us here. Rumbold lived for only three days before passing into Paradise. Meanwhile, he spoke fluent Latin, repeated his Paternoster and Credo (unlike the child in *Pearl* – cf lines 483-5) and exhorted his elders to holiness (cf. Loxton, *op. cit.*, p. 138). Like St Nicholas, he exemplifies the Prioress's statement that:

> . . . by the mouth of children thy bountee
> Parfourned is, for on the brest soukynge
> Somtyme shewen they thyn heriynge.

(VII, 457-9)

(Incidentally, the Clerk of Oxenford would have found in the cathedral's NE. transept [close to the shrine of St William of Perth] the tomb of Bp. Walter de Merton, founder of the oldest college in his university.) The search for such associations remains a harmless pastime so long as it is realized that they are of no value for an appreciation of *The Canterbury Tales*.

27. Ranging in scope from Harold F. Brooks, *Chaucer's Pilgrims: the Artistic Order of the Portraits in the Prologue* (London, 1962) to Jill Mann, *Chaucer and Medieval Estates Satire: The Literature of Social Classes in the General Prologue to the Canterbury Tales* (Cambridge, 1973). See also E. T. Donaldson's essay 'Chaucer the Pilgrim' in his *Speaking of Chaucer* (London, 1970), pp. 1-12.
28. See below, Ch. 2, p. 27.
29. Cf. esp. I, 80, 87-8, 97-8; V, 1-3.
30. This has been disputed by Terry Jones, *Chaucer's Knight: The Portrait of a Medieval Mercenary* (London, 1980). But Jones's arguments have been effectively countered by Maurice Keen, 'Chaucer's Knight, the English Aristocracy and the Crusades' in V. J. Scattergood and J. W. Sherborne (edd.), *English Court Culture in the Later Middle Ages* (London, 1983), pp. 45-61.
31. On levels of style in *KnT*, see A. J. Gilbert, *Literary Language from Chaucer to Johnson* (London, 1979), pp. 29-42.
32. See below, Ch. 3, p. 56.
33. See below, Ch. 3, n. 3.
34. (Oxford, 1974).
35. For example, Bennett's researches have admirably complemented those of Beichner (see below, Ch 3, n. 20) on Chaucer's use of the name, Absolon, in the Miller's Tale. T. W. Craik, in his lively study, *The Comic Tales of Chaucer* (London, 1964), states that the name was 'surely never given to an English child at baptism!' (p. 12). But Bennett observes that the name does occur in records of the city of Oxford — though the name is not recorded (interestingly enough) for any member of the university (Bennett, *op.cit.*, p. 42). 'Nicholas' is, of course, the appropriate name for the university scholar (see above, n. 26).
36. Bennett, *op. cit.*, p. 19.
37. For arguments concerning the propriety of this tale to its narrator, see M. Copland, '*The Reeve's Tale*: Harlotrie or Sermonyng?', *MÆ* 31 (1962), pp. 14-32; V. A. Kolve, *Chaucer and the Imagery of Narrative,* pp. 219 ff.
38. See Penn R. Szittya, 'The Green Yeoman as Loathly Lady: the Friar's Parody of the Wife of Bath's Tale', *PMLA*, 90 (1975), pp. 386-94.
39. Cf. P. Ruggiers, *The Art of the Canterbury Tales* (Madison, Wisc., 1965), pp. 122-3; R. M. Haines, 'Fortune, Nature and Grace in Fragment C', *ChR*, 10 (1975-76), pp. 220-35.
40. J. E. Grennen, 'Saint Cecilia's Chemical Wedding: the Unity of the Canterbury Tales, Fragment VIII', *JEGP*, 65 (1966), pp. 466-81; B. A. Rosenberg, 'The Contrary Tales of the Second Nun and the Canon's Yeoman', *ChR*, 2 (1968), pp. 278-91. (These tales are juxtaposed in Ellesmere; *CYT* does not appear in Hengwrt.)
41. Text in D. S. Brewer (ed.), *Chaucer: The Critical Heritage*

(London, 1978), i, 166.

42. i.e. *KnT* and *Second Nun's Tale* (see below, Ch. 2, p. 27).

43. The Man of Law seems to propose to tell a tale in prose (cf. II, 96) and proceeds to relate one in 'rhyme royal' stanzas; the narrator of the Merchant's Tale speaks as if he were a religious (cf. IV, 1251); the Shipman as if he were a woman (VII, 11-19).

44. The most committed advocate of the propriety of tales to tellers is R. M. Lumiansky, *Of Sondry Folk* — see above, n. 2.

45. See below Ch 7, p. 158.

46. See below, Ch 4, pp. 101-2.

47. See below, Ch 6, pp. 127 ff.

48. See below, Ch 2, pp. 49-51.

49. A convenient summary of discussions critical of the Franklin and his tale (together with some rejoinders) is given in C.A. Owen, Jr., *Pilgrimage and Storytelling*, p. 240 and nn. 45 and 46. The question of the Franklin's social rank has been sensibly dealt with by G. Morgan (ed.), *Geoffrey Chaucer: the Franklin's Prologue and Tale* (London, 1980), pp. 10-15.

50. R. B. Burlin, *Chaucerian Fiction* (Princeton, 1977), p. 198.

51. See below, Ch. 6, n. 46.

52. R. B. Burlin, 'The Art of Chaucer's Franklin', *Neophilologus*, 51 (1967), repr. (with revisions) in J. J. Anderson (ed.), *Chaucer: The Canterbury Tales: A Casebook* (London, 1974), pp. 183-208, see esp. p. 201.

53. See below, Ch 3, p. 67.

54. See below, Ch 3, p. 71.

55. G. L. Kittredge, 'Chaucer's Discussion of Marriage', *MP* 9 (1911-12), pp. 435-67; repr. in Anderson, *Casebook*, pp. 61-92, and in R. Schoeck & J. Taylor, *Chaucer Criticism: The Canterbury Tales* (Notre Dame, Indiana, 1960), pp. 130-59 (on pp. 158-9 there is a convenient list of contributions to the critical debate about the 'marriage debate'). See also Kittredge's *Chaucer and his Poetry*, pp. 185-211.

56. Kittredge, *Chaucer and his Poetry*, p. 190.

57. *The Structure of the Canterbury Tales* (London, 1983), p. 72. The most celebrated compilation of this kind is the *Summa Theologiae* by St Thomas Aquinas (1225-74). Dr Cooper observes that a *summa* amounted to something more than an encyclopaedia: 'it was intended to show the wholeness, the unity, of all creation and all abstract or intellectual thought in all their diversity'.

58. See below, Ch. 2, p. 27.

59. See Dieter Mehl, *The Middle English Romances of the Thirteenth and Fourteenth Centuries* (London, 1967), esp. pp. 13-22; E. Vinaver, *The Rise of Romance* (Oxford, 1971), esp. Ch. 1; J. Stevens, *Medieval Romance: Themes and Approaches* (London, 1973), esp. Chs 1 & 11.

60. On Chaucer's prose, see Margaret Schlauch, 'The Art of Chaucer's Prose' in D. S. Brewer (ed.), *Chaucer and Chaucerians* (London and Edinburgh, 1966), pp. 140-63; Diane Bornstein, 'Chaucer's *Tale of Melibee* as an Example of the *Style Clergial*', ChR, 12 (1977-78), pp. 236-54.

61. *Chaucer: The Canterbury Tales*, trans. N. Coghill (Harmondsworth, 1951), p. 28.

62. *Chaucer: The Canterbury Tales*, ed. A. C. Cawley (Everyman's Library, London, 1958).

63. The most convenient simple treatment of the subject is Helge Kökeritz, *A Guide to Chaucer's Pronunciation* (Stockholm and New Haven, 1954). On Chaucer's language generally, see R. W. W. Elliott, *Chaucer's English* (London, 1974).

64. E.g. J. G. Southworth, *Verses of Cadence, an Introduction to the Prosody of Chaucer and his Followers* (Oxford, 1954); *The Prosody of Chaucer and his Followers, Supplementary Chapters to Verses of Cadence* (Oxford, 1962); I. Robinson, *Chaucer's Prosody: A Study of the Middle English Verse Tradition* (Cambridge, 1971).

65. This stanza is transcribed into broad phonetic script in Kökeritz, *op. cit.*, p. 27.

66. See N. F. Blake (*ed. cit.*, pp. 560-1). This MS (together with a few others) contains only the first four lines of the Knight's speech, which then incorporates the latter part of the address to the Monk attributed to the Host in most MSS. The Host enters with his address to the Nun's Priest. In Hengwrt the final 'tragedye' of the Monk's Tale is that of 'Hugelyn'. There can, however, be no doubt about the authenticity of the longer version of this Prologue; see *A Variorum Edition of the Works of Geoffrey Chaucer*, Vol. II, Pt. 9, NPT, ed. D. A. Pearsall (Norman, Oklahoma, 1984), pp. 85-7.

# NOTES TO CHAPTER 2

1. See J.D. Burnley, '*Fine Amor*: Its Meaning and Context', *RES*, n.s. 31 (1980), pp. 129-48.

2. See Chaucer's 'Moral Balade', *Gentilesse*. Also his favourite line, 'For pitee renneth soone in gentil herte' (*CT*, I, 1761, &c); for other occurrences, see Robinson's note on this line.

3. For a suggestion as to how it might have been completed, see V.A. Kolve,'From Cleopatra to Alceste: An Iconographic Study of *The Legend of Good Women*', in J.P. Hermann and J.J. Burke, Jr. (edd.), *Signs and Symbols in Chaucer's Poetry* (University of Alabama Press, 1981), pp. 130-78.

4. On Chaucer's adaptation of *Il Teseida*, see P. Boitani, *Chaucer and*

Boccaccio (Oxford, 1977), Ch. 1 *et passim*; N. Havely, *Chaucer's Boccaccio* (Woodbridge and Totowa, N.J., 1980); P. Boitani (ed.), *Chaucer and the Italian Trecento* (Cambridge, 1983), esp. pp. 89-113 (essay by J.A.W. Bennett), pp. 185-201 (essay by Boitani).

5.  For suggested reasons for this curious fact, see Boitani (ed.), *Chaucer and the Italian Trecento*, pp. 91 & 159.

6.  For this view of Criseyde, see I. Bishop, *Chaucer's Troilus and Criseyde: A Critical Study* (University of Bristol Press, Bristol, 1981).

7.  Compare, for example, *TC*, III, 1-49, with *CT*, I, 1918-54.

8.  I. Bishop, '*Troilus and Criseyde* and *The Knight's Tale*' in Boris Ford (ed.), *The New Pelican Guide to English Literature*, Vol. I, *Medieval Literature*, Part i, *Chaucer and the Alliterative Tradition* (Harmondsworth, 1982), pp. 174-87.

9.  The standard ed. is by D.S. Brewer (London and Edinburgh, 1960). The most detailed study is J.A.W. Bennett, *The Parlement of Foules: An Interpretation* (Oxford, 1957).

10. Lines 129-520. See Guillaume de Lorris and Jean de Meun, *Le Roman de la Rose*, ed. Félix Lecoy, 3 vols, *CFMA*, 92, 95, 98 (Paris, 1965-70). Modern English trans. by Harry W. Robbins, ed. C.W. Dunn (New York, 1962). In the ME *Romaunt of the Rose* (included in Robinson's ed. of Chaucer), the passage begins at line 132.

11. On the *topos* of the *locus amoenus*, see Bennett, *op. cit.*, p. 70.

12. See *Roman*, 15891 ff.

13. Ed. T. Wright, *Anglo-Latin Satirical Poets of the Twelfth Century*, II (London, 1872). Trans. D.M. Moffat, *Yale Studies in English*, 36 (1908; repr. Hamden, Connecticut, 1972). The poem is discussed in C.S. Lewis, *The Allegory of Love* (Oxford, 1936), pp. 105-9; E.R. Curtius, *European Literature and the Latin Middle Ages*, trans. W.R.Trask (London, 1953), Ch. 6, esp. pp. 117-22; P. Piehler, *The Visionary Landscape: A Study in Medieval Allegory* (London, 1971), Ch. 4; G.D. Economou, *The Goddess Natura in Medieval Literature* (Cambridge, Mass., 1972), esp. pp. 72-97, and see Ch. 5 for a discussion of *PoF*. An indispensable article is R.H. Green, 'Alan of Lille's *De Planctu Naturae*', *Speculum*, 31 (1956), pp. 649-74, who was the first to demonstrate that Nature's complaint about man's sexual conduct is not restricted to a specific denunciation of sodomy. See also Economou, *op. cit.*, p. 87.

14. On this point I disagree with D.S. Brewer, *ed. cit.*, p. 11.

15. Commentators – including Bennett (cf. *op. cit.*, p. 165) — have not discerned this suitor's strategy. Bennett, however, makes some illuminating comparisons with *KnT* in his preceding paragraphs.

16. The idea is ultimately from Aristotle, *Rhetoric*, II, i. See also J.J. Murphy (ed.), *Three Medieval Rhetorical Arts* (Berkeley, Los

Angeles, London, 1971), p. xvi; T. Hunt, 'The Rhetorical Background to the Arthurian Prologue' in D.D.R. Owen (ed.), *Arthurian Romance: Seven Essays* (Edinburgh and London, 1970), pp. 1-23.

17. [Cicero], *Ad Herennium*, text ed. with trans. by H. Caplan (Loeb Classical Library; London, 1954, repr. 1964), pp. 20-2. Throughout the Middle Ages this was one of the most influential treatises on rhetoric, partly because it was attributed (incorrectly) to Cicero.

18. On Emelye's reluctance to marry, see J.A.W. Bennett, 'Some Second Thoughts on *The Parlement of Foules*' in E. Vasta and Z.P. Thundy (edd.), *Chaucerian Problems and Perspectives; Essays Presented to Paul E. Beichner* (Notre Dame, Indiana, and London, 1979), pp. 132-46, esp. pp. 142-3.

19. See below, pp. 152-3.

20. See J.M. Steadman, *Disembodied Laughter* (Berkeley, Los Angeles, London, 1972).

21. See A.J. Minnis, *Chaucer and Pagan Antiquity* (Woodbridge, 1982), in which *KnT* is discussed on pp. 108-43.

22. G.L. Kittredge, *Chaucer and his Poetry*, (Cambridge, Mass., 1915), p. 109.

23. E.g. at I, 155-322; II, 610-58, 1555-end; IV, 141-219, 680-730.

24. As noted by P. Boitani, *Chaucer and Boccaccio* (Oxford, 1977), p. 10. This monograph contains the most detailed and illuminating comparison of the two poems. See also P. Boitani (ed.), *Chaucer and the Italian Trecento* (Cambridge, 1983), pp. 185-6.

25. *KnT* is so divided in Ellesmere and several other MSS.

26. The play is ed. by G.R. Proudfoot (London and Nebraska, 1970). Its relation to *KnT* is discussed by Ann Thompson, *Shakespeare's Chaucer* (Liverpool, 1978), esp. Ch. 5. She refers to the lost plays on pp. 29-30, 168.

27. E.g. Muscatine, *Chaucer and the French Tradition*, p. 181; Allen and Moritz, *A Distinction of Stories*, p. 30.

28. In the course of an interesting discussion of the symbolic significance of this location, V.A. Kolve notes an inconsistency in Chaucer's description, when considered on the literal level. See *Chaucer and the Imagery of Narrative: The First Five Canterbury Tales* (London, 1984), p. 130.

29. Ann Thompson (*Shakespeare's Chaucer*, p. 168) comments on the absurdity of the plot, and cites similar opinions by earlier critics.

30. A feature of Chaucer's representation that is overlooked by Thompson in her comparison, *op. cit.*, pp. 172-6.

31. For an adverse view of the conduct of Theseus (as well as of the tale's narrator), see Terry Jones, *Chaucer's Knight* — see above, Ch. 1, n. 30, for details and for reply to his contentions.

32. On the iconographic significance of the prison/garden juxta-position, see Kolve, *Chaucer and the Imagery of Narrative*, Ch. III, *passim*.

33. One assumes that the narrator is conveniently overlooking Theseus's liaison with Ariadne, whom he abandoned on the island of Naxos; cf. *LGW*, 1886-2227.

34. See J.A. Burrow, 'Chaucer's *Knight's Tale* and the Three Ages of Man' in his *Essays on Medieval Literature* (Oxford, 1984), pp. 27-48.

35. *The Two Noble Kinsmen*, III, vi; cf. V, iv.

36. See Kolve's account of the use, throughout these descriptions, of the traditional iconography of 'the children of the planets', *Chaucer and the Imagery of Narrative*, pp. 115 ff.

37. See above, pp. 33-4.

38. On the *consolatio mortis*, see I. Bishop, *Pearl in its Setting* (Oxford, 1968), Ch. 1, and see esp. pp. 21-2 for an account of those employed in *KnT*; also my 'Chaucer and the Rhetoric of Consolation', *MÆ*, 52 (1983), pp. 38-50, esp. pp. 43-5.

39. See I. Bishop, '*Solacia* in *Pearl* and in Letters of Edward III Concerning the Death of his Daughter, Joan', *N&Q*, 229 (December 1984), pp. 454-6.

40. Aristotle, *Rhetoric*, I, i; II, xx-xxvi. Trans. by E.C. Welldon (London, 1886), pp. 5-6; 190-223. For use of the term in medieval 'Arts of Preaching' (*Artes Praedicandi*), see J.J. Murphy, *Rhetoric in the Middle Ages: A History of Rhetorical Theory from St Augustine to the Renaissance* (Berkeley, Los Angeles, London, 1974), pp. 327, 350-2. Cf. the essay by Margaret Jennings, 'The *Ars componendi sermones* of Ranulph Higden' in J.J. Murphy (ed.), *Medieval Eloquence* (Berkeley, Los Angeles, London, 1978), pp. 112-26, esp. pp. 120-1.

41. See below, Ch. 6, pp. 127-8.

42. For this technical phrase, cf. Milton, *Paradise Lost*, viii, 82; also C.S. Lewis, *The Discarded Image* (Cambridge, 1964), p. 14.

43. See above, p. 45 and n. 39.

44. See *Marie de France: Lais*, ed. A. Ewert (Oxford, 1947). For a prose trans., see E. Mason, *Lays of Marie de France and Others* (Everyman's Library, No. 557; London, 1911).

45. Cf. *Sir Orfeo*, ed. A.J. Bliss (Oxford, 1954); *Sir Launfal*, ed. A.J. Bliss (London and Edinburgh, 1960).

46. Jennifer R. Goodman, 'Chaucer's *Squire's Tale* and the Rise of Chivalry', *SAC*, 5 (1983), pp. 127-36, esp. p. 136.

47. Goodman describes *SqT* as a 'composite romance left unfinished by design' (p. 135). She is thinking of such a composite work as *Generydes*.

48. The phrase is applied to the Green Knight by J.A. Burrow, *A Reading of Sir Gawain and the Green Knight* (London, 1965), p. 18.

49. One of the traditional five parts of rhetoric was *Pronunciatio*, which was concerned with expressive gestures and facial expression as well as oral delivery.

50. See N. Orme, 'The Education of the Courtier' in V.J. Scattergood and J.W. Sherborne (edd.), *English Court Culture in the Later Middle Ages* (London 1983), pp. 63-85, esp. pp. 69-72. See also discussion of *PhT* below, Ch. 7.

51. On the use of 'gent' in Chaucer's works, see E.T. Donaldson, *Speaking of Chaucer* (London, 1970), p. 22. In contemporary alliterative poetry the word retained its prestigious status: see e.g. the exx. from *Pearl* and *Piers Plowman* cited by *MED* under 'gent' adj., 1(a).

52. See A. McI. Trounce, 'The English Tail-Rhyme Romances', *MÆ*, I (1932), pp. 87-108, 168-82; II (1933), pp. 34-57, 189-98; III (1934), pp. 30-50.

53. *Libaeus Desconus*, EETS, 261 (1969), ed. M. Mills. See the same editor's *Six Middle English Romances* (London, 1973) for texts of some other romances for popular audiences.

54. G.L. Brook (ed.), *The Harley Lyrics* (Manchester, 1948), No. 7 (pp. 37-9).

55. See T. Burton, '"The Fair Maid of Ribblesdale" and the Problem of Parody', *EC*, 31 (1981), pp. 282-98.

56. See Trounce, *MÆ*, I (1932), p. 107.

57. In addition to notes in Robinson's ed., see: Susie I. Tucker, 'Sir Thopas and the Wild Beasts', *RES*, n.s. 10 (1959), pp. 54-6; E.T. Donaldson, *Speaking of Chaucer*, pp. 14-15, 20-2; J.A. Burrow, *Essays on Medieval Literature*, pp. 60-78.

58. See Laura H. Loomis, 'The Tale of Sir Thopas', in W.F. Bryan and Germaine Dempster (edd.), *Sources and Analogues of The Canterbury Tales* (London, 1941), pp. 486-559.

59. The standard ed. is by Tolkien and Gordon (revised N. Davis, Oxford, 1967). For text with partly modernized spelling and marginal glosses, see *Pearl, Cleanness, Patience, Sir Gawain and the Green Knight*, ed. A.C. Cawley and J.J. Anderson (Everyman's Library; London, 1976).

60. *Essays on Medieval Literature*, pp. 61-5.

61. One reason for the anonymity may be the desire to protect the reputation of Gawain and 'his olde curteisye' (*CT*, V, 95 — and see above, p. 50). For, as the analogues to *WBT* suggest, if one were to return to 'Fairye' (cf. V, 96), one would find that the perpetrator of the rape was indeed Arthur's famous nephew. See S. Eisner, *A Tale of Wonder: A Source Study of The Wife of Bath's Tale* (Wexford, 1957), pp. 55 ff.

62. See above, p. 27.

63. See above, p. 33.

64. J.A. Burrow remarks of Chaucer's description of this tournament

that he adopts 'the uncharacteristic manner of writing, close to that of traditional alliterative verse, as if to mark an alien matter': *Ricardian Poetry* (London, 1971), p. 56.

## NOTES TO CHAPTER 3

1.  See above, p. 33.
2.  See *A Variorum Edition of the Works of Geoffrey Chaucer*, Vol. II, Pt. 3: *The Miller's Tale*, ed. T.W. Ross (Oklahoma Univ. Press, Norman, 1983). A Survey of Criticism is included on pp. 7-49.
3.  For a comprehensive study of the genre, see Per Nykrog, *Les Fabliaux* (Copenhagen, 1957), who argues that such tales were intended for the entertainment of an upper-class audience. For a brief survey of discussions of the audience for fabliaux, see Ross, *Variorum* ed., pp. 7-11. For specimens of fabliaux, see (apart from relevant sections of Bryan and Dempster, *Sources and Analogues*), L.D. Benson and T.M. Anderson (edd.), *The Literary Context of Chaucer's Fabliaux: Texts and Translations* (Indianapolis, 1971).
4.  Few commentators agree with N. Coghill's opinion that the recurrence of this line is merely accidental. See his essay, 'Chaucer's Narrative Art in *The Canterbury Tales*', in D.S. Brewer (ed.), *Chaucer and Chaucerians* (London, 1966), pp. 114-39, esp. p. 115. Nevertheless, the warning is salutary. I am not nearly so sure, for example, that the obscene *rime riche* on *queynte* (I, 3275-6) was inspired by the innocent *rime riche* at I, 2333-4.
5.  See J.A.W. Bennett, *Chaucer at Oxford and at Cambridge* (Oxford, 1974), pp. 15, 24, 68.
6.  On account of the reference to Noah's wife at I, 3540. The most helpful ed. of The Towneley (Wakefield) Play of Noah is in K. Sisam (ed.), *Fourteenth Century Verse and Prose* (Oxford, 1921), No. xvii; see esp. pp. 195-9.
7.  L.C. Martin (ed.), *Marlowe's Poems* (London, 1931), p. 35.
8.  On resemblances of *MilT* to ancient comedy and to traditions of the medieval Feast of Fools, see A. David, *The Strumpet Muse* (Bloomington and London, 1976), pp. 93 ff.
9.  *Roman de la Rose*, lines 21346-end.
10. Cf. *Romaunt of the Rose*, lines 349-412 (Elde is here a female personification).
11. On prescriptions by medieval rhetoricians for writing portraits of women, see Edmond Faral, *Les Arts Poétiques du XIIᵉ et du XIIIᵉ Siècles* (Paris, 1924), esp. pp. 75 ff., and pp. 214-15 (for the relevant passage in Geoffrey of Vinsauf's *Peotria Nova*). For trans. of *Poetria Nova*, see J.J. Murphy (ed.), *Three Medieval Rhetorical Arts* (Berkeley, Los Angeles, London, 1971), esp. pp. 53 ff. See also

D.S. Brewer, 'The Ideal of Feminine Beauty', *MLR*, 50 (1955), pp. 257-69. For Chaucer's response here to these conventions, see Muscatine, *Chaucer and the French Tradition*, pp. 228-30; D.S. Brewer, 'Towards a Chaucerian Poetic', *PBA*, 60 (1974), pp. 219-52, esp. p. 250. Also K.S. Kiernan, 'The Art of the Descending Catalogue and a Fresh Look at Alisoun', *ChR*, 10 (1975-76), pp. 1-16. I do not share Kiernan's enthusiasm (pp. 4-5) for the Harley Lyric, 'Blow, Northerne Wynd'.

12.  Cf. G.L. Brook (ed.), *The Harley Lyrics* (Manchester, 1948), No. 3, line 22; No. 9, lines 3-4.

13.  See below, pp. 152-3, and cf. I Bishop, *Chaucer's Troilus and Criseyde*, pp. 19-21.

14.  See Faral, *ed. cit.*, p. 120.

15.  Brook (ed.), *The Harley Lyrics*, No. 4, line 14.

16.  See above, p. 52, and n.55, for ref. to article by T. Burton. And see article by Kiernan (n. 11, above) for instances of comic descriptions. He does not mention 'The Fair Maid'; Brewer, in his pioneering article (*MLR*, 50, esp. pp. 260-1), examines it only in so far as it illustrates the conventional ideal.

17.  First Sestiad, 5-50 (L.C. Martin, *ed. cit.*, pp. 27-30).

18.  *De Planctu Naturae*, Prosa 12, Metrum 2 (pp. 5-18 in Moffat's trans.). See above, Ch. 2, p. 31 and n. 13.

19.  On the history of the decasyllabic line between Chaucer and Marlowe, see Karen Lynn, 'Chaucer's Decasyllabic Line and the Myth of the Hundred Year Hibernation', *ChR*, 13 (1978-79), pp. 116-27.

20.  See P.E. Beichner, 'Characterization in *The Miller's Tale*' in R. Schoeck and J. Taylor (edd.), *Chaucer Criticism: The Canterbury Tales* (Notre Dame, Indiana, 1960), pp. 117-29, esp. pp. 119-23.

21.  On wafer-sellers as bawds, see Bennett, *Chaucer at Oxford and at Cambridge*, p. 45.

22.  For the text of the relevant portion of the play presented at Coventry by the 'Shearmen and Taylors', see R.G. Thomas (ed.), *Ten Miracle Plays* (London, 1966), pp. 74-90 (esp. p. 85).

23.  On the shifting meanings of this epithet, see Beichner, *art. cit.*, esp. pp. 124-7.

24.  See E.T. Donaldson, 'Idiom of Popular Poetry in The Miller's Tale' in his *Speaking of Chaucer*, pp. 13-29, esp. pp. 19-20.

25.  On this phrase, see Bennett, *Chaucer at Oxford and at Cambridge*, pp. 12-13, 117-19.

26.  For the music of this famous song, see J. Stevens, '*Angelus ad Virginem*: the History of a Medieval Song' in P.L. Heyworth (ed.), *Medieval Studies for J.A.W. Bennett* (Oxford, 1981), pp. 297-328.

27.  *Romaunt of the Rose*, lines 3113-66. On the meaning of *Danger*, see C.S. Lewis, *The Allegory of Love* (Oxford, 1936), Appendix II (pp. 364-6).

28. See Janette Richardson, *'Blameth Nat Me'*: *A Study of Imagery in Chaucer's Fabliaux* (The Hague, Paris, 1970), pp. 100-22.
29. Text in B. Dickins and R.M. Wilson (edd.), *Early Middle English Texts* (Cambridge, 1951), No. XX, pp. 103-9. Also Carleton Brown (ed.), *English Lyrics of the XIIIth Century* (Oxford, 1932), No. 43, pp. 68-74. On its imagery, see further I. Bishop, 'Lapidary Formulas as Topics of Invention: Thomas of Hales to Henryson', *RES*, n.s. 37 (1986), pp. 469-77, esp. 469-71.
30. On the character of the Merchant and Chaucer's detailed representation of the commercial world, see V.J. Scattergood, 'The Originality of *The Shipman's Tale*', *ChR*, 11 (1976-77), pp. 210-31.
31. See J.R.R. Tolkien, 'Chaucer as Philologist: *The Reeve's Tale*', *Transactions of the Philological Society* (London, 1934), pp. 1-70.
32. See above, Ch. 1, p. 22.
33. *Chaucer and the French Tradition*, p. 204.
34. *Ibid.* This assertion is repeated by T. Whittock, *A Reading of the Canterbury Tales* (Cambridge, 1968), p. 99. *MED* cites this instance as an example of *disparage* v. sense 2. But surely the technical connotation of its sense 1 is evoked here. For the usual social register of the term, see also exx. under *disparage* n. Cf. especially Chaucer's use of the noun in the Clerk's Tale (IV, 908) and — in view of my remarks below about 'nations' and xenophobia — see use of the verb in *WBT* (III, 1069).
35. '. . . qui non sunt de natione regni Anglie'. See F.R.H. Du Boulay, *An Age of Ambition: English Society in the Late Middle Ages* (London, 1970), p. 21. See also J.W. Baldwin, *Masters, Princes and Merchants: The Social Views of Peter the Chanter and his Circle* (Princeton, N.J., 1970), i. pp. 248-9.
36. Du Boulay, *op cit.*, pp. 18-19, where *ReeveT.* is specifically cited. See also Bennett, *op. cit.*, pp. 99-100. He notes (p. 99) that there is no reason for necessarily supposing that Aleyn and John were either poor or of inferior social class. See also his remarks on the dialect of the clerks (and of the Reeve himself), pp. 100-3.
37. The poems in MS. BL Cotton Nero A.x. are written in NW. Midland dialect; yet *Pearl* and *Gawain* are the work of an author who is no less educated, sophisticated and courtly than Chaucer himself. It should be noted, moreover, that the clerks are able to pay in cash for their enforced night's lodging.
38. IV, xii (27); xvii (34). See *On Christian Doctrine*, trans. D.W. Robertson, Jr., The Library of Liberal Arts, No. 80 (New York, 1958), pp. 136, 142-3.

190

## Notes to Chapter 4

1. See the section on 'Curriculum Authors' in E. R. Curtius (trans. W. R. Trask), *European Literature and the Latin Middle Ages* (London, 1953), pp. 48-54.
2. See Ch. 8 below, pp. 164 ff..
3. On the academic *accessus* to the works of *auctoures*, see A. J. Minnis, *Medieval Theory of Authorship: Scholastic Literary Attitudes in the Later Middle Ages* (London, 1984), esp. pages listed under *accessus* in 'Index of Latin Terms' (p. 312). Also P. Miller, 'John Gower, Satiric Poet' in A. J. Minnis (ed.), *Gower's Confessio Amantis: Responses and Reassessments* (Woodbridge, 1983), pp. 79-105, esp. pp. 81 ff.
4. For a list of discussions of Chaucer's notion of 'tragedye', see I. Bishop, *Chaucer's Troilus and Criseyde*, n. 30 (on pp. 109-10).
5. See above, Ch. 1, p. 4 and n. 12.
6. G. C. Macaulay (ed.), *The English Works of John Gower*, EETS, e.s. No. 81 (1900, reprinted 1957), p. 151. On Gower's use of *exempla*, see C. Runacres, 'Art and Ethics in the *Exempla* of *Confessio Amantis*' in Minnis (ed.), *Gower's Confessio &c.* (cf. n. 3 above), pp. 106-34.
7. See below, p. 87.
8. See I. Bishop, *Chaucer's Troilus and Criseyde*, pp. 12-14.
9. *PL*, 172; coll. 855-7. See further Beryl Smalley, *English Friars and Antiquity in the Early Fourteenth Century* (Oxford, 1960).
10. Gail McMurray Gibson, 'Resurrection as Dramatic Icon in the Shipman's Tale' in J. P. Hermann and J. J. Burke, Jr. (edd.), *Signs and Symbols in Chaucer's Poetry*, pp. 102-12; and see review in *RES*, n.s. 35 (1984), pp. 357-9.
11. On the differences between allegory and *exemplum*, see J. A. Burrow, *Medieval Writers and their Work* (Oxford, 1982), Ch. 4, 'Modes of Meaning'.
12. *Roman de la Rose*, lines 6489 ff.
13. On the differing order of the Monk's *exempla* in various MSS., see Robinson's 2nd ed., pp. 746-7.
14. See F. Warren (ed.), *The Dance of Death*, EETS, No. 181 (1929).
15. See P. Godman, 'Chaucer and Boccaccio's Latin Works' in Piero Boitani (ed.), *Chaucer and the Italian Trecento*, pp. 269-95.
16. Robinson, 2nd ed., p. 331. But Chaucer misunderstands the reference to Perseus (see above, p. 82).
17. D. L. Lepley, 'The Monk's Boethian Tale', *ChR*, 12 (1977-78), pp. 162-70.
18. The most illuminating among recent comparisons is Piero Boitani, 'The *Monk's Tale*: Dante and Boccaccio', *MÆ*, 45 (1976), pp. 50-69. He refers to the more important among previous discussions.

19. Cf. *Inf.*, xxxiii, 4-6, with *Aen.*, ii, 3-4.
20. Boitani, *art. cit.*, (*MÆ*, 65), pp. 63-4.
21. As Charles A. Owen, Jr., puts it, in the course of one of the most perceptive accounts of the Pardoner and his tale: 'The *exemplum* has swallowed the sermon of which it is ordinarily a part, and then the sermon proceeds to spawn new *exempla*.' *Pilgrimage and Storytelling* &c., p. 175.
22. Germaine Dempster, *Dramatic Irony in Chaucer* (1932, repr. New York, 1959), pp. 72-9. She is particularly concerned with the relationship between the tale and its sources — a subject that I do not discuss in the following pages, which reproduce (with minor modifications) my article, 'The Narrative Art of *The Pardoner's Tale*', *MÆ*, 36 (1967), pp. 15-24.
23. 'Old Age and *Contemptus Mundi* in the Pardoner's Tale', *MÆ*, 33 (1964), pp. 121-30.
24. 'The Old Man in The Pardoner's Tale', *RES*, n.s. 2 (1951), pp. 49-55.
25. Steadman, *art. cit.*, p. 127.
26. *Ibid.*, p. 123.
27. For an example of such an explanation, see the separate ed. of the tale by Carleton Brown (Oxford, 1935), pp. xv-xx. Brown's arguments are discussed and rejected by G. G. Sedgewick, 'The Progress of Chaucer's Pardoner, 1880-1940', *MLQ*, I (1940), pp. 431-58. But Sedgewick's own solution — that the Pardoner contrives to introduce references to as many sins as possible, whether relevant to the *exemplum* or not, in order to affect his audience's consciences — seems to me hardly more satisfactory. Scholars who have thought the digression to be irrelevant have made much of the fact that the Pardoner resumes his narrative at 661 with the words: 'Thise riotoures thre of whiche I telle' — although he has never mentioned them before. A better knowledge of ME idiom might have diminished their allegations of inconsistency. The demonstrative was used not infrequently in ME to introduce a new subject or character, and the simple present was often used, as in OE, to express futurity (cf. *CT*, I, 3278, or *Pearl*, 524). The line could therefore be rendered idiomatically as follows: 'The story I am going to tell you concerns three revellers.'
28. This has indeed been acknowledged by a number of scholars. But insufficient emphasis has been placed upon the fact that, according to the logic of Chaucer's version of the story, the catastrophe could hardly have taken place, if the rioters had not been subject to all three of these sins, as well as to Avarice.
29. *Romeo and Juliet*, V, i, 42 ff.
30. Thomas of Hales, 'A Luue Ron', line 24. For edd., see above, Ch. 3, p. 71, n. 29.
31. The taverner refers to him as 'child' at 686. The fact that he is

referred to as 'this boy' at 670 is probably not an indication of his age; the word is employed in its older sense of 'servant'. See E. J. Dobson, 'The Etymology and Meaning of *Boy*', *MÆ*, 9 (1940), pp. 121-54; also *MED boie* n. (1), senses 1 & 4.

32.  I, 3935; cf. 4300-6. And see above, Ch. 3, p. 74.
33.  I, 3969, 3972; cf. 4211 ff. And see above, Ch. 3, p. 75.
34.  *Pearl*, line 64.
35.  See VI, 788-92. They are thieves because the treasure was not theirs in the first place and also because they plot to take it from each other by force. Notice especially the use of 'slyly' (792), 'ful prively' (797), 'subtilly' (798) — a singularly ironical use of the word — and '"Shal it be conseil?"' (819).
36.  VI, 895 ff.
37.  VI, 710.
38.  I Cor. 15: 54. Cf. Hosea 13: 14. Part of this verse is quoted at *Piers Plowman*, B. xviii, 35 (ed. Schmidt, p. 221), to describe the consequence of the Crucifixion: 'O mors, ero mors tua!'
39.  Rom. 6: 23.
40.  In *Paradiso*, xxix, 91-126, Dante introduces a powerful denunciation of the exhibitionism indulged in by contemporary preachers, which is worth considering in relation to the Pardoner's performance. On the way in which the art of rhetoric was adapted for preaching during the 13th and 14th centuries, see Th.-M. Charland, *Artes Praedicandi: Contribution à l'Histoire de la Rhétorique au Moyen Age* (Paris and Ottowa, 1936); J. J. Murphy, *Rhetoric in the Middle Ages: A History of Rhetorical Theory from St Augustine to the Renaissance* (Berkeley, Los Angeles, London, 1974), Ch. VI *passim*. See p. 345 for a list by Robert de Basevorn of requisites for a genuine preacher.
41.  *EETS*, 225, pp. 123 ff.
42.  See below, Ch. 5, p. 110.
43.  Langland recognized that the simoniacal behaviour of a pardoner made him the spiritual counterpart of a prostitute: c.f. *Piers Plowman*, B, v, 639-end (ed. Schmidt, p. 65).
44.  The Pardoner's ethical situation may be fittingly analysed in terms of the distinction between 'making' and 'doing' which Aristotle (*Nicomachean Ethics*, VI, 4 & 5) introduces into his discussion about the difference between Art and *Phronēsis* (the virtue that directs human conduct). The modern Thomist, Jacques Maritain, considers some of the implications of this distinction with reference to scholastic terminology: see his *Art and Scholasticism*, trans. J. F. Scanlan (London, 1943), esp. pp. 5-8.
Chaucer's remark (*LGW* Prol., F, 165-6) 'for vertu is the mene / As Etik seith' seems to allude to Aristotle's famous doctrine in Book II. The complete text of the *Ethics* was available in the West after

Grosseteste's Latin translation (c. 1246-47): cf. N. Kratzmann *et al.* (edd.), *The Cambridge History of Later Medieval Philosophy* (Cambridge, 1982), p. 659. Chaucer's knowledge of the doctrine of the 'mean' may, however, be derived from a *florilegium* rather than the *Ethics* itself.

45. *CT*, III, 1483-503, esp. 1483-5 and 1497-9.
46. The contrary view (that the sacrament was thereby rendered inefficacious) was a Wycliffite heresy. When Margery Kempe was examined, under suspicion of heresy, in All Hallows, Leicester, in 1417, she demonstrated her orthodoxy by stating her opinion on this very point (cf. *EETS*, 212 [1940 for 1939], p. 115, lines 8-20).
47. The use of the words *multiplie* (365) and *multipliyng* (374) should be compared with their use (with an added technical nuance) throughout *CYT*. See below, Ch. 5, p. 115 and n. 15.
48. Discussion of the implications of these lines was initiated by Kittredge, *Chaucer and his Poetry*, pp. 216 ff.
49. For contrasting views on the Pardoner and his tale, see D. R. Faulkner (ed.), *Twentieth Century Interpretations of the Pardoner's Tale* (Englewood Cliffs, N.J., 1973). Also A. David, *The Strumpet Muse*, pp. 193-204; D. Pearsall, 'Chaucer's Pardoner: The Death of a Salesman', *ChR*, 17 (1983), pp. 357-65.
50. For evidence (if needed) that one did not even mention *coillons* in polite society, see the lover's reply to Reason in *Roman de la Rose*, 6901 ff. The present instance is the earliest use of the word in English recorded by *MED*.


# NOTES TO CHAPTER 5

1. Cf. description of the Yeoman in *GP* (I, 101-17). Green was still the huntsman's colour in parts of Western Europe in the early-nineteenth century. In the cycle of lyrics by Wilhelm Müller, which Schubert set as *Die Schöne Müllerin*, this is the point of the poems called 'Die Liebe Farbe' and 'Die Böse Farbe'.
2. Ed. F.M. Mack, *EETS*, 193.
3. *Ibid.*, p. 30.
4. *Ibid.*, p. 32.
5. *Ibid.*, p. 38.
6. *Ibid.*, p. 30.
7. *Ibid.*
8. Ed. P. Hodgson, *EETS*, 218, p. 22.
9. Ed. E.V. Gordon (Oxford, 1953); here quoted from A.C. Cawley and J.J. Anderson (edd.), *Pearl, Patience, Cleanness, Sir Gawain and the Green Knight* (Everyman's Library, London, 1976).

10. See I. Bishop, *Pearl in its Setting*, Ch. 3, 'The Conduct of the Debate'.

11. See above, Ch. 3, pp. 63-4.

12. Ed. A.V.C. Schmidt, William Langland, *The Vision of Piers Plowman* (Everyman's Library, London, 1978), p. 262.

13. On the authenticity of *CYT* (which does not appear in Hengwrt MS. — see above, p. 6), cf. P. Brown, 'Is "The Canon's Yeoman's Tale" Apocryphal?', *ES*, 64 (1983), pp. 481-90.

14. Cf. Bennett, *Chaucer at Oxford and at Cambridge*, p. 41.

15. On the technical meanings of *multiplicacioun*, see A.V.C. Schmidt (ed.), *Chaucer: General Prologue and Canon's Yeoman's Tale* (London, 1974), p. 154, n. on [his] line 116.

16. See I. Bishop, *Pearl in its Setting*, esp. pp. 96-8.

17. *EETS*, 225, p. 95. There is a translation of *Ancrene Riwle* (based upon a different MS.) by M. Salu (London, 1955).

18. Text from D. Pearsall (ed.), *Piers Plowman by William Langland: An Edition of the C-text* (London, 1978), p. 102 (I have modernized the spelling). In Skeat's Parallel Text ed. of 1886, the Passus is numbered VI (vol. i, p. 121).

19. On the possibility that Pars Secunda was composed first, even before the Canterbury scheme had evolved, see A.E. Hartung, *ChR*, 12 (1977-78), pp. 111-28.

20. *Pace* Muscatine (*Chaucer and the French Tradition*, p. 214). To Muscatine belongs the credit of being the first notable critic to perceive the tale's symbolic possibilities. This perhaps causes him to underestimate its 'realism'.

21. In the present context it is relevant to compare Langland's discussion of *mede*, and its relationship to the ideal of justice, in *PP*, B, ii-iv. On this subject, see Myra Stokes, *Justice and Mercy in Piers Plowman: A Reading of the B-Text Visio* (Beckenham, Kent, 1984), esp. pp. 125 ff.

## NOTES TO CHAPTER 6

1. See above, Ch. 1, p. 15.

2. Cf. Martianus Capella, *De Nuptiis Philologiae et Mercurii*, ed. F. Eyssenhardt (Lipsiae, 1866). Chaucer refers to this fifth-century treatise 'On the Nuptials of Mercury and Learning (Philology)' at *MerchT*, IV, 1732-5, and *HoF*, 985. See further C.S. Lewis, *The Allegory of Love* (Oxford, 1936), pp. 78-82; *The Discarded Image* (Cambridge, 1964), pp. 107-8. Also E.R. Curtius, *European Literature &c.*, pp. 38 ff. (See below, p. 204, for trans.)

3. See H.E. Sandison, *The Chanson d'Aventure in Middle English* (Bryn Mawr, Penn., 1913).

4. *Piers Plowman*, B.Prol. 60 (ed. Schmidt, p. 3).

5. See esp. *Piers Plowman*, B. iii, 332-end (ed. Schmidt, pp. 34-5). The

orthodox, 'spiritual' gloss on Alys's favourite text ('*Crescite et multiplicamini*' — Gen. 1: 28) was — it must be admitted — given by another woman, Margery Kempe, when questioned at York by 'a gret clerke' (see *EETS*, 212 [1940 for 1939], p. 121, lines 1-10).

6. Ed. E.G. Stanley (London and Edinburgh, 1960), lines 51 ff.; 1667-1716.
7. Ed. Sir I. Gollancz (London, 1930).
8. On the source of this tale, see above, Ch. 2, n. 61.
9. See his essay 'On Fairy-Stories', in C.S. Lewis (ed.), *Essays Presented to Charles Williams* (London, 1947), pp. 38-89, esp. p. 43.
10. See above, p. 46. The following paragraphs follow fairly closely Section vi of my article, 'Chaucer and the Rhetoric of Consolation', *MÆ*, 52 (1983), pp. 38-50, esp. pp. 47-9. See p. 39 of that article for exx. of special pleading in Shakespeare (including the one cited here).
11. Text in D.S. Brewer (ed.), *Chaucer: The Critical Heritage* (London, 1978), i, 171. The earliest comment inspired by the passage (together with Chaucer's balade 'Gentilesse') is in the poem by Henry Scogan (probably the addressee of Chaucer's *Envoy*), part of which is reproduced in Brewer, *ibid.*, p. 60. This takes the lecture on 'gentilesse' as a piece of 'straight' moralizing — which it indeed is, if abstracted from its context.
12. See above, Ch. 2, pp. 45-6.
13. Tony Slade, 'Irony in the Wife of Bath's Tale', *MLR*, 64 (1969), pp. 241-7 (esp. p. 245). Reprinted in J.J. Anderson (ed.), *Chaucer: The Canterbury Tales: A Casebook* (London, 1974), pp. 161-71 (esp. p. 168).
14. See Aristotle, *Rhetoric*, I, xv, 3 (trans. E.C. Welldon, London, 1886, p. 106).
15. See below, Ch. 8, p. 173. For a contrary view of the significance of the hag's speech, see D.S. Brewer, 'Towards a Chaucerian Poetic', *PBA*, 60 (1974), pp. 219-52, esp. p. 251. Although I sympathize with the general principle that Brewer there enunciates, I believe that this particular instance is an exception that *probes* the rule — in the spirit in which *WBPT* unsettles other cherished assumptions. However, see n. 11 above.
16. Pandarus works upon Criseyde in a similar manner, as she lies in bed, at *TC*, iii, 750-931.
17. See F.N.M. Diekstra (ed.), *A Dialogue Between Reason and Adversity: A Late Middle English Version of Petrarch's 'De Remediis'* (Assen, 1968).
18. Chaucer could have found the legend in Dante's *Paradiso*, xi. See also *Sacrum Commercium Beati Francisci cum Domina Paupertate*, discussed in E. Auerbach, *Scenes from the Drama of European Literature* (New York, 1959), pp. 79-98.

19. Carleton Brown (ed.), *Religious Lyrics of the XIVth Century*, rev. by G.V. Smithers (Oxford, 1952), No. cvi.

20. See esp. J. Burke Severs, *The Literary Relationships of Chaucer's Clerkes Tale* (New Haven, 1942).

21. These are discussed by Elizabeth Salter, *Chaucer: The Knight's Tale and the Clerk's Tale* (London, 1962), pp. 42 ff.

22. See Robinson (2nd ed.), p. 114.

23. See J. MacQueen, *Robert Henryson: A Study of the Major Narrative Poems* (Oxford, 1967), Ch. 4.

24. Ed. MacEdward Leach, *EETS*, 203.

25. See N. Orme, 'Chaucer and Education', *ChR*, 16 (1981-82), pp. 38-59, esp. p. 42.

26. The ME *Ipomedon A* (ed. E. Kölbing, Breslau, 1889) follows the French original fairly closely. On relations between versions, see Dieter Mehl, *The Middle English Romances of the Thirteenth and Fourteenth Centuries* (London, 1967), pp. 56-68. Two ME versions of *Guy of Warwick* (ed. J. Zupitza, *EETS*, e.s. 42, 49, 59; Cambridge version, e.s. 25, 26) keep fairly close to the original (see Mehl, pp. 220-7). Chaucer mentions 'sir Gy' in *Thopas*, VII, 899.

27. See esp. J. Burke Severs, *op. cit.*, pp. 235-6.

28. See above, p. 33.

29. Used only here by Chaucer. The noun *daf* is used in *ReeveT* (I, 4208) — for its context, see above, p. 78.

30. See above, Ch. 2, pp. 29 ff., and also p. 132.

31. On the importance of *fantasye*, see J.A. Burrow, *Essays in Medieval Literature*, Ch. 3, 'Irony in The Merchant's Tale'.

32. Cf. Parson's Tale, X, 858-60; also 904-5.

33. See above, Ch. 3, p. 59.

34. On the use of biblical language and imagery in Absolon's speech, see R.E. Kaske, 'Patristic Exegesis in the Criticism of Medieval Literature: The Defense' in Dorothy Bethurum (ed.), *Critical Approaches to Medieval Literature* (New York, 1960), pp. 27-60, esp. pp. 52 ff.

35. '. . . an attractive, but hysterical, rather silly woman' — R.B. Burlin, 'The Art of Chaucer's Franklin', in J.J. Anderson (ed.), *Casebook*, pp. 183-208, esp. p. 195. Burlin later slightly modified this assessment of her: 'a . . . human and engaging, if somewhat hysterical and even occasionally silly woman', *Chaucerian Fiction*, p. 200. She is accused of Pride by E.B. Benjamin, 'The concept of order in the *Franklin's Tale*', *PQ*, 38 (1959), pp. 119-24, esp. p. 120.

36. The following paragraphs are based fairly closely upon Section V of my article, 'Chaucer and the Rhetoric of Consolation'.

37. For a discussion of the differences between medieval and modern theories of 'psychology', and of their relevance to the behaviour of Chaucer's characters, see G. Morgan (ed.), *Geoffrey Chaucer: The*

*Franklin's Tale* (London, 1980), esp. pp. 1-4, 9-10, 16-25. But Dr Morgan does not discuss the crucial lines, V, 779-83, or the term 'derke fantasye' (844) — both considered below.

38.  See the article by Benjamin (ref. in n. 35 above). For further discussion of her first 'compleynte', see G. Joseph, *The Franklin's Tale*: Chaucer's Theodicy', *ChR*, I (1966), pp. 20-32; W.B. Bachman, 'To maken illusioun: the philosophy of magic and the magic of philosophy in the Franklin's Tale', *ChR*, 12 (1977), pp. 55-67. R.B. Burlin thinks this complaint 'a piece of metaphysical foolishness', *Chaucerian Fiction*, p. 205.

39.  See G. Leff, *Bradwardine and the Pelagians* (Cambridge, 1957), pp. 54-5. For a different account of Bradwardine's theology, see H.A. Oberman, *Archbishop Thomas Bradwardine: A Fourteenth Century Augustinian* (Utrecht, 1957).

40.  Bradwardine, *De Causa Dei Contra Pelagium*, ed. by Lord Henry Savile (London, 1618), p. 296. Cf. Leff, *op. cit.*, p. 60.

41.  *De Causa Dei*, p. 295.

42.  *Essay on Man*, i, 291.

43.  As demonstrated by Leff, *op. cit.*, pp. 57 ff.

44.  Some recent commentators, however, have questioned the view that Nominalist philosophy is sceptical and its theology fideistic. See the discussion of Holcot by H.A. Oberman, *The Harvest of Medieval Theology: Gabriel Biel and Late Medieval Nominalism* (Cambridge, Mass., 1963), pp. 242-8.

45.  *Chaucer and his Poetry* (Cambridge, Mass., 1915), pp. 207-11.

46.  Most notably D.W. Robertson, Jr., *A Preface to Chaucer* (Princeton, 1962), pp. 470-72; and see above Ch. 1, p. 13, and n. 51. See also section on 'Marriage' in A.C. Spearing (ed.), *The Franklin's Prologue and Tale* (Cambridge, 1966), pp. 26-32.

47.  On *FrankT* as a 'Breton lai', see above, Ch. 2, p. 49.

48.  English readers are most likely to know these stories in the 15th-century versions by Malory, [*Works*, ed. E. Vinaver; London, O.U.P., 1954], whose account of Lancelot and Guinevere is unforgettable. But his narrative of Tristan is surpassed by the 13th-century German version by Gottfried von Strassburg (English trans. by A.T. Hatto — together with trans. of the even earlier French version by Thomas — Harmondsworth, 1960). The nature of *fine amor* in the Tristan story is complicated by the motif of the love potion. Chaucer includes 'Tristram' and 'Isaude' in a catalogue of doomed lovers at *PoF*, 290; and see below, n. 49. He mentions Lancelot in *SqT*, V, 287 (see above, Ch. 2, p. 50) and *NPT*, VII, 3212.

49.  Cf. Chaucer's facetious remark in 'To Rosemounde', line 20.

50.  Cf. e.g. *Piers Plowman*, Prol. 93 (ed. Schmidt, p. 4); xv, 31 (ed. Schmidt, p. 176); also the lyric attrib. William of Shoreham, No. 32 in Carleton Brown (ed.), rev. G.V. Smithers, *Religious Lyrics of*

*the XIVth Century* (Oxford, 1952), line 22 (with reference to the devil's legal claim on fallen man). Numerous other exx. cited by *MED* under *chalenge* v. sense 4; and cf. *chalenge* n. sense 4.

## Notes to Chapter 7

1. On 'affective' devotion, see Douglas Gray, *Themes and Images in the Medieval English Religious Lyric* (London, 1972), pp. 18 ff.
2. Cf. the rubric in Hengwrt MS.: 'Here beginneth the Prioresse Tale of Alma Redemptoris Mater' (N.F. Blake, *ed. cit.*, p. 474).
3. See Florence H. Ridley, *The Prioress and the Critics* (University of California, Berkeley, 1965).
4. The phrase comes from Mirk's *Festial*: see I. Bishop, *Pearl in its Setting*, pp. 109 and 116.
5. See Marie P. Hamilton, 'Echoes of Childermas in the Tale of the Prioress', in E. Wagenknecht (ed.), *Chaucer: Modern Essays in Criticism* (New York, 1959), pp. 88-97. Also *Pearl in its Setting*, Ch. 7.
6. On medieval education of girls of good family, see N. Orme, 'Chaucer and Education', *ChR*, 16 (1981-82), pp. 38-59, esp. p. 45; and above, Ch. 2, n. 50, for Orme's paper, 'The Education of the Courtier' in Scattergood and Sherborne.
7. On the responsibilities of baptismal sponsors, see *Piers Plowman*, B, ix, 75-79 (ed. Schmidt, p. 94). For an example of a treacherous 'maister' who had charge of the education of a royal minor, see the legend of St Kenelm, discussed below, p. 156.
8. See above, pp. 45 & 48, and I. Bishop, '*Solacia* in *Pearl* and in Letters of Edward III Concerning the Death of his Daughter, Joan', *N&Q*, 229 (December 1984), pp. 454-6.
9. See above, Ch. 3, pp. 63-4.
10. For similar characterization of Nature in *PoF*, see above, Ch. 2, p. 31.
11. Ch. 3, pp. 63-4.
12. *Roman de la Rose*, lines 12541-14546.
13. See Robinson's note on VI, 117.
14. As noted by C.S. Lewis, *The Discarded Image*, p. 195.
15. *Roman de la Rose*, lines 5589-794.
16. For a somewhat different explanation of the tale's failure, see Sheila Delany, 'Politics and the Paralysis of Poetic Imagination in The Physician's Tale', *SAC*, 3 (1981), pp. 47-60. Also N. Coghill, 'Chaucer's Narrative Art' in D.S. Brewer (ed.), *Chaucer and Chaucerians* (London and Edinburgh, 1966), pp. 126-8.
17. Cf. *Piers Plowman*, B, x, 307-8 (ed. Schmidt, p. 111).

18. The best ed. of this particular legend is in J.A.W. Bennett and G.V. Smithers (edd.), *Early Middle English Verse and Prose* (Oxford, 1968), pp. 96-107.
19. *Ibid.*, p. 101, line 104.
20. For a well-informed and well-balanced discussion of this controversial matter, see A.B. Friedman, 'The Prioress's Tale and Chaucer's Anti-Semitism', *ChR*, 9 (1974), pp. 118-29 — in addition to Ridley (see n. 3 above).
21. See N. Cohn, *The Pursuit of the Millennium* (London, 1957), esp. p. 72.
22. Cf. the lyric attrib. William of Shoreham, No. 32 (lines 53-4), in Carleton Brown (ed.), rev. G.V. Smithers, *Religious Lyrics of the XIVth Century* (Oxford, 1952).

# Notes to Chapter 8

1. See above, Ch. 4, p. 80.
2. E.g. J. Speirs, *Chaucer the Maker* (London, 1951), p. 189: 'the poem develops as a tragi-comic allegory of the Fall ...' Also D. Holbrook in B. Ford (ed.), *The New Pelican Guide to English Literature*, Vol. 1, Pt. 1: *Chaucer and the Alliterative Tradition* (Harmondsworth, 1982), pp. 163-73, esp. pp. 167-8: 'Chauntecleer is Adam ...'.
3. E.T. Donaldson, *Speaking of Chaucer*, p. 150. See also Jill Mann, 'The *Speculum Stultorum* and The Nun's Priest's Tale', *ChR*, 9 (1974), pp. 262-82.
4. For a survey of critical opinion of this tale, see *Variorum* ed., Vol. 2, Pt. 10, *MancT*, ed. D.C. Baker (Norman, Oklahoma, 1984), pp. 19-38.
5. For a shrewd and comprehensive summary of critical comment on this tale, see *Variorum* ed., Vol. 2, Pt. 9, *NPT*, ed. D. Pearsall (Norman, Oklahoma, 1984), pp. 30-82.
6. N. Coghill, *The Poet Chaucer* (London, 1949), p. 156.
7. T. Whittock, *A Reading of the Canterbury Tales* (Cambridge, 1968), p. 285.
8. For some interesting suggestions about the type of tale Chaucer intended it to be, see V.J. Scattergood, 'Perkyn Revelour and the Cook's Tale', *ChR*, 19 (1984), pp. 14-23.
9. V.J. Scattergood, 'The Manciple's Manner of Speaking', *EC*, 24 (1974), pp. 124-46.
10. For a judicious summary of discussions concerning the narrator of *NPT*, see Pearsall, *ed. cit.* (see above, n. 5), pp. 32-42.
11. See above, Ch. 2, p. 27.
12. Cf. *Piers Plowman*, B. Prol., 193-4 (ed. Schmidt, p. 8).

13. The following pages are based closely upon my article, 'The Nun's Priest's Tale and the Liberal Arts', *RES*, n.s. 30 (1979), pp. 257-67.

14. For a critical summary of 'interpretations' of this tale, see *Variorum* ed., Vol. 2, Pt. 9, *NPT*, ed. D. Pearsall (Norman, Oklahoma, 1984), pp. 50-64.

15. Cf. H. Davis, *The Satire of Jonathan Swift* (New York, 1947), p. 32.

16. *Gemma Animae*, I, cxliv, *PL*, 172, col. 589.

17. On the Liberal Arts, see E.R. Curtius, *European Literature &c.*, pp. 36 ff.; C.S. Lewis, *The Discarded Image*, pp. 185-97.

18. On levels of style, see A.J. Gilbert, *Literary Language from Chaucer to Johnson*, esp. Introduction and Ch. 1.

19. On medieval organs in England, see C. Clutton and A. Niland, *The British Organ* (London, 1963), pp. 45 ff. Also E.J. Hopkins, *The English Medieval Church Organ* (Exeter, 1888). On early organs in general, see J. Perrot (trans. N. Deane), *The Organ* (London, 1971); he discusses the three types of organ mentioned here in his Ch. 14 and cf. pp. 277, 285-6.

20. See Clutton and Niland, *op. cit.*, p. 47.

21. On the Wells clock, see C.F.C. Beeson, *English Church Clocks* (London and Chichester, 1971); p. 22 for its date; p. 48 for description of its original movement; p. 112 for description of its jacks and automata. See p. 46 for Salisbury clock of 1386. This is supposed to be the earliest clock with its original movement (partly replaced) still working. It is currently displayed in the cathedral's N nave aisle. Another early clock (1485-89) still in working order (and in its original position) may be seen in the chapel of Cotehele Manor, Cornwall. (A visit to Cotehele will immediately transport the reader back into the physical environment of *The Canterbury Tales* — especially that of the Miller's and Reeve's tales. Not only does the Manor retain its dovecote and medieval barn, but also its [later] water-mill [still in working order] in a group with a blacksmith's forge, wheelwright's and carpenter's shop.)

22. Cf. V, 189-90 — of the crowd in the *SqT* who are astonished by the magic horse.

23. See C. Cipolla, *Clocks and Culture* (London, 1967), p. 43.

24. On this distinction, see above, Ch. 1, n. 12.

25. See Beryl Smalley, *English Friars and Antiquity in the Early Fourteenth Century* (Oxford, 1960); J.B. Allen, *The Friar as Critic* (Nashville, 1971).

26. For classical and medieval accounts of the relationship between allegory and irony, see I. Bishop, *Pearl in its Setting*, pp. 62-5.

27. E.g. B.F. Huppé and D.W. Robertson, Jr., *Fruyt and Chaf: Studies in Chaucer's Allegories* (London, 1963). And see review in *MÆ*, 32, pp. 238-42, for criticism of their methods.

28. For Latin text, see Edmond Faral, *Les Arts Poétiques du XII^e et du*

*XIII<sup>e</sup> Siècles* (Paris, 1924). An English trans. is included in *Three Medieval Rhetorical Arts*, ed. J.J. Murphy (Berkeley, Los Angeles, London, 1971).

29. The largest medieval encyclopaedia was the thirteenth-century *Speculum Maius* (Great Mirror) by Vincent of Beauvais.

30. See F.N. Robinson, *Chaucer's Works*, 2nd ed., p. 690, for discussion of this possibility; also R. Hazelton, 'The Manciple's Tale: Parody and Critique', *JEGP*, 62 (1963), pp. 1-31.

31. *Complete Works*, ed. G.C. Macaulay (Oxford, 1899-1902), Vol. IV: 'Some of them bray in the beastly manner of asses, some bellow the lowings of oxen. Some give out horrible swinish grunts, and the earth trembles from their rumbling.' Trans. by E.W. Stockton, *The Major Latin Works of John Gower* (Seattle, 1962) pp. 67-8.

32. See I. Bishop, *Pearl in its Setting*, p. 41, and esp. n. 2 (on p. 137), for discussion of *NPT* in relation to medieval debates.

33. See M. Hamm, 'Heigh Ymaginacioun', *MLN*, 69 (1954), pp. 394-5; R.A. Pratt, 'Some Latin Sources of the Nonnes Preest on Dreams', *Speculum*, 52 (1977), pp. 538-70, esp. pp. 564 ff. Pratt notes an alternative explanation of the phrase by Norman Davis and suggests that the term is ambivalent.

34. See I. Bishop, *Pearl in its Setting*, pp. 62-6.

35. See I. Bishop, *Chaucer's Troilus and Criseyde*, pp. 81-9.

36. I.e. the allusion to 'Daun Burnel the Asse' (3312 ff.). It is misleading because the fox employs it in order to urge Chauntecleer to crow, but omits to mention that the point of Nigel of Longchamp's anecdote is that the wise cock displayed his 'subtiltee' by refraining from crowing.

37. See W. A. Pantin, *The English Church in the Fourteenth Century* (Cambridge, 1955), Chs 9 & 10.

# List of Works Cited

This list is not a complete bibliography of the subject; it is confined to works cited in the notes. It is arranged as follows:

## I. PRIMARY SOURCES (EDITIONS AND TRANSLATIONS)
   A. Chaucer's Works.
   B. Other Authors and Texts.

## II. SECONDARY SOURCES
   A. Studies of Chaucer and his Works.
   B. Other Literary and Historical Studies.
(Anthologies and collections of texts are included in Section II under the editors' names.)

## I. PRIMARY SOURCES (EDITIONS AND TRANSLATIONS)
## A. *Chaucer's Works*
(i)  Editions of Complete Works

Skeat, W.W. (ed.), *The Works of Geoffrey Chaucer*, 6 vols. (Oxford, 1894-1900).

Robinson, F.N. (ed.), *The Complete Works of Geoffrey Chaucer* (2nd ed., London, 1957).
   [A third edition is scheduled for publication shortly: L.D. Benson (general editor), *The Riverside Chaucer* (Based on *The Works of Geoffrey Chaucer*, ed. by F.N. Robinson) (Houghton Mifflin, Boston, 1987).]

Ruggiers, P.G. (General Editor), *A Variorum Edition of the Works of Geoffrey Chaucer* (Norman, Oklahoma, 1982—). See under (iii), below, for details.

(ii)  Complete Editions of *The Canterbury Tales*

Manly, J.M. (ed.), *The Canterbury Tales* (New York, 1928).

Manly, J.M. and Rickert, Edith (edd.), *The Text of The Canterbury Tales*, 8 vols. (Chicago, 1940).

Cawley, A.C. (ed.), *Geoffrey Chaucer: Canterbury Tales* (Everyman's Library, London, 1958). [A convenient glossed edition (but without detailed notes or apparatus), using Robinson's text.]

Pratt, R.A. (ed.), *Chaucer's Tales of Canterbury* (Boston, 1974).

Ruggiers, P.G. (ed.), *The Canterbury Tales: A Facsimile and Transcription of the Hengwrt Manuscript* (Norman, Oklahoma, 1979).

Blake, N.F. (ed.), *The Canterbury Tales of Geoffrey Chaucer edited from the Hengwrt Manuscript* (London, 1980).

Verse Translation:

Coghill, N., *Geoffrey Chaucer: The Canterbury Tales Translated into Modern English* (Harmondsworth, 1951).

(iii)  Editions of Separate Tales

Spearing, A.C. (ed.), *The Franklin's Prologue and Tale* (Cambridge, 1966).

Morgan, G. (ed.), *Geoffrey Chaucer: The Franklin's Prologue and Tale* (London, 1980).

Schmidt, A.V.C. (ed.), *The General Prologue to the Canterbury Tales and the Canon's Yeoman's Prologue and Tale* (London, 1974).

Baker, D.C. (ed.), *The Manciple's Tale: A Variorum Edition of the Works of Geoffrey Chaucer*, Vol. 2, Pt. 10 (Norman, Oklahoma, 1984).

Ross, T.W. (ed.), *The Miller's Tale: Variorum Ed.*, Vol. 2, Pt. 3 (Norman, Oklahoma, 1983).

Pearsall, D.A. (ed.), *The Nun's Priest's Tale: Variorum Ed.*, Vol. 2, Pt. 9 (Norman, Oklahoma, 1984).

Brown, Carleton (ed.), *Chaucer; The Pardoner's Tale* (Oxford, 1935).

(iv)  Other Works

Brewer, D.S. (ed.), *Geoffrey Chaucer: The Parlement of Foulys* (London and Edinburgh, 1960).

## B.  *Other Authors and Texts*

Alain de Lille, *De Planctu Naturae* [in T. Wright (ed.), *Anglo-Latin Satirical Poets of the Twelfth Century*, ii; London, 1872].

—— trans. D.M. Moffat, Yale Studies in English, No. 36 (1908, repr. Hamden, Connecticut, 1972).

*Amis and Amiloun*, ed. MacEdward Leach, EETS, 203.

*Ancrene Riwle: The English Text of the Ancrene Riwle*, ed. from Cotton MS. Nero A. XIV by Mabel Day, EETS, 225.

—— trans. by Mary B. Salu (London, 1955).

Aristotle, *Rhetoric*, trans. E.C. Welldon (London, 1886).

*Artes Poeticae*. See Section II B below, *under* Faral and *under* Murphy, *Three Medieval Rhetorical Arts*.

Augustine, St, *On Christian Doctrine [De Doctrina Christiana]*, trans. D.W. Robertson, Jr. (New York, 1958).

Bradwardine, Archbishop Thomas, *De Causa Dei Contra Pelagium*, ed. Lord Henry Savile (London, 1618).

Capella [see under Martianus Capella, below].

Chrétien de Troyes, *Le Chevalier de la Charette [Lancelot]*, ed. M. Roques, *CFMA* (1958).

—— *Arthurian Romances*, trans. with introd. and notes by D.D.R. Owen (Everyman's Library, London, 1987).

[Cicero], *Rhetorica ad Herennium*, text ed. with trans. by H. Caplan (Loeb Classical Library; London, 1954, repr. 1964).

*The Cloud of Unknowing and The Book of Privy Counselling*, ed. Phyllis Hodgson, EETS, 218.

*The Dance of Death*, ed. F. Warren, EETS, 181.

*A Dialogue Between Reason and Adversity: A Late Middle English Version of Petrarch's 'De Remediis'*, ed. F.N.M. Diekstra (Assen, 1968).

Fletcher, J. and Shakespeare, W., *The Two Noble Kinsmen*, ed. G.R. Proudfoot (London and Nebraska, 1970).

Gottfried von Strassburg, *Tristan, with surviving fragments of the Tristan of Thomas*, trans. A.T. Hatto (Harmondsworth, 1960).

Gower, John, *Complete Works*, ed. G.C. Macaulay (London, 1899-1902), 4 vols. (Vol. 4, *Latin Works*).

—— *English Works*, ed. G.C. Macaulay, *EETS*, e.s. 81, 82.

—— *The Major Latin Works of John Gower*, trans. E.W. Stockton (Seattle, 1962).

Guillaume de Lorris and Jean de Meun, *Le Roman de la Rose*, ed. Félix Lecoy, 3 vols., CFMA, 92, 95, 98 (Paris, 1965-70).

—— Trans. into Modern English by Harry W. Robbins, ed. C.W. Dunn (New York, 1962).

*Guy of Warwick*, ed. J. Zupitza, *EETS*, e.s. 42, 49, 59; Cambridge version, *EETS*, e.s. 25, 26.

*The Harley Lyrics*, ed. G.L. Brook (Manchester, 1948).

Honorius ('of Autun'), *Opera*, *PL*, 172.

*Ipomedon*, ed. E. Kölbing (Breslau, 1889).

Jean de Meun [see under Guillaume de Lorris].

Kempe: *The Book of Margery Kempe*, ed. by Hope Emily Allen and S.B. Meech, *EETS*, 212.

Langland, William, *The Vision of Piers Plowman: A Complete Edition of the B-Text*, ed. A.V.C. Schmidt (Everyman's Library, London, 1978).

—— *Piers Plowman by William Langland: An Edition of the C-Text*, ed. by D.A. Pearsall (London, 1978).

—— *The Vision of William Concerning Piers the Plowman In Three Parallel Texts Together with Richard The Redeless*, ed. W.W. Skeat, 2 vols. (London, 1886).

*Libaeus Desconus*, ed. M. Mills, *EETS*, 261.

Malory: *The Works of Sir Thomas Malory*, ed. E. Vinaver (Oxford Standard Authors, London, 1954).

Marie de France, *Lais*, ed. A. Ewert (Oxford, 1947).

—— *Lays of Marie de France and Others*, trans. E. Mason (Everyman's Library, London, 1911).

Marlowe, Christopher, *Marlowe's Poems*, ed. L.C. Martin (London, 1931).

Martianus Capella, *De Nuptiis Philologiae et Mercurii*, ed. F. Eyssenhardt (Lipsiae, 1866), trans. by W.H. Stahl *et al.* (New York, 1971-7).

*The Owl and The Nightingale*, ed. E.G. Stanley (London and Edinburgh, 1960).

*Pearl*, ed. E.V. Gordon (Oxford, 1953).

—— *Pearl, Patience, Cleanness, Sir Gawain and the Green Knight*, ed.

A.C. Cawley and J.J. Anderson (Everyman's Library, London, 1976).

*Piers Plowman* [see under Langland, William]

*Rhetorica ad Herennium* (see under [Cicero])

*Saint Kenelm* (from *South English Legendary*), included in Bennett and Smithers [see below, Section II (B), under Bennett]

*Seinte Marherete*, ed. F.M. Mack, *EETS*, 193.

Shakespeare, W. [see Fletcher, John].

*Sir Launfal*, ed. A.J. Bliss (London and Edinburgh, 1960).

*Sir Orfeo*, ed. A.J. Bliss (Oxford, 1954).

*Sir Gawain and the Green Knight*, ed. J.R.R. Tolkien and E.V. Gordon, revised N. Davis (Oxford, 1967).

—— *Pearl, Patience, Cleanness, Sir Gawain and the Green Knight*, ed. A.C. Cawley and J.J. Anderson (Everyman's Library, London, 1976).

Thomas of Hales, *A Luve-Ron*, text in Dickins and Wilson, also in Carleton Brown (ed.), *English Lyrics of the XIIIth Century* [see below, Section II (B) under Dickins, and Brown, respectively].

*Winner and Waster*, ed. Sir I. Gollancz (London, 1930).


## II. Secondary Sources
### A. Studies of Chaucer and his Works

Allen, J.B. and Moritz, T.A., *A Distinction of Stories: The Medieval Unity of Chaucer's Fair Chain of Narratives for Canterbury* (Columbus, Ohio, 1981).

Anderson, J.J. (ed.), *Chaucer: The Canterbury Tales: A Casebook* (London, 1974).

Anderson, T.M. (ed.) [see Benson, L.D., below]

Bachman, W.B., 'To maken illusioun: the philosophy of magic and the magic of philosophy in the Franklin's Tale', *ChR*, 12 (1977), pp. 55-67.

Baldwin, R., *The Unity of The Canterbury Tales*, Anglistica, 5 (Copenhagen, 1955).

Beichner, P.E., 'Characterization in *The Miller's Tale*', in Schoeck and Taylor, *Chaucer Criticism* [q.v., below].

Benjamin, E.B., 'The Concept of Order in the Franklin's Tale', *PQ*, 38 (1959), pp. 119-24.

Bennett, J.A.W., *The Parlement of Foules: An Interpretation* (Oxford, 1957).

—— *Chaucer at Oxford and at Cambridge* (Oxford, 1974).

—— 'Some Second Thoughts on *The Parlement of Foules*', in Vasta and Thundy [see under Vasta, below].

—— 'Chaucer, Dante and Boccaccio' in Boitani, *Chaucer and the Italian Trecento* [q.v., below].

Benson, L.D., 'The Order of The Canterbury Tales', *SAC*, 3 (1981), pp. 77-120.

—— [and Anderson, T.M. (edd.)], *The Literary Context of Chaucer's Fabliaux: Texts and Translations* (Indianapolis, 1971).

Bishop, I., 'The Narrative Art of *The Pardoner's Tale*', *MÆ*, 36 (1967), pp. 15-24 (repr. in J.J. Anderson [ed.], *Chaucer . . . Casebook* [q.v., above]).

—— 'The Nun's Priest's Tale and the Liberal Arts', *RES*, n.s. 30 (1979), pp. 257-67.

—— *Chaucer's Troilus and Criseyde: A Critical Study* (Bristol University Press, Bristol, 1981).

—— '*Troilus and Criseyde* and *The Knight's Tale*' in B. Ford (ed.), *Chaucer and the Alliterative Tradition* [q.v., below].

—— 'Chaucer and the Rhetoric of Consolation', *MÆ*, 52 (1983), pp. 38-50.

Blake, N.F., *The Textual Tradition of The Canterbury Tales* (London, 1985).

Boitani, P., '*The Monk's Tale*: Dante and Boccaccio', *MÆ*, 45 (1976), pp. 50-69.

—— *Chaucer and Boccaccio* (Oxford, 1977).

—— (ed.), *Chaucer and the Italian Trecento* (Cambridge, 1983).

Bornstein, Diane, 'Chaucer's *Tale of Melibee* as an Example of *Style Clergial* ', *ChR*, 12 (1977-78), pp. 236-54.

Brewer, D.S. (ed.), *Chaucer and Chaucerians* (London and Edinburgh, 1966).

—— 'Towards a Chaucerian Poetic', *PBA*, 60 (1974), pp. 219-52.

—— (ed.), *Chaucer: The Critical Heritage*, 2 vols. (London, 1978).

Brooks, H.F., *Chaucer's Pilgrims: the Artistic Order of the Portraits in the Prologue* (London, 1962).

Brown, P., 'Is "The Canon's Yeoman's Tale" Apocryphal?', *ES*, 64 (1983), pp. 481-90.

Burrow, J.A. [see under Section II (B)]. There are chapters on the Knight's Tale, the Merchant's Tale, and Sir Thopas, in his *Essays on Medieval Literature*.

Bryan, W.F. and Dempster, G. (edd.), *Sources and Analogues of Chaucer's Canterbury Tales* (London, 1941).

Burke, J.J. (ed.) [see under Hermann, J.P., below].

Burlin, R.B., 'The Art of Chaucer's Franklin', *Neophilologus*, 51 (1967), repr. (with author's revisions) in Anderson, J.J., *Chaucer . . . Casebook* [q.v., above].

—— *Chaucerian Fiction* (Princeton, 1977).

Coghill, N., *The Poet Chaucer* (London, 1949).

—— 'Chaucer's Narrative Art in *The Canterbury Tales*', in Brewer (ed.), *Chaucer and Chaucerians* [q.v., above].

Cooper, Helen, *The Structure of The Canterbury Tales* (London, 1983).

Copland, M., '*The Reeve's Tale*: Harlotrie or Sermonyng?', *MÆ*, 31 (1962), pp. 14-32.

Craik, T.W., *The Comic Tales of Chaucer* (London, 1964).

Crow, M.M. [and Olson, C.C.] (edd.), *Chaucer Life-Records* (Oxford, 1966).

David, A., *The Strumpet Muse* (Bloomington and London, 1976).

Delany, Sheila, 'Politics and the Paralysis of Poetic Imagination in The Physician's Tale', *SAC*, 3 (1981), pp. 47-60.

Dempster, Germaine, *Dramatic Irony in Chaucer* (1932, repr. New York, 1959).

—— [and see under Bryan, W.F., above].

Donaldson, E.T., *Speaking of Chaucer* (London, 1970).

Eisner, S., *A Tale of Wonder: A Source Study of the Wife of Bath's Tale* (Wexford, 1957).

Elliott, R.W.W., *Chaucer's English* (London, 1974).

Faulkner, D.R. (ed.), *Twentieth Century Interpretations of the Pardoner's Tale* (Englewood Cliffs, N.J., 1973).

Ford, B. (ed.), *The New Pelican Guide to English Literature*, Vol. 1: *Medieval Literature*: Pt. 1; *Chaucer and the Alliterative Tradition* (Harmondsworth, 1982).

Friedman, A.B., 'The Prioress's Tale and Chaucer's Anti-Semitism', *ChR*, 9 (1974), pp. 118-29.

Gibson, Gail M., 'Resurrection as Dramatic Icon in the Shipman's Tale' in Hermann and Burke (edd.), *Signs and Symbols* [q.v., below, under Hermann].

Godman, P., 'Chaucer and Boccaccio's Latin Works' in Boitani (ed.), *Chaucer and the Italian Trecento* [q.v., above].

Goodman, Jennifer R., 'Chaucer's *Squire's Tale* and the Rise of Chivalry', *SAC*, 5 (1983), pp. 127-36.

Greenfield, S.B., 'Sittingbourne and the Order of the Canterbury Tales', *MLR*, 48 (1953), pp. 51-2.

Grennen, J.E., 'Saint Cecilia's Chemical Wedding: the Unity of the Canterbury Tales, Fragment VIII', *JEGP*, 65 (1966), pp. 466-81.

Haines, R.M., 'Fortune, Nature and Grace in Fragment C', *ChR*, 10 (1975-76), pp. 220-35.

Hamilton, Marie P., 'Echoes of Childermas in the Tale of the Prioress', in Wagenknecht (ed.), *Chaucer* . . . [q.v., below].

Hamm, M., 'Heigh Ymaginacioun', *MLN*, 69 (1954), pp. 394-5.

Hartung, A.E., 'The "Pars Secunda" and the Development of *The Canon's Yeoman's Tale*', *ChR*, 12 (1977-78), pp. 111-28.

Haveley, N., *Chaucer's Boccaccio* (Woodbridge and Totowa, N.J., 1980).

Hazelton, R., '*The Manciple's Tale*: Parody and Critique', *JEGP*, 62 (1963), pp. 1-31.

Hermann, J.P. and Burke, Jr., J.J. (edd.), *Signs and Symbols in Chaucer's Poetry* (University of Alabama Press, 1981).

Holbrook, D., 'The Nun's Priest's Tale' in B. Ford (ed.), *Chaucer and the Alliterative Tradition* [q.v. above].

Howard, D.R., *The Idea of The Canterbury Tales* (Berkeley, 1976).

Huppé, B.F. [see Robertson, D.W., below].

Jones, Terry, *Chaucer's Knight: The Portrait of a Medieval Mercenary* (London, 1980).

Jordan, R.M., *Chaucer and the Shape of Creation* (Cambridge, Mass., 1967).

Joseph, G., 'The Franklin's Tale: Chaucer's Theodicy', *ChR*, 1 (1966), pp. 20-32.

Keen, Maurice, 'Chaucer's Knight, the English Aristocracy and the Crusades' in Scattergood and Sherborne (edd.), *English Court Culture* . . . [q.v., below, Section II (B)].

Kiernan, K.S., 'The Art of the Descending Catalogue, and a Fresh Look at Alisoun', *ChR*, 10 (1975-76), pp. 1-16.

Kittredge, G.L., 'Chaucer's Discussion of Marriage', *MP*, 9 (1911-12), pp. 435-67. [Repr. in Anderson (ed.), *Chaucer . . . Casebook* (q.v., above) and Schoeck and Taylor (edd.), *Chaucer Criticism* . . . (q.v., below)].

—— *Chaucer and His Poetry* (Cambridge, Mass., 1915).

Kökeritz, Helge, *A Guide to Chaucer's Pronunciation* (Stockholm and New Haven, 1954).

Kolve, V.A., 'From Cleopatra to Alceste: An Iconographic Study of *The Legend of Good Women*' in Hermann and Burke (edd.), *Signs and Symbols* . . . [q.v., above, under Hermann].

—— *Chaucer and the Imagery of Narrative: The First Five Canterbury Tales* (London, 1984).

Lepley, D.L., 'The Monk's Boethian Tale', *ChR*, 12 (1977-78), pp. 162-70.

Loomis, Laura H., 'The Tale of Sir Thopas' in Bryan and Dempster (edd.), *Sources and Analogues* . . . [q.v., above, under Bryan, W.F.].

Lumiansky, R.M., *Of Sondry Folk: The Dramatic Principle in The Canterbury Tales* (Austin, Texas, 1955).

Lynn, Karen, 'Chaucer's Decasyllabic Line and the Myth of the Hundred Year Hibernation', *ChR*, 13 (1978-79), pp. 16-27.

Mann, Jill, *Chaucer and Medieval Estates Satire: The Literature of Social Classes in the General Prologue to the Canterbury Tales* (Cambridge, 1973).

—— 'The *Speculum Stultorum* and the Nun's Priest's Tale', *ChR*, 9 (1974), pp. 262-82.

Minnis, A.J., *Chaucer and Pagan Antiquity* (Woodbridge, 1982).

Moritz, T.A. [see Allen, J.B., above].

Muscatine, C., *Chaucer and the French Tradition* (Berkeley and Los Angeles, 1957).

Norton-Smith, J., *Geoffrey Chaucer* (London, 1974).

Olson, Clair C. [see Crow, M.M., above].

Orme, N., 'Chaucer and Education', *ChR*, 16 (1981-82), pp. 38-59.

Owen, C.A., Jr., *Pilgrimage and Storytelling in the Canterbury Tales: the Dialectic of 'ernest' and 'game'* (Norman, Oklahoma, 1977).

Owen, W.J.B., 'The Old Man in The Pardoner's Tale', *RES* n.s. 2 (1951), pp. 49-55.

Payne, R.O., *The Key of Remembrance: A Study of Chaucer's Poetics* (New Haven and London, 1963).

Pearsall, D.A., 'Chaucer's Pardoner: The Death of a Salesman', *ChR*, 17 (1983), pp. 357-65.

—— *The Canterbury Tales* (London, 1985).

Pratt, R.A., 'Some Latin Sources of the Nonnes Preest on Dreams', *Speculum*, 52 (1977), pp. 538-70.

—— [and Young, K.], 'The Framework of the *Canterbury Tales*' in Bryan and Dempster, *Sources and Analogues* ... [see above, under Bryan, W.F.].

Richardson, Janette, *'Blameth Nat Me': A Study of Imagery in Chaucer's Fabliaux* (The Hague, Paris, 1970).

Ridley, Florence H., *The Prioress and the Critics* (University of California, Berkeley, 1962).

Robertson, D.W., Jr., *A Preface to Chaucer* (Princeton, 1962).

—— (and Huppé, B.F.), *Fruyt and Chaf: Studies in Chaucer's Allegories* (London, 1963).

Robinson, I., *Chaucer's Prosody: A Study of the Middle English Verse Tradition* (Cambridge, 1971).

Rosenberg, B.A., 'The Contrary Tales of the Second Nun and the Canon's Yeoman', *ChR*, 2 (1968), pp. 278-91.

Ruggiers, P., *The Art of the Canterbury Tales* (Madison, Wisc., 1965).

Salter, Elizabeth, *Chaucer: The Knight's Tale and the Clerk's Tale* (London, 1962).

Scattergood, V.J., 'The Manciple's Manner of Speaking', *EC*, 24 (1974), pp. 124-46.

—— 'The Originality of The Shipman's Tale', *ChR*, 11 (1976-77), pp. 210-31.

—— 'Perkyn Revelour and the *Cook's Tale*', *ChR*, 19 (1984), pp. 14-23.

Schlauch, Margaret, 'The Art of Chaucer's Prose' in Brewer (ed.), *Chaucer and Chaucerians* [q.v., above].

Schoeck, R. and Taylor, J. (edd.), *Chaucer Criticism: The Canterbury Tales* (Notre Dame, Indiana, 1960).

Sedgewick, G.G., 'The Progress of Chaucer's Pardoner, 1880-1940', *MLQ*, 1 (1940), pp. 431-58. (Repr. in Schoeck and Taylor [see above] and in Wagenknecht [see below].

Severs, J. Burke, *The Literary Relationships of Chaucer's Clerkes Tale* (New Haven, 1942).

Slade, Tony, 'Irony in the Wife of Bath's Tale', *MLR*, 64 (1969), pp. 241-7. (Repr. in Anderson, *Chaucer ... Casebook* [q.v., above]).

Southworth, J.G., *Verses of Cadence, An Introduction to the Prosody of Chaucer and his Followers* (Oxford, 1954).

—— *The Prosody of Chaucer and his Followers, Supplementary Chapters to Verses of Cadence* (Oxford, 1962).

Speirs, J., *Chaucer the Maker* (London, 1951).

Steadman, J.M., 'Old Age and *Contemptus Mundi* in the Pardoner's Tale', *MÆ*, 33 (1964), pp. 121-30. (Repr. in Faulkner [q.v., above]).

—— *Disembodied Laughter* (Berkeley, Los Angeles, London, 1972).

Szittya, Penn R., 'The Green Yeoman as Loathly Lady: the Friar's Parody of the Wife of Bath's Tale', *PMLA*, 90 (1975), pp. 386-94.

Taylor, J. [see Schoeck, R., above].

Thompson, Ann, *Shakespeare's Chaucer* (Liverpool, 1978).

Thundy, Z.P. [see Vasta, below].

Tolkien, J.R.R., 'Chaucer as Philologist: *The Reeve's Tale*', *Transactions of the Philological Society* (London, 1934).

Tucker, Susie I., 'Sir Thopas and the Wild Beasts', *RES* n.s. 10 (1959), pp. 54-6.

Vasta, E. (and Thundy, Z.P.), (edd.), *Chaucerian Problems and Perspectives: Essays Presented to Paul E. Beichner* (Notre Dame, Indiana and London, 1979).

Wagenknecht, E. (ed.), *Chaucer: Modern Essays in Criticism* (New York, 1959).

Whittock, T., *A Reading of the Canterbury Tales* (Cambridge, 1968).

Young, K. [see Pratt, R.A. (joint article in Bryan and Dempster, *Sources and Analogues . . .* )]

## B. *Other Literary and Historical Studies*

Allen, J.B., *The Friar as Critic* (Nashville, 1971).

Auerbach, E., *Scenes from the Drama of European Literature* (New York, 1959).

Baldwin, J.W., *Masters, Princes and Merchants: The Social Views of Peter the Chanter and his Circle*, 2 vols. (Princeton, N.J., 1970).

Beeson, C.F.C., *English Church Clocks* (London and Chichester, 1971).

Bennett, J.A.W. [and Smithers, G.V.], (edd.), *Early Middle English Verse and Prose* (Oxford, 1968).

Bethurum, Dorothy (ed.), *Critical Approaches to Medieval Literature* (New York, 1960).

Bishop, I., '*Pearl' in its Setting: A Critical Study of the Structure and Meaning of the Middle English Poem* (Oxford, 1968).

—— 'Solacia in *Pearl* and in Letters of Edward III Concerning the Death of his Daughter, Joan', *N&Q*, 229 (December 1984), pp. 454-6.

—— 'Lapidary Formulas as Topics of Invention: Thomas of Hales to Henryson', *RES*, n.s. 37 (1986), pp. 469-77.

Brewer, D.S., 'The Ideal of Feminine Beauty', *MLR*, 50 (1955), pp. 257-69.

Brown, Carleton (ed.), *English Lyrics of the XIIIth Century* (Oxford, 1932).

—— *Religious Lyrics of the XIVth Century*, rev. by G.V. Smithers (Oxford, 1952).

Burnley, J.D., '*Fine Amor:* Its Meaning and Context', *RES* n.s. 31 (1980), pp. 129-48.

Burrow, J.A., *A Reading of Sir Gawain and the Green Knight* (London, 1965).

—— *Ricardian Poetry: Chaucer, Gower, Langland, and the 'Gawain' Poet* (London, 1971).

—— *Medieval Writers and Their Work* (Oxford, 1982).

—— *Essays on Medieval Literature* (Oxford, 1984).

Burton, T., '"The Fair Maid of Ribblesdale" and the Problem of Parody', *EC*, 31 (1981), pp. 282-98.

Charland, Th.-M., *Artes Praedicandi: Contribution à l'Histoire de la Rhétorique Au Moyen Age* (Paris and Ottowa, 1936).

Cipolla, C., *Clocks and Culture* (London, 1967).

Clutton, C. (and Niland, A.), *The British Organ* (London, 1963).

Cohn, N., *The Pursuit of the Millennium* (London, 1957).

Curtius, E.R., *European Literature and the Latin Middle Ages*, trans. W.R. Trask (London, 1953).

Davis, H., *The Satire of Jonathan Swift* (New York, 1947).

Dickins, B. [and Wilson, R.M.], (edd.), *Early Middle English Texts* (Cambridge, 1951).

Dobson, E.J., 'The Etymology and Meaning of *Boy*', *MÆ*, 9 (1940), pp. 121-54.

Du Boulay, F.R.H., *An Age of Ambition: English Society in the Late Middle Ages* (London, 1970).

Economou, G.D., *The Goddess Natura in Medieval Literature* (Cambridge, Mass., 1972).

Faral, Edmond, *Les Arts Poétiques du XII^e et XIII^e Siècles* (Paris, 1924).

Gilbert, A.J., *Literary Language from Chaucer to Johnson* (London, 1979).

Gray, Douglas, *Themes and Images in the Medieval English Religious Lyric* (London, 1972).

Green, R.H., 'Alain of Lille's *De Planctu Naturae*', *Speculum*, 31 (1956), pp. 649-74.

Heyworth, P.L. (ed.), *Medieval Studies for J.A.W. Bennett* (Oxford, 1981).

Hopkins, E.J., *The English Medieval Church Organ* (Exeter, 1888).

Hunt, Tony, 'The Rhetorical Background to the Arthurian Prologue', in D.D.R. Owen (ed.), *Arthurian Romance* . . . [q.v., below].

Jennings, Margaret, 'The *Ars Componendi Sermones* of Ranulph Higden' in J.J. Murphy (ed.), *Medieval Eloquence* [q.v., below].

Kaske, R.E., 'Patristic Exegesis in the Criticism of Medieval Literature: the Defense' in Dorothy Bethurum (ed.), *Critical Approaches* . . . [q.v., above].

Kratzmann, N. [*et al.*], (edd.), *The Cambridge History of Later Medieval Philosophy* (Cambridge, 1982).

Leff, G., *Bradwardine and the Pelagians* (Cambridge, 1957).

Lewis, C.S., *The Allegory of Love* (Oxford, 1936).

—— (ed.), *Essays Presented to Charles Williams* (London, 1947).

—— *The Discarded Image* (Cambridge, 1964).

Loxton, H., *Pilgrimage to Canterbury* (Newton Abbot, 1978).

MacQueen, J., *Robert Henryson: A Study of the Major Narrative Poems* (Oxford, 1967).

Maritain, Jacques, *Art and Scholasticism*, trans. by J.F. Scanlan (London, 1943).

Mehl, Dieter, *The Middle English Romances of the Thirteenth and*

*Fourteenth Centuries* (London, 1967).

Miller, P., 'John Gower, Satiric Poet' in A.J. Minnis (ed.), *Gower's Confessio Amantis* . . . [q.v., below].

Mills, M. (ed.), *Six Middle English Romances* (London, 1973).

Minnis, A.J. (ed.), *Gower's Confessio Amantis: Responses and Reassessments* (Woodbridge, 1983).

—— *Medieval Theory of Authorship: Scholastic Literary Attitudes in the Later Middle Ages* (London, 1984).

Murphy, J.J. (ed.), *Three Medieval Rhetorical Arts* (Berkeley, Los Angeles, London, 1971).

—— *Rhetoric in the Middle Ages: A History of Rhetorical Theory from St Augustine to the Renaissance* (Berkeley, Los Angeles, London, 1974).

—— (ed.), *Medieval Eloquence* (Berkeley, Los Angeles, London, 1978).

Newman, J., *West Kent and the Weald* in 'The Buildings of England' series, General Editor, N. Pevsner (Harmondsworth, 1969).

Niland, A. [see Clutton, C., above].

Nykrog, Per, *Les Fabliaux* (Copenhagen, 1957).

Oberman, H.A., *Archbishop Thomas Bradwardine: A Fourteenth Century Augustinian* (Utrecht, 1957).

—— *The Harvest of Medieval Theology: Gabriel Biel and Late Medieval Nominalism* (Cambridge, Mass., 1963).

Orme, N., 'The Education of the Courtier' [in Scattergood and Sherborne (edd.), *English Court Culture* (q.v., below)].

Owen, D.D.R. (ed.), *Arthurian Romance: Seven Essays* (Edinburgh and London, 1970).

Pantin, W.A., *The English Church in the Fourteenth Century* (Cambridge, 1955).

Paré, G. (*et al.*), *La Renaissance du XII^e Siècle: Les Ecoles et l'Enseignement* (Paris, Ottowa, 1933).

Perrot, J., *The Organ*, trans. N. Deane (London, 1971).

Piehler, P., *The Visionary Landscape: A Study in Medieval Allegory* (London, 1971).

Runacres, C., 'Art and Ethics in the *Exempla* of *Confessio Amantis*' in A.J. Minnis (ed.), *Gower's Confessio* . . . [q.v., above].

Sandison, H.E., *The Chanson d'Aventure in Middle English* (Bryn Mawr, Penn., 1913).

Scattergood, V.J. [and Sherborne, J.W.], (edd.), *English Court Culture in the Later Middle Ages* (London, 1983).

Sherborne, J.W. [see Scattergood, V.J., above].

Sisam, K. (ed), *Fourteenth Century Verse and Prose* (Oxford, 1921).

Smalley, Beryl, *English Friars and Antiquity in the Early Fourteenth Century* (Oxford, 1960).

Smithers, G.V. (ed.) [see Bennett, J.A.W., above].

Stevens, J., *Medieval Romance: Themes and Approaches* (London, 1973).

—— 'Angelus ad Virginem: the History of a Medieval Song' in Heyworth, P.L., Medieval Studies . . . [q.v., above].

Stokes, Myra, Justice and Mercy in Piers Plowman: A Reading of the B-Text Visio (Beckenham, Kent, 1984).

Thomas, R.G. (ed.), Ten Miracle Plays (London, 1966).

Tolkien, J.R.R., 'On Fairy-Stories', in C.S. Lewis (ed.), Essays Presented to Charles Williams [q.v., above].

Trounce, A. McI., 'The English Tail-Rhyme Romances', MÆ, 1-2 (1932-34).

Vinaver, E., The Rise of Romance (Oxford, 1971).

Wilson, R.M. (ed.), [see Dickins, B., above].